Popular Culture and Representations of Literacy

Routledge Studies in Literacy

EDITED BY DAVID BARTON, *Lancaster University, U.K.*

1. Women, Literacy and Development
Edited by Anna Robinson-Pant

2. Literacy and Globalization
Reading and Writing in Times of Social and Cultural Change
Uta Papen

3. Popular Culture and Representations of Literacy
Bronwyn T. Williams and Amy A. Zenger

Popular Culture and Representations of Literacy

Bronwyn T. Williams and
Amy A. Zenger

Routledge
Taylor & Francis Group
New York London

Routledge
Taylor & Francis Group
711 Third Avenue,
New York, NY 10017

Routledge
Taylor & Francis Group
2 Park Square
Milton Park, Abingdon
Oxon OX14 4RN

© 2007 by Taylor & Francis Group, LLC
Routledge is an imprint of Taylor & Francis Group, an Informa business

First published in paperback 2011

ISBN13: 978-0-415-36095-1 (hbk)
ISBN13: 978-0-415-51411-8 (pbk)

No part of this book may be reprinted, reproduced, transmitted, or utilized in any form by any electronic, mechanical, or other means, now known or hereafter invented, including photocopying, microfilming, and recording, or in any information storage or retrieval system, without written permission from the publishers.

Trademark Notice: Product or corporate names may be trademarks or registered trademarks, and are used only for identification and explanation without intent to infringe.

Library of Congress Cataloging-in-Publication Data

Williams, Bronwyn T.
 Popular culture and representations of literacy / Bronwyn T. Williams and Amy A. Zenger.
  p. cm. -- (Routledge studies in literacy ; 3)
 Includes bibliographical references and index.
 ISBN 978-0-415-36095-1 (hardback : alk. paper)
 1. Literacy--United States. 2. Popular culture--United States. 3. Motion pictures--Social aspects. 4. Motion pictures--Plots, themes, etc.. I. Zenger, Amy A. II. Title.

LC149.W455 2007
302.2'244--dc22   2006033134

Visit the Taylor & Francis Web site at
http://www.taylorandfrancis.com

and the Routledge Web site at
http://www.routledge-ny.com

Contents

Acknowledgments	vii
Introduction	1
1 Literacy in everyday life, literacy on the screen	3
PART I **Representations of literacy and identity**	19
2 The pragmatic and the sentimental: Literacy and gender roles	21
3 Who's allowed to read and write? Literacy and social class	41
4 Writing others: Images of race and literacy	63
PART II **Literacy and social contexts**	83
5 Control and action: Literacy as power	85
6 The perils of misreading: Literacy as danger	105
PART III **Literacy myths in the movies**	125
7 The passions of the romantic author: Literacy as individualism	127
8 The triumph of the word: Literacy as salvation and commodity	145

vi *Contents*

Conclusion 161

9 **Life is not like the movies (or is it?): Literacy on film and in our lives** 163

References 171
Filmography 177
Index 181

Acknowledgments

We would like to thank David Barton, the series editor, for his support for this project. In addition we are grateful to all of the helpful people at Routledge Press, including our editor, the always-patient Terry Clague. We also want to thank Helen McDougall and Katherine Carpenter for their help with the details and production of this book.

We are also grateful to the colleagues and friends who have encouraged us in this research, especially Mary Hallet, whose innovative uses of documentary film in writing classrooms have often inspired us. We are also grateful to Patricia Sullivan for her friendship and support for both of us as scholars as well as her expertise and insights into issues of popular culture. We also thank Tom Newkirk for his insights on literacy and patient wisdom that have been a constant and calming guide for both of us for many years. In addition we appreciate the suggestions and comments from the people who attended the conference presentations we did based on this research while it was in process.

Parts of Chapter Two originally appeared in the article "Who Reads and Writes in Hollywood? Reading Representations of Literacy in Contemporary Movies" in *The International Journal of Learning*, vol. 11. (2004).

The images in the book are used with the following permissions:

Introduction: © Paramount Pictures/Photofest, page 1.

Section I: Representations of Literacy and Identity, page 19, © Paramount/Everett Collection.

Section II: Literacy and Social Contexts, page 83, © Warner Brothers/Photofest.

Section III: Literacy Myths in the Movies, page 125, © Focus Features/Everett Collection.

Conclusion, page 161, © Columbia Pictures/Everett Collection.

Amy: I would like to acknowledge the Graduate School of the University of New Hampshire for offering me a Summer Fellowship to fund my first study of representations of literacy in the movies. I would also like to thank Cinthia Gannet, Paula Salvio, and Kate Tirabassi for their discussions and insights into film and literacy.

viii *Acknowledgments*

In this project, as with every one of my accomplishments, I am indebted to my adventurous, intelligent, and amiable family, which includes my parents, Richard Zenger and Edna Zenger, as well as Rebecca, Robin, Mary Ann, John, Gabrielle, Beatrix Rose, Isobel Josephine, Matthew, and Ian. Last but not by any means least, I am grateful for the wisdom and humor of my husband, Stephen, who loves to go to the movies as much as I do.

Bronwyn: I want to thank the members of my 2005 "Popular Culture and Literacy" graduate seminar for their valuable insights into this research and into the work of exploring the links between literacy and popular culture: Marina Ajanovic, Cindy Britt, Kate Brown, Stephanie Fleischer, Alanna Frost, Dan Keller, Deanna McGaughey-Summers, Julie Myatt, Stephen Neaderhiser, Robbie Ritchie, James Romesburg, and Susan Wright. I also want to thank Rhys Brydon-Williams for his work in compiling the Filmography for the book.

My love of movies came from my father, Reese M. Williams. My love of teaching from my mother, Louise Williams. What I learned from them is present in this book. I am lucky enough to have two sons, Griffith and Rhys, who share both my love of movies and my love of reading and writing. I am grateful to them for their help in pointing out literacy moments in movies throughout this project. My favorite time of the week for years has been Friday Family Film Night. Finally, I am grateful every day for the intellectual insights and love of my wife and favorite movie-going companion, Mary. We'll always have Paris...

Introduction

Tom Cruise in Mission: Impossible (1996). ©Paramount Pictures/Photofest

1 Literacy in everyday life, literacy on the screen

We start by taking you to the White House at the end of *X2: X-Men United* (2003), a popular Hollywood action blockbuster, as the President prepares to address the nation.

The President of the United States (Cotter Smith) strides purposefully down the halls of the White House, surrounded by a phalanx of aides. In his hand he holds a copy of a speech that he is reading aloud, pausing to ask an aide about the choice of a word: "Do we like this word, 'annihilation'?" His aide assures him it is the appropriate word. The President arrives in the Oval Office, sits behind his desk, and begins his televised address about a looming crisis, a "growing threat within our own population." We are given a shot of the speech from the President's point of view, so we can see the words he is reading scrolling up the teleprompter screen.

No sooner has the President begun to speak when the lights go out, lightning flashes outside, and time seems to stop for everyone but the President and the X-men (and women) who have suddenly appeared in the Oval Office. Professor Xavier (Patrick Stewart), leader of the X-men, dressed impeccably in a gray suit, introduces his colleagues as the very mutants about whom the President was about to warn the country, but assures the President they mean him no harm.

President: Who are you people?
Xavier: We are mutants. My name is Charles Xavier. Please sit down.
President: I'd rather stand.

Xavier turns to a young woman (Anna Paquin) and asks her to hand a file to the President saying:
These files were taken from the private offices of William Stryker (the movie's villain) (Brian Cox).

President: How did you get this?
Xavier: Well, let's just say I know a little girl who can walk through walls.

4   *Popular culture and representations of literacy*

Xavier tells the President he has been deceived about the threat—that it is not the mutants the country should fear, but a nefarious secret government project. Time continues to stand still, as the President studies the file pensively. The lights then go back on, time resumes, and the mutants have vanished from the room. The President looks back up at the words on the teleprompter but pauses, as if rethinking what he will say next...

And so the world is saved again. But was it the X-Men or was it literacy? Instrumental in the scene, yet almost unnoticed in the special effects, dramatic tension, and earnest acting is the way literacy practices figure centrally in what is happening on screen. The scene centers around two literacy events, the meanings of which change as the context of the events changes as a result of what happens among the characters. It begins with the President reading a hard copy the text of the speech he is about to give and discussing the appropriateness of the language. Then he begins to read the speech from the teleprompter as he sits at his desk in the Oval Office. After the arrival of the X-men, the plea of Professor Xavier only becomes persuasive when he presents the President with the "secret" file, which details, in writing, the persecution of the mutants by a rogue general. The two literacy events—the President reading a speech and then a file—are straightforward. What is more important is the way the meaning of those events shifts as the events unfolding in the scene change the context of how the speech and file are read.

The "literacy event" of reading a speech only tells part of the story. As David Barton and Mary Hamilton (1998) have pointed out, literacy events are only the observable part of "literacy practices," which go beyond observable units of behavior to include "values, attitudes, feelings, and social relationships" (6). Thus, cultural context is vital to interpreting literacy practices. The "secret file" is a staple of so many film thrillers, either as the goal of the plot or, as in this case, the deus ex machina that saves the heroes from the villains. What is actually written in the file almost becomes less important than its talisman-like presence as the container of "truth." (In fact, as in the case of most "secret files" in movies, we never actually get to read them, but the contents are summarized by one of the characters.) In *X2*, once that file, and the truth it contains, changes from being secret to sitting in the hands of power, the meaning of reading the file changes as well. As the scene ends it is clear that the words in the file have now made the words on the teleprompter empty, if not dangerous.

There is nothing extraordinary about the role literacy plays in this scene in this action film. The list of films that include presidential speeches or secret files is long. The question is not whether literacy practices are present in contemporary popular culture, in this case movies. It is much harder to find a movie without literacy represented in it than it is to find one where people are reading or writing. The more important and useful question

Literacy in everyday life, literacy on the screen 5

is how do we in the audience interpret the literacy practices we find in popular culture? What do such representations tell us about how literacy is perceived in the culture at large?

Most movies are filled with scenes of people of all ages, sexes, races, and social classes reading and writing in a wide variety of contexts and for a wide variety of purposes. In the literacy practices represented, class and gender are marked, institutional hierarchies identified and reinforced, cultural power hoarded or shared, individual and social desire enacted or denied. Though often portrayed as incidental to main narratives in individual films, when taken together across a number of different films, representations of literacy practices construct and contest submerged narratives and counter-narratives about literacy. Yet scenes showing reading and writing on film go largely unnoticed, even by literacy scholars, despite the fact that these images recreate and reinforce pervasive concepts and perceptions of literacy, perceptions that inevitably influence both how we teach reading and writing and how our students respond to print literacy and to writing classes.

This book addresses how everyday literacy practices are represented in popular culture, specifically in mainstream, widely distributed contemporary movies. Though we often watch such movies without connecting the acts we are seeing to the ideas we—and our students—have about literacy, the pervasive representations of literacy have an effect on our cultural conceptions of reading and writing, from issues of identity to institutional practices. What is important about the way literacy practices are portrayed in films is not that they are different from dominant conceptions of literacy and culture, but that they reproduce such conceptions so seamlessly, and often in ways that escape our explicit attention.

OBSERVING CULTURE ON FILM

Popular culture and film have been theorized and studied from a variety of perspectives, including a rich tradition of cultural studies that examines how films are not just the product of the explicit intent of the filmmakers, but represent and reproduce ideological functions of larger culture. Cultural studies film scholarship examines how movies support and reproduce a culture's dominant values and social orders. The cultural construction of identity, particularly in terms of gender, race, social class, and sexuality, has been a focus of much of the work in cultural studies film criticism. As Andrew Light (2003) points out, movies, like other popular culture texts, create complex portrayals of how we see ourselves and others that don't "merely represent individuals and groups but also help to actually create understandings of who we think we are, how we regard others, and how members of groups identify and understand their group membership and their obligations to that group" (9). The mainstream films made at any

6 Popular culture and representations of literacy

cultural moment reflect to the audience a recognizable world with characters who act in a comprehensible and recognizable manner. Even in fantasy and science fiction, for example, the clothes hairstyles, furniture, not to mention the characters' identities and relations with one another, reflect the cultural moment in which the films were made. Just by looking at the clothes, set design, and casting, it is just as easy to place a film like *Forbidden Planet* (1956) in the fifties, *Star Wars* (1977) in the seventies, and *The Matrix* (1999) in the nineties as it would be with any domestic drama. Though we know movies are fictional, we accept the world, characters, and actions we see in movies as consistent with the ideological truths and values that shape our lives. Literacy, as Brian Street (1995, 2001) has argued so forcefully, is also a product of ideology and defined by cultural norms and expectations just as much as by aspects of identity, politics, and economics. Theory and research on literacy as an ideological construct have increasingly focused on examining the web of "associations between cultural conventions, literacy practices, notions of self, person and identity and struggles over power" (Street 1995, 135).

In this project, we are working in the tradition of cultural studies film criticism to examine how movies represent and reproduce the ideological nature of literacy as a social phenomenon. The literacy practices displayed on the screen and consumed by the public are part of the ideological construction of what is considered literacy, what social goals it serves in what institutions, how it is perpetuated, how it shapes concepts of identity, and what cultural power is determined by who is considered literate. Like many elements of culture and ideology, however, literacy practices in mainstream movies often pass unnoticed because they are so naturalized, so normalized. Literacy practices, though they often don't stand out in the narrative because they reproduce the dominant values and power relationships, are an integral part of the construction of culture and ideology. Of course, ideology is not seamless, and not adopted uniformly by every person in a culture. As in any text, there are often contradictions and paradoxes in how literacy practices are represented and read in movies. Even so, "the best forms of ideological critique, whatever their interest, attend to the complex ways in which films make their appeals to us as viewers in the multiple and specific places in which we as social subjects incorporate cinemas into our everyday lives" (Tinkcom and Villarejo 2001, 3). Our goal is to examine how film, as an integral part of culture and ideology, shapes and maintains our conceptions of literacy and identity.

Another theoretical tradition that shapes our work in this book comes from our backgrounds in rhetoric. By bringing to this study a rhetorical approach to reading and interpreting literacy representations in film, we can examine such moments as situated acts of expression that exist in comprehensible and ideological combinations of appeals. Both the production and consumption of movies are rhetorical, social acts that involve directing audiences toward some purpose by employing familiar rhetorical con-

Literacy in everyday life, literacy on the screen 7

ventions. In any mainstream movie, stories are told, arguments formed, and identification, in the Burkean sense, is sought with the audience. Films are complex rhetorical texts that draw on rhetorics of words, images, and movement to create these narratives and arguments. Mainstream filmmakers work within genres and try to fulfill certain audience expectations (so people will pay to see the work) and so also work within dominant ideologies, whether consciously or not. Audiences watching the same films read them with the same expectations and within the same ideologies.

It is important to note, that, while we find the pervasive patterns of how literacy practices are represented to be significant in helping to shape and maintain certain ideological constructions of literacy, we do not believe that people consume such representations without thought or without adapting them to their experiences and contexts. Popular culture is not a force that people in their daily lives are unable to resist, like so many mindless cultural dupes. Rather than thinking about the audience in a theatre as sitting helpless and mesmerized before the images on the screen, it is more useful to employ Margaret Morse's metaphor, in her discussion of television, of the popular culture "membrane" whose "function is to link the symbolic and immaterial world on the monitor with an actual and material situation of reception" (1998, 18). Movies work in much the same way, and we recognize that popular culture is not uniform in either its production or its consumption; instead people balance their experiences and readings of such texts against their individual and group lived experiences. Rhetorical theory allows the flexibility to read a film as an "isolated, substantive, and symbolic form of expression, but also through more general cultural, psychological, and rhetorical frames, ones that guide interpretation and that shape our understanding of what meanings film makes possible" (Blakesley 2003, 8). Throughout this book we are mindful that the representations of literacy practices we see on film will, in readings by others, be subject to a different set of interpretations that allow for adoption or resistance, or both at the same time.

Finally, by working in the traditions of cultural and rhetorical studies we also work in an interdisciplinary tradition. Consequently, we draw on a range of theoretical approaches to examine the literacy practices on film. Throughout the book we employ different theoretical lenses (such as feminist, materialist, postcolonial, critical race, narrative, genre, and others) to approach different issues or interpretations of what we see on the screen. We will address these theories and their applications throughout the book as they become relevant.

No one doubts that popular mass media have an influence on our perceptions of gender or class or race or sexual orientation or any other cultural construction. We should not doubt, then, that such media are influencing perceptions and practices of writing and reading. If we are to research and teach reading and writing, at any level, we need to understand how and

8 Popular culture and representations of literacy

why students and the culture at large regard literacy practices as they do and then be able to address such perceptions.

THE GLOBAL POWER OF FILM

Our initial approach to this project was to study representations of literacy in many forms of popular culture, including television, magazines, the Internet, advertising, and video games. Very quickly, however, we realized that to try to cover so many forms of mass-produced popular culture would either result in a huge, unfocused book or one that risked treating different genres and media too superficially to be useful. It was at this point we decided to sharpen our focus to contemporary, mainstream movies. Using movies as our field of study provides several advantages beyond allowing us to explore one form of popular culture in significant depth.

Movies remain a popular and pervasive form of popular culture, both in the United States and around the world. Also, mainstream Hollywood movies, of the kind we are discussing in the book, circulate as easily around the globe as any medium or cultural form and dominate the global film industry. Thus, though we are often discussing movies made in the United States, we understand that the audience watching and interpreting these movies may be sitting in a theatre or watching a DVD anywhere from London to Beirut to Hong Kong. Even when U.S. films are not being watched, they often have an effect on other films that are being made. Though they may not always be our proudest cultural export, there is no denying the global appeal of mainstream U.S. films. This border-crossing quality makes contemporary film a more intriguing and flexible form of popular culture to study than some forms, such as radio and television that may be more influenced by local cultures.

Also, with a history dating back more than century, the genre and formal qualities of film have had time to develop in ways that reveal both patterns and conflicts. Film has also developed into a form that has clearly been used for a variety of purposes, from straightforward diverting entertainment, to propaganda, to complex aesthetic and philosophical inquiry. These qualities give film a richer history and more diverse set of uses and texts than some newer popular culture forms such as the Internet.

Finally, the narrative, naturalistic conventions of most mainstream movies make them intriguing, if not necessarily reliable, mirrors of our culture and ideology. The representations of literacy on film are not always real, but often reflect dominant cultural attitudes about reading and writing. At the same time, because "there is no simple division between the cinema which functions as an instrument of dominant ideology, and the cinema which facilitates challenges to it" (Mayne 2002, 29), we can also see literacy practices portrayed on the screen that run counter to the dominant narrative and culture,.

Literacy in everyday life, literacy on the screen 9

Even as we focus our project on mainstream films, the kinds of issues and themes we are going to discuss can be easily extrapolated to other forms of popular culture. For example, the representations of literacy and how they connect to issues of gender, race, and social class can be seen as easily on an episode of *ER* or *The Simpsons* as they can be in movies. Similar connections could be made to representations of literacy in advertising, music, the Internet or other forms of popular culture.

When we have mentioned this project to friends and colleagues, their first thoughts are often films in which literacy is foregrounded and triumphant. Films that explicitly forground literacy often convey highly positive messages about it. Films about literacy also often reinforce the belief that literacy is an autonomous set of skills that one can, and should, adopt to join the dominant culture. Such messages can make triumph-of-literacy movies appealing to many writing teachers, because they echo the meta-narratives that permeate public policy about literacy education, and education as well. We agree that it is important to analyze the literacy practices in such films, and their representations of literacy as salvation or commodity, and we do so in Chapter Eight.

Yet, scholars in literacy studies have pointed out that even as practices and pedagogies in schools construct institutional definitions of literacy (Street 1995), important literacy practices also exist outside of schools (Barton and Hamilton 1998; Gregory and Williams 2000). In the same vein, we also believe that there is a great deal to be learned from movies that are not explicitly about teaching reading or writing. We consequently decided to study situated literacy practices in films that had been disseminated widely and endorsed by mainstream producers, critics, and theatres. There is much to be learned in how literacy is represented as everyday aspects of characters' lives whether in social dramas, romantic comedies, fantasies, or action blockbusters.

We began our research by viewing a broadly inclusive group of films, ranging widely across the years and including films produced in countries outside of the United States. After this initial exploration, we focused our attention within a narrower field, studying Hollywood-produced movies that were in wide release—in other words, had at least five or more copies on the new release shelves of chain video stores such as Blockbuster or Hollywood video—so that we would be watching movies that were also being watched by the culture at large. Though our work also extends to some films produced in countries other than the United States, we have focused most of this project on Hollywood movies. More than simply offering some coherence and focus for the research, it also reflects the dominance of the American movie industry in global popular culture. Like it or not, Hollywood-produced films are watched around the world and, with the exception of the Indian film industry, crowd out movies produced in other countries. Consequently, the representations of literacy practices in Hollywood movies reach more than American audiences. Even though these

10   *Popular culture and representations of literacy*

representations may be read differently in different cultures, we believe it is still useful to examine in detail the ways in which literacy is portrayed in these movies and hope that scholars and teachers in other cultures can use our observations as a place to begin further discussions of how these representations are read and reproduced by their audiences.

We also had to come up with a definition of literacy. On the one hand, we did not want to follow the common trend of using literacy as a synonym for any knowledge or cultural competence. This book will not include discussions of concepts such as emotional literacy or technological literacy or environmental literacy. Instead we decided to note when written words or the act of reading or writing them showed up in a movie, whether on a piece of paper, television or computer screen, street sign, newspaper, letter, book, business card, and so on. At the same time, we knew we must recognize that communication in our contemporary culture is multimodal and that we needed to be aware of how theories of multiliteracies influence literacy practices. As Barton and Hamilton (1998) note, "people use written language in an integrated way as a part of a range of semiotic systems" (9). We also then noted when written words might be working in concert with images or gesture or spoken words to create meaning for the characters and the audience.

When we started to watch contemporary Hollywood films, we noticed immediately a wide variety in the extent to which literacy was represented. In some films, such as *America's Sweethearts* (2001), we are shown virtually no reading or writing events, even when the story takes place in an environment rife with them. In others, the presence of reading and writing is much more pervasive. *Bridget Jones' Diary* (2001), of course, is constructed entirely around the conceit of the diary and also represents other literacy events of many different sorts. Films we studied also varied in the formal means by which they represent literacies. *The Royal Tennenbaums* (2001), for example, is structured as a narrative into "chapters" and at the beginning of each of these "chapters" the screen is designed to look like the page of a storybook that "opens" to the film action. In this usage, the film consciously hearkens back to older films in which the film screen mimics the book page, the calendar page, or newspaper headline to visually prop the film action. More typically, we see characters reading or writing for purposes that make narrative sense.

Most surprising, however, was the prevalence of literacy practices in most movies we watched. Though the plots did not always hinge on such moments, we began to see many characters reading and writing in many forms. Sometimes these literacy events were interesting as individual moments of reading and writing that we wanted to analyze. More often, however, we saw the literacy events throughout the film as creating a kind of narrative about literacy that existed in addition to the primary narrative of the film. Most of the time these narratives about literacy, and the arguments and assumptions they made about how and why people read and

Literacy in everyday life, literacy on the screen 11

write, were submerged in the more explicit narratives of the film. In fact the narratives about literacy did not always support the assumptions and arguments of the primary narrative. As we watched movies ranging from fantasy blockbusters to teen comedies to domestic dramas, we began to see patterns connected to these representations that often crossed genres. These patterns shaped the book's organization into sections addressing Representations of Literacy and Identity, Literacy and Social Contexts, and Literacy Myths in the Movies and the chapters within each section on specific issues of representation such as race, gender, social class, power, danger, and individualism.

Perhaps the greatest difficulty in writing this book, however, has not been analysis, but deciding on the films to use in each chapter to illustrate the issues raised by that analysis. The presence of literacy practices in films is so pervasive that we were faced with the difficult task of finding films that would be particularly useful and clear as examples. Again we chose depth over breadth. We decided it would often be more useful to focus on a few films in each chapter as case studies, making connections as necessary to other movies. A detailed focus on a film or two in each chapter allows us a more nuanced and thoughtful analysis that we feel confident readers can extend to other movies. The exceptions to this approach are the chapters that focus on one genre of films, such as James Bond movies, that reproduce the same scenes of literacy over and over again. We make no claim that the movies we are studying are the best films made in recent years, or even always films we particularly like, but they are popular films that offer representative insights into the portrayal of literacy practices in popular culture.

Because we draw on cultural and rhetorical theories in our approach to film, it is also important to outline our theoretical approach to literacy.

SOCIAL THEORIES OF LITERACY

Brian Street's well-known challenge to what he called the "autonomous model" of literacy—that literacy is a set of neutral, stand-alone decoding skills—helped begin a conversation about the situated and contextual nature of literacy, a new approach that regards it as a social phenomenon, inextricable from issues of culture, epistemology, and identity (2001). Given that literacy is a social act, then the meaning and importance of it will necessarily vary depending on the cultural context. For our project we draw specifically on the work of David Barton and Mary Hamilton (1998), who propose a "social theory of literacy" that emphasizes the need to think of literacy as a "social practice". They define "literacy practices" as the "general cultural ways of utilizing written language which people draw on in their lives" (6), which allows for "a powerful way of conceptualizing the

12 *Popular culture and representations of literacy*

link between the activities of reading and writing and the social structures in which they are embedded and which they help shape" (6).

It is important to pause for a moment and clarify the terms we are using. Barton and Hamilton call any moment of observable reading or writing— like the scene in *X2* where the President is reading from a teleprompter—a "literacy event." The concept of an "event," drawing from Bakhtin and from sociolinguistics, emphasizes that literacy is always situated in a cultural context. In addition, texts, however written or read, are essential to literacy events. But "literacy events" only tell part of the story. They are only the observable part of "literacy practices." For Barton and Hamilton, literacy practices go beyond observable units of behavior to include "values, attitudes, feelings, and social relationships" (6). A social theory of literacy combines events, texts, and practices to define literacy as "a set of social practices; these can be inferred from events which are mediated by written texts" (8).

In order to study how literacy is represented on film, then, we need to look at more than simply the actions of a character reading or writing, but to also situate those actions in the context of issues of social structures, identity, and power. Thus cultural context is vital to interpreting literacy practices. In the *X2* clip, for example, the meaning and power of the file of papers changes as its status changes from "secret" file to "stolen" file to "Presidential" file.

To help define literacy as a social practice, Barton and Hamilton offer a set of points (7) that can be used as a useful framework for revisiting the *X2* scene that opened this chapter.

Literacy is best understood as a set of social practices; these can be inferred from events which are mediated by written texts. The social practices in the scene center around the persuasion of the President at a moment of national crises. The events that mediate these practices are the reading of the speech, on paper and the teleprompter, and the explanation and reading of the "secret" file.

There are different literacies associated with different domains of life. Though this concept will be illustrated more clearly in the rest of the book when we can address entire films, the domain in which the *X2* clip takes place is crucial to the meaning given to literacy events. That the scene is set in the domain of government and political power means that any literacy event has the potential to have far-reaching political implications; setting the scene on a mountain top or at a kitchen table or in a shopping mall would clearly alter the meaning and impact of the reading either the file or the speech.

It also means that the language and rhetorical strategies that will be used will be more formal and carefully constructed, as we can see when the President ponders the appropriateness of individual words before giving the speech.

Literacy in everyday life, literacy on the screen 13

Literacy practices are patterned by social institutions and power relationships, and some literacies are more dominant, visible, and influential than others. The President reads the speech, but it is clear from his questions about the language that he has not written it. Yet the act of the President reading the words aloud on a televised broadcast from the Oval Office invests the speech with the authority and importance of the social institution of the presidency. Few people would be able or willing to stop such an event or alter the reading of the speech. That's why the mutants have to stop time and sneak into the room under the cover of an appropriately dramatic thunderstorm. Yet, is also significant that, once the mutants are in the room, it is Xavier who does the talking. His character may be a mutant, but he is still a white male in a suit speaking standardized English with an upper-class accent to another white male in a suit. Xavier is even sure to introduce himself with the title "professor" and never touches the file himself, having a young woman hand it over in the same way a secretary would for an executive. The legitimacy of the information in the file, and the reason that the President is persuaded to read the file, comes from the social and power attributes that Xavier presents in his performance of identity. The President might be much less likely to read the file had it been presented to him by the young girl who actually stole it.

Literacy practices are purposeful and embedded in broader social goals and cultural practices. The goal of the speech that the President begins to give is the security of the country. The meaning for the President changes, however, when he reads the file which illustrates that another goal—social tolerance—may be more at issue. There are also two well-known cultural practices at work in the scene. An "Oval Office address" usually given only in times of national emergency and coming from the center of presidential power, is invested with a sense of power and gravitas that, again, means any words said during the address will have a substantial political and emotional impact on the country. At the same time, "secret government files" are texts that are commonly discussed if rarely seen. Politicians and bureaucrats refer to them as totems of national security while investigators, political opponents, and conspiracy theorists invoke them as the repositories of misdeeds and uncomfortable truths. Stealing such a file is illegal, but making the file public with the goal of promoting social justice changes the meaning of the theft from one of legality to one of righteousness. Both the "Oval Office address" and the "secret government file" are well known in daily life and well represented in popular culture. Most people have probably seen more Oval Office addresses by fictional presidents in movies than they have the real thing by sitting presidents. Even fewer people have seen authentic classified government documents, but recognize them easily as a trope in movie thrillers.

Literacy is historically situated. Again, the meaning of an Oval Office speech is grounded in a history of such speeches, as well as in the history of the White House as the center of executive power in the United States.

14 *Popular culture and representations of literacy*

The history of secret files as the places where governments (whether U.S. governments or governments of other countries) hide their misdeeds, has been shaped by such scandals as the Pentagon Papers, Watergate, and the Iran-Contra Affair. In these scandals, as in others, the evidence of government misdeeds and abuses of power were often revealed or substantiated by previously secret documents. Often, as in the Pentagon Papers, these documents were revealed against the wishes of the government. Hence the mutants understand the importance of intervening in an Oval Office speech that will set both national policy and emotions in a moment of crisis. They also understand the power of a secret file as written evidence of the charges they are making. In the same way the historical context of the secret file shapes the President's reading of it.

Literacy practices change and new ones are frequently acquired through processes of informal learning and sense making. Though this concept is not seen specifically in this scene, there are other films in which we have begun to see the "secret file" move from paper to computer disk, such as *Mission: Impossible* (1996). Certainly presidential speeches and how people respond to them have changed over time with the introduction of speech writers, television, teleprompters, and shifts in public rhetorical practices.

We recognize the multiple, overlapping literacy practices that exist in communities, and argue that such literacy practices "are as fluid, dynamic, and changing as the lives and societies of which they are a part" (Barton and Hamilton 1998, 12). The consequence of this approach to literacy studies has been to move research beyond the classroom to consider how literacy develops and functions in different settings and domains of life.

Yet what remains to be explored more fully is how popular culture—a significant element in most people's lives—has influenced perceptions of and responses to literacy practices. A social theory of literacy allows us to see that even in films that are not about the traditional triumph of literacy, literacy practices large and small in vastly varied contexts still fill the screen. It was these cinematic literacy representations that intrigued us. In the films we watched, one could see the ways in which literacy acts "as display, as threat, and as ritual" (Barton and Hamilton 1998, 11). If literacy practices are as much about "values, attitudes, feelings, and social relationships" (6) as the decoding or inscribing of words on a page, then looking to popular movies to see how they are represented provides us with a fascinating mirror into the dominant literacy practices in our culture. Popular movies are not only fictional, but are certainly not always what passes for a "realistic" portrayal of any aspect of contemporary life. Yet movies reflect and reproduce our dominant cultural beliefs and practices, and allow us to slow them down and watch them with a care and recursiveness not available in the real world, For these reasons, they bear watching, to see what they have to tell about literacy practices.

THE CONTENTS OF THIS BOOK

Section I of the book focuses on Representations of Literacy and Identity in film. Chapter Two, "The Pragmatic and the Sentimental: Literacy and Gender Roles," addresses how movies construct gender roles in terms of literacy. For example, using literacy to express emotions or to establish emotional relationships is often presented as the domain of women. Men, on the other hand, are more often shown using reading and writing in pragmatic and instrumental ways, as tools of commerce and power. On the other hand, more sentimental portrayals of literacy, though still tying men to professional writing, allow men to transcend traditional male gender roles and find an avenue for expressions of emotion on the page that they may not be interested in risking in person. Women can also use literacy to escape gender roles, often by using writing to prove intellectual ability that has been doubted by other characters, as in *Divine Secrets of the YaYa Sisterhood* (2002) or *Erin Brockovitch* (2001). It is also worth noting that in popular children's films (e.g., *Harriet the Spy* (1996), *Atlantis* (2001), *Beauty and the Beast* (1991)) literacy practices are almost always the performed by nerds and outcasts, rather than by physically attractive or action-oriented heroes.

In Chapter Three, "Who's Allowed to Read and Write? Literacy and Social Class," we focus on how film representations of everyday literacy practices construct class and class aspirations. This chapter focuses on the films *Changing Lanes* (2002), *Catch Me if You Can* (2002), and *Office Space* (1999) to illustrate how literacy is represented as a marker of social class. In these movies, the way class is marked by literacy practices is either enforced by social institutions to frustrate character's aspirations, or used to attribute particular virtues and admirable qualities to characters that allow for blurring social class boundaries.

Chapter Four, "Writing Others: Literacy and Race," examines the ways in which constructions of race are depicted on film through social relationships and artifacts involving literacy. In some (somewhat subtle) instances, white males achieve self-knowledge by connecting with non-whites through literacy (*About Schmidt* (2002), *The Green Mile* (1999)). The chapter focuses analysis on two films: *Holes* (2003) and *The Mummy* (1999). A discussion of *Holes* looks at the ways that literacy achievement and under-achievement have been tied to race. In *The Mummy*, the dramatization of race is more overt. Literacy and literacy artifacts are central to this film, which follows an expedition of white European academics defying threatening hordes of Oriental races to search for an ancient Book of Life.

The second section of the book examines how theories of Literacy and Social Contexts are played out in contemporary movies. The power of literacy is the focus of Chapter Five, "Control and Action: Literacy as Power." In this chapter, we look at how literacy functions as power in the hugely popular genre of action films. Rather than focus only on one or two films,

16   *Popular culture and representations of literacy*

here we examine action films as a genre, to illustrate how representations of literacy practices can fulfill similar, and expected, narrative conventions in one action film after another. The scenes of reading and writing in action films, whether in a popular series such as the James Bond movies or a single film, such as *The Peacemaker* (1997), get repeated as set pieces that not only fulfill genre conventions, but also act as particular markers about the character of the action hero and his relationship with society.

Although literacy is often portrayed in movies as leading to empowerment and salvation, representations of literacy as a power that is darker, even overtly dangerous sometimes appear in the same film. In Chapter Six, "The Ambiguity of Texts: Literacy as Danger," we look at the darker images of literacy in movies. In films such as *Harry Potter and the Chamber of Secrets* (2002) literacy is imbued with mystical power that echoes ancient and medieval perceptions. Yet this mystical and powerful literacy is also deeply dangerous if not properly controlled. In these films, texts, and those who control them, are often not to be trusted; those who can decode texts risk unleashing great dangers if they fail to properly interpret what they are reading. Indeed the real literacies of power in such films are often represented in contrast to more ordinary school or scholarly literacy.

The final section of the book is concerned with how Literacy Myths in the Movies are portrayed in movies and the implications of our research for teaching writing and reading. Chapter Seven focuses on "The Passions of the Romantic Author: Literacy as Individualism." In this chapter, we discuss how films about "authors"—in this chapter meaning creative literary writers—separate them from most people. Their writing, rather than connecting them to others, tends to set them apart. The act of writing, rather than a social act drawn from and driven by social contact, is instead an interior and unique activity, driven by an interior genius, in the tradition of Romantic individualism. Such films portray writing as mysterious, and unavailable to the average person, and generally focus not on the writing, but on the quirky, individualistic, and troubled behaviors of the "writer." When audiences are shown these repeated representations of writing as an elite activity that comes at a high personal cost, as the creation of genius, not craft, or as an individual, not a social activity, it is perhaps easier to understand some of the conceptions of writing and teaching writing that continue to dominate the culture and students in the classroom.

Chapter Eight is devoted to the kinds of films that people often think of most readily in relation to literacy and the movies. In "The Triumph of the Word: Literacy as Salvation and Commodity," we take a different look at these kinds of movies. The triumph of literacy—and the problems of illiteracy—have been dominant themes in a wide array of films over the years, including *Educating Rita* (1983), *Il Postino* (1994), *The Dead Poets' Society* (1989), *Dangerous Minds* (1995), and *My Big Fat Greek Wedding* (2002), to name only a few. Triumph-of-literacy films usually convey the message that literacy results in positive developments such as political empower-

Literacy in everyday life, literacy on the screen 17

ment, social mobility, material gain, moral enlightenment, and individual agency. Such messages can make such movies appealing to many writing teachers, because they echo the meta-narratives that permeate literacy education from kindergarten through college. Scholars such as historian Harvey Graff (1987) are critical of unhistoricized and unproblematized representations of literacy that portray it as being value-neutral, as always beneficial, and as being simple to learn, for example. Triumph-of-literacy films often reinforce the "myth" that literacy is an autonomous set of skills that one can, and should, adopt to join the dominant culture.

In the concluding chapter, "Life is Not Like the Movies (Or Is it?): Literacy on Film and in Our Lives," we pull together some ideas about literacy that we have seen consistently throughout the films we have studied. In addition, we turn from the movie screen to the classroom and beyond, to discuss the implications of paying attention to the representations of literacy practices in popular culture.

As we watch movies, we internalize representations of literacy, which, in turn, reinforce how we respond to literacy practices and to ideas about literacy pedagogy when we leave the theatre. If we watch films carefully for who reads and writes, in what settings, and for what social goals, we can see a reflection of the dominant functions and perceptions that shape our conceptions of literacy in our culture. To address such perceptions is not a matter of "bringing" popular culture into the classroom; it has already entered through the front door. Such perceptions influence public debates about literacy instruction, teachers' expectations of what will happen in their classrooms, and certainly students' ideas about what reading and writing should be. Studying the representations of how people read and write in popular culture is an important step toward a better understanding of how contemporary society conceives of and values literacy practices. That in itself is reason enough to settle in and go to the movies.

Part I
Representations of literacy and identity

Samuel L. Jackson in Changing Lanes (2002). ©Paramount/Everett Collection.

2 The pragmatic and the sentimental
Literacy and gender roles

In her memoir of growing up in New York and New Jersey in the 1940s and 1950s, Louise DeSalvo (1996) reflects on her life at the age of sixteen by recalling a film that had obsessed her at the time—Alfred Hitchcock's *Vertigo* (1958). DeSalvo writes that she and her friends went to the movies every Saturday, no matter what was showing, not to see the movies, but simply to hang out with girlfriends and to meet boys (170). *Vertigo* was different from other films for her. Its story of passion and betrayal mesmerized DeSalvo, and she felt compelled to watch the movie over and over—eight times in one week. "I have to watch this movie closely," she recalls thinking. "Maybe it has something to tell me" (177). For the young DeSalvo, the film reflects tangled choices facing her in her own life. For the mature DeSalvo, *Vertigo* provides a glimpse into the beginnings of her life as a writer, showing the conflicting demands and dizzying emotions that the practice of writing helped her to address. The film even contributes its name to the title of De Salvo's memoir.

Whether or not our experiences have been as intense or compulsive as the one De Salvo describes, most of us could, like her, reveal a great deal about ourselves by reminiscing about identifications we recall in our lives as filmgoers. We could list movies that we have watched over and over for one reason or another. We could reminisce about characters that we wished we could be like, talk about the vivid scenes we can still remember because they horrified us or delighted us, and quote bits of dialogue that have seeped into our everyday conversations, like "Go ahead, make my day," or "I don't think we're in Kansas any more." Our film autobiographies would undoubtedly have a lot to tell us about the identities we have forged for ourselves, about how we live our lives as blacks or whites, as upper class or working class, and as men or women.

Today the concept of identity, including gender, "is operating," in the words of Stuart Hall (1996), "'under erasure' in the interval between reversal and emergence; an idea which cannot be thought in the old way, but without which certain key questions cannot be thought at all" (2). The reemergence of feminism and the development of film studies as a discipline have coincided with the groundswell of theorizing that questions of the

22 *Popular culture and representations of literacy*

"old way" of thinking about identity and crosses virtually all intellectual fields. The "old way" assumes that individual identity could be defined in terms of a core, or essence, that remains always the same, is always stable and is always "identical" to itself across time and place. The "old way" conceives of identity as something we are born with that then receives an overlay of social and cultural elaboration, resting upon it more or less like a suit of clothing: culture is added, and underneath we assume there is something we might be able to discover through introspection. Today, however, theorists argue that identities are produced only *within* culture, not prior to it. According to various postmodern theories, identity no longer has an essential content, but is defined instead as a "subject position" produced by a tangle of social discourses, a slot available for us to fill. What does it mean to "be a man" or to be "a woman"? The meaning of "masculinity" and "femininity" is not innate and is never fixed, but is defined by an ever-ongoing series of discursive negotiations that change across cultures and across history.

As Stuart Hall's comment indicates, however, we still need to hold on to identity as a concept; even though it has been "erased" by our denial that it has any real content apart from its construction within social discourses, identity is still a powerful organizer of social realities. Gender, race, nationality, and class, to name only the most salient identities, still operate to categorize individuals within hierarchies of power. Feminists argue, for example, that patriarchy is a political system—though unnamed—that works to separate people along gender lines into those who count as full citizens—persons within the body politic—and those who do not. As far as literacy is concerned, one of the most striking differences between males and females may be the discrepancy between literacy rates among men and women. In global terms, women are more likely than men to be categorized as illiterate (Ramdas 1989), and in the most impoverished communities, girls are more likely than boys to leave school at a young age or not to attend school at all (631). Beyond this very broad, fundamental distinction, though, literacy researchers also know that the purposes of literacy, technologies of literacy, and sites of literacy can be marked according to gender. Girls and boys, and women and men engage with different genres of reading and writing, value different purposes for reading and writing, and perform differently in assessments of literacy. Relinquishing the concept of identity altogether would leave us at a kind of impasse, and make it impossible to study these gendered differences that are so important for us to consider.

This chapter, which is concerned with gender in relation to literacy, and the next two chapters, which are concerned with literacy in relation to class and race, are situated within that "interval between reversal and emergence" that Hall describes. One reason it is important to stress this "erased" nature of the concept of identity is that it shifts the nature of what we are looking at—gender, in this case—from a static object to a dynamic *process.* Conceiving of identity in terms of socially or discursively constructed categories has pressured theorists to explain the process by which individuals come to assume identities and to form an individual sense of self—to identify themselves and to act as male or female. The general concept of identification, as theorized in "Ideology and Ideological State Apparatuses," an influential essay by Louis Althusser (1971), is that identities are presented to individuals who then respond to these "calls." From the moment they are born, individuals are "called" or "invited" through material practices to identify with the socially constructed categories of identity—to *become* masculine or feminine, for example. How identification really works, according to Hall, is still an open question, though it is being addressed by many theorists. But the idea of identification recognizes identity as a dynamic process of continually becoming, rather than a static matter of simply being.

Representation has assumed a new importance in postmodern theories of identity, because representation in its many guises does the cultural work of negotiating the meanings of social categories like race, gender, or class at any particular time and place—of inviting identification. In traditional conceptions, representation—the image or narrative, or even language itself—is conceived as being a copy, or mirror, of an original that exists "in the world." According to this traditional conception, the value of a mimetic representation lies in its ability to evoke an original. But in current constuctivist conceptions of representation, the relationship between the representation and "reality" changes. Constructivist theorists argue that meaning does not exist outside of language or representation; rather, meaning is made within the process of representation itself. Images of men or women, for example, are not simply mirrors of a fixed set of values that exist in culture. As feminist critic Teresa de Lauretis (1987) writes, "The representation of gender *is* its construction" (3).

In this chapter, we draw on the theories of representation and identification that inform film criticism and cultural studies to consider how literacy practices and events are represented as gendered actions in the movies. Like gender itself, literacy is not foregrounded in most films, but appears without fanfare in the course of film narratives. On one hand, literacy events are employed to further the narrative action and to disclose aspects of character, including gender identities; film narratives, on the other hand, inflect the meaning of each scene of literacy.

IMAGES OF WOMEN AND MEN IN THE MOVIES

Representations in popular culture can take innumerable forms: narratives in films, novels, and television series; visual representations in advertisements, paintings, and magazine covers, and fashion, to name only a few. Feminists quickly recognized film as a powerful medium for producing

24 Popular culture and representations of literacy

and circulating representations of masculinity and femininity, and gender theory has been very strongly intertwined with film theory since the first resurgence of the feminist movement in the late 1960s and early 1970s. Criticism of film representations of women has been very productive for feminist theorists, and feminist criticism has shaped and influenced the development of film studies. Film lends itself naturally to feminist critique; one of the most marked differences between what it has meant to "be a man" and to "be a woman" in Western culture has been visual, after all. A simplistic distinction between the sexes has been that men are expected to *do* and to *act*, while women are expected to *be*, and to *be looked at*. Hollywood films put the bodies of actors on display, especially female bodies.

Feminist film critics first sought to show that the images of women presented in movies for entertainment were ideological products, implicated in the system of patriarchy—that they were visions of women produced by men for consumption by men (Byars 1991). Feminist critics interrogated the portrayals of women in popular movies to dismantle the idea that film representations of women were "natural." They scrutinized the production and distribution of films and analyzed film images as visual texts to show the constructedness of these representations. Feminist film theorists also developed film theories tracing "the gaze" as it functioned to create the film image, as a dynamic within films that show characters in the act of looking and being looked at; and as a dynamic functioning in audiences viewing the film (Byars 1991, 34).

Connections between gender and literacy have also been the focus of research since the 1970s. Feminist scholars and compositionists have produced a complex body of theory and research on women and writing. One approach, initiated in the work of Sandra Gilbert and Susan Grubar (1979), has been to study how gender operates through textuality, for example, by observing that the authorship of certain public genres has been traditionally limited to men. Another approach attempts to address whether there are definable differences (socially constructed or not) in the ways that women and men compose texts (Chodorow 1978; Belenky, et. al. 1986; Gilligan 1982). If some privileged genres of linear, objective expository writing are defined as "male," for example, female writers might find it more difficult to produce this kind of prose. Some theorists, like Helene Cixous (1975) and Susan Griffin (1982), argue that women compose texts in new forms in order to use writing itself as a means to intervene in patriarchal structures of gender encoded in texts and language. Most of the research on gender and writing has been driven by the desire to undermine a system of male dominance, but new work also studies the literacies of boys. In a recent book, *Misreading Masculinity*, Thomas Newkirk (2002) has argued that the predilections boys bring with them into the classroom are often at odds with the curriculum acceptable in schools, and this may be hurting their growth as readers and writers.

The pragmatic and the sentimental   25

Gender is such a fundamental social category that it is impossible for any film not to represent it consciously or unconsciously, explicitly or implicitly. The study of gender representation in film has broadened with the evolution of film studies as a discipline and the adoption of cultural studies approaches to reading film. Interest in the construction of masculine identities, and theorizing gay and lesbian film and film identities have been added to feminists' initial concern with the objectification of women. Gender is represented and can be read on a number of different levels in relation to film. Movie genres themselves are often identified as being intended for male or female audiences (hence the so-called "chick flick"). Sometimes, as in *Tootsie* (1982), *Thelma and Louise* (1991), or *Boys Don't Cry* (1999), movies consciously focus on gender as a social issue. Finally, gender is always represented in movies through relationships among the characters, narrative development, and visual presentation, which in itself can be richly layered and complex. Film actors are carefully selected in part for their appearance, and their bodies can be further manipulated to portray a gender ideal by dieting, body building, surgery, make-up, and wardrobe. Film techniques themselves, such as lighting, camera angle, and the framing of shots are also used to sculpt the images of "maleness" and "femaleness" that appear on the movie screen.

Our premise in this book is that popular representations of literacy—in film, in this case—can influence what we think we are doing when we are reading and writing, inside and outside of the classroom. In the vast majority of Hollywood films, however, neither gender nor literacy is very likely to appear as an explicit theme. Popular films rarely address, or even refer to the most fundamental issue of literacy, that is, to both men's and women's lack of access to literacy. When images of illiteracy or low literacy do turn up in the movies, they are commonly framed in terms of class or race, rather than gender (*Shawshank Redemption* (1994), *Dangerous Minds* (1995), *Stanley and Iris* (1990), *Il Postino* (1994)). Occasionally, however, movies do deal with differences in men's and women's access to higher education. The most memorable of these films in the minds of most people may be *Educating Rita* (1983), the story of an emotionally bankrupt university professor (Michael Caine) and a female student (Julie Walters). More recently, *Legally Blonde* (2001) appropriates negative stereotypes of women and constructs a narrative that turns the stereotypes on their heads: the woman's (supposedly limited) intellectual capacities and (supposedly limited) interest in public issues are triumphant in a realm in which they would, under ordinary circumstances, never succeed. In *Legally Blonde*, Elle Woods (Reese Witherspoon), a Barbie-like caricature of feminine literacies and aspirations, confounds all expectations by getting herself accepted into that bastion of male privilege, Harvard Law School. Expert in beauty treatments, shopping, and social protocol, and emotionally subsumed by the relationship she has with her boyfriend, Elle is able to find ways to valorize what the film defines as "women's ways of

26 Popular culture and representations of literacy

knowing" in order to be successful in a masculinized world. The humor in *Legally Blonde* is generated by exploiting gendered differences in literacy and by acknowledging the unequal access those differences create for women to attend elite institutions and to have the powerful careers schools like this make possible. *Educating Rita* and *Legally Blonde* place gender and literacy at the center of the narrative, but the films are unusual in this respect.

In the following section, we proceed inductively, analyzing images of situated literacy in a single film, *As Good As It Gets* (1997), and making general inferences about what the images reveal about literacy imagined as a set of practices that are gendered.

IMAGES OF LITERACY AND GENDER

A romantic comedy that came out in 1997, *As Good As It Gets* stars Jack Nicholson and Helen Hunt. It was nominated for several Oscar awards, and won in two categories: Best Actor in a Leading Role and Best Actress in a Leading Role. Nicholson plays Melvin Udall, a successful writer of romance novels. Melvin is wealthy but socially isolated, a truly unlikable character who is portrayed as a misogynist, a racist, and a homophobe, besides being unkind to animals. He suffers from Obsessive Compulsive Disorder but refuses to take his medication, and he locks himself into his apartment to write. Hunt plays Carol Connelly, a waitress in the restaurant that Melvin patronizes. She is the only employee at the restaurant who is tough enough and direct enough to deal with Melvin's frequently offensive behavior. Carol is a single mother struggling to care for her son, who has a serious case of asthma. When her son's illness causes Carol to miss work, Melvin pays to get him good medical treatment. Melvin's good deed, however, is motivated only by his selfish desire to ensure that Carol will always be available to wait on him at the restaurant. Through an uneasy series of events, mediated for the most part by Melvin's neighbor, Melvin and Carol forge a tentative relationship that appears to be as close as either of them is able to get to romance.

As Good As It Gets implicitly engages with gender representations as it appears to struggle to redefine what it means to be a white male in a time when whiteness and masculinity have come under concerted attack by feminist and race critics. In Melvin we see the beleaguered core subject of the patriarchal system—a white, middle-aged, middle-class, New York-dwelling male. The casting of Jack Nicholson in this role further exaggerates the masculine identity of the character. Over the course of his career, in such films as *Five Easy Pieces* (1970), *One Flew over the Cuckoo's Nest* (1975), and *Chinatown* (1974), Nicholson has forged a masculine persona that defines a particularly gritty and intractable version of masculinity. In

As Good As It Gets, Melvin's character performs a nasty version, verging on caricature, of the white, Western male as he has come to be seen in the wake of multiculturalism—or perhaps as he may *feel* he is represented by others, once the comforting obliviousness conferred by privilege has been torn away by his critics. Melvin exhibits stagy, outrageous intolerance towards a gay man, a black man, a Panamanian housekeeper, a Jewish couple, and women—in short, towards many identities that have been historically "othered" in Western societies.

Although in reality othering often occurs silently and even unconsciously, and may be difficult for the oppressors themselves to detect, Melvin is vocal and loud in his expression. He gratuitously heaps homophobic insults on his neighbor, Simon, is almost comically terrified of the black art dealer who shows Simon's paintings, and gets a couple to vacate a table he wants in a restaurant by making loud, anti-Semitic pronouncements within their hearing. When a gushing female fan asks Melvin, "How do you write women so well?" he tells her: "I think of a man. Then I take away reason and accountability." The film chronicles the transformation of this man—who gets variously called by other characters "you sick fuck," "you absolute horror of a human being," and "that awful man"—into a more tolerant and more tolerated member of the community.

Melvin's attraction to Carol functions as a catalyst to begin rehabilitating him in his relationships with others. It is because of her that he agrees to drive Simon to see his parents and ask them for money, and it is for her that he pays for medical care for her son. He is shoved unwillingly by threats and coercion into other changes, taking care of Simon's dog while Simon is in the hospital, for example. The dog he had once thrown down the garbage chute becomes Melvin's adoring companion. Simon, who is at first horrified by Melvin, later tells him, "I love you" when Melvin offers him a room to stay in until he is able to get back on his feet after his stay in the hospital. Eventually, even Carol grudgingly starts to think of Melvin as her "boyfriend" even though she had once ridden a bus across town in the middle of the night to tell him that this would never happen.

The focus of *As Good As It Gets* is on the emotional interactions among the characters, not on literacy, but scenes in which people compose texts or read them appear as integral parts of the narrative throughout the film. Images of Melvin at work as an author appear very early, for example, as the film credits are shown, and function to establish Melvin's character. As the scene opens, we hear Melvin voicing the lines of his novel as he composes, savoring each sentimental sentence as it materializes. The leisurely cadence of Melvin's voice is matched by the slow movement of the camera as it pans across the meticulously ordered spaces of the interior of his apartment, past jars of jelly beans separated by color, past unlabeled bottles of water arrayed in perfect alignment, to arrive at a close-up of his face, illuminated by the bluish light of his computer screen. He intones:

28 *Popular culture and representations of literacy*

Somewhere in the dark, she had confessed and he had forgiven.

"This is what you live for," he said. "Two heads on a pillow, where all is approval and there is only the safety of being with each other"...

At last she was able to define love. Love was....love was.....

At this point, Melvin is interrupted by an insistent knock on his apartment door. It is the neighbor, Simon. In the scenes immediately preceding this one, Melvin had pushed Simon's terrier down the garbage disposal chute in their building. When Simon had come searching for his pet, and Melvin had expressed very obviously insincere concern, Simon was prompted to remark witheringly, "You don't love anything, Mr. Melvin."

Now the building superintendent has discovered Simon's dog, and Simon has come to confront Melvin. Although he is guilty of the deed Simon is charging him with, Melvin responds to the interruption with outraged (and outrageous) conviction about the importance of his work, and a very evident sense that writing entitles him to absolute privacy. "Do you realize that I *work* at *home*?" he demands, sidestepping the issue of the abused dog entirely. Melvin insults Simon to reinforce an ultimatum: "Don't knock on this door...not for any reason."

Later in the film we also see Carol at home in *her* apartment, composing a letter to Melvin to thank him for the gift of medical treatment that has brought about such a huge improvement in her son's health and, coincidentally, in her own life, since she is no longer compelled to nurse her son constantly. Carol is with her mother in the kitchen. As the scene opens, we see a page of Carol's handwritten letter, scribbled on lined notebook paper, and we hear Carol's mother exclaiming, "You are *not* still writing that thank-you note!" Carol responds by telling her mother that she has to finish the letter or she'll "go nuts." Carol asks how to spell "conscience," and she continues to work on the sheaf of paper as her mother explains the baby-sitting arrangements she has made so that they can go out. Carol uses the genre of the thank-you note to work out what is to her a complex problem. She recognizes the economy of gift giving but doesn't want to be beholden to Melvin so much that she cannot refuse his attentions. Thank-you notes express appreciation, yet tend to formalize and conventionalize feeling. They also tend to be short, and often are written on a card purchased for the occasion. Carol's letter, however, spills over the boundaries of thank-you note expectations both in volume and sincerity. For her, the thank you note is an available means to clarify her own purposes and meanings in the relationship, and she pushes it to serve her own ends.

As Carol's mother becomes more insistent, Carol stops writing and focuses on their emotionally charged conversation. She confesses that the improvement in her son's health had revealed a sense of emptiness in her own life; once he no longer requires her constant attention, she is forced to recognize that she misses having a man in her life. Annoyed at the intrusion into her letter writing, Carol presses her mother to tell her what it is that

The pragmatic and the sentimental   29

her mother wants. Her mother says, "I want to go out, like people do!" and Carol acquiesces. She stops writing, leaves her son with the baby-sitter, and goes out with her mother.

Comparing these two scenes of Melvin and Carol engaged in writing reveals interesting ways in which composing is defined not only by individual character, but also by various identities, including gender. Take the two spaces in which they are writing, for example. Both are similar in that they are at home, inside of their apartments. In this respect, both writing spaces can be defined as private, not public. But other differences tend to reinscribe a public/ private separation of the genders. Even though Melvin is at home when he is writing, his being in the apartment has been represented as pathological in the film when he is shown obsessively locking his apartment door five times exactly before sitting down to write. Furthermore, as a space, Melvin's apartment doesn't bear out the emotional or social connotations of the private domain, because he seems to lack the ability to form friendships or any kind of intimate relationship (even with Simon's pet dog). In fact, in terms of economic production, Melvin's apartment, especially his office, might more appropriately be seen as a public space, because he is writing a commercial work for public consumption. He composes on a computer in a room set aside for his work. Melvin feels entitled to react angrily when he is interrupted by personal matters forcing themselves into his workspace—which happens to be at home—and hampering his work—which happens to be writing.

Carol, on the other hand, is writing not in a room that is not specially designated for composing, but on a space she has cleared on the kitchen table. She writes by hand on lined notebook paper that she might have taken from her son's school supplies. She is writing a personal letter, not a text for which she will be paid. She is motivated by emotion, not just because of her own feelings, but out of love for her son. Unlike Melvin, whose sterile environment and antisocial actions contrast with the intimate scene he is describing, Carol appears to be emotionally caught up in what she is trying to say. She is ambivalent in her feelings of gratitude towards Melvin, and grapples with the moral issues. She is baffled by the spelling of "conscience," and her list of attempts to spell the word appears on the film screen. Besides the emotional importance of the letter, Carol's relational connections are indicated visually by the fact that as she writes, three other people appear within the frame of the shot: her mother, standing next to her at the kitchen table, and her son and the baby-sitter, seen in the background, through a doorway.

In terms of the film narrative, each of these scenes develops the characters and the problems they face. The challenge for Melvin's character is to construct a world for himself that contains emotional relationships with other people. The text of Melvin's novel is interesting in terms of gender because it suggests a romance novel—a genre that is predominantly authored by and read by women, not men. Given his character, we would

30 *Popular culture and representations of literacy*

have expected that he would be writing something more identified with males, a spy thriller or hard bitten detective story, perhaps. The contradiction does ironically highlight his emotional isolation, however. He uses writing to isolate himself personally. He also demonstrates a kind of pleasure and satisfaction in the act of writing. He needs, in a sense, to find a way to access the private domain, to allow others to enter his apartment as well as his life. Melvin begins to change as a person when he uses the money he earns as a writer to help Carol's son, and, later, to help Simon.

The challenge for Carol's character is to find a way to live more for herself and what she wants and needs than for others and their needs. For her, writing is shown as an anomalous activity. Her mother sees Carol's struggle with letter writing as problematic, and she succeeds in getting her daughter to stop. Later, when Carol gives her letter to Melvin, he refuses to read it. She forces him to hear what she wants to say by opening the letter and reading it to him out loud in the restaurant, much to his embarrassment. Both the writing and the reading of Carol's letter emerge as evidence of her emotional strength and integrity; reading and writing simply do not appear to be part of what she is expected to do. When she does engage in them, however, it is as part of an activity in which she is assumed to be very competent: personal relationships.

As viewers of *As Good As It Gets*, we easily read how the literacy in scenes like those described further the narrative, since they reveal character and personal issues. Presented as they are, woven into the narrative of the film, the individual literacy events depicted do not pretend to present coherent statements about literacy. They do, however, begin to disclose underlying assumptions about the relation of literacy to gender that appear to be both reflected in and constructed by these film representations. Representations of male characters reading and writing link them to literacy as a powerful commodity. Melvin, a publishing author, is shown writing a novel, an activity for which he receives, we are led to understand, a great deal of money; the doctor who comes to Carol's apartment is shown interpreting and taking action on the little boy's medical records in a way that seems miraculous to Carol and her mother; and Simon's work as an artist, although it is not reading and writing precisely, also shows him engaging in a kind of "composing" that is a public form of production and earns him a living. Representations of women associate them with writing and reading as private, emotionally charged activities. Carol is shown struggling to write the letter to Melvin, and showing the doctor her son's medical reports, and the art gallery assistant is shown reading the bad news very gently to Simon.

Assumptions about gendered differences suggested by images of literacy in *As Good As It Gets* show up again and again across many different films. In *Bridget Jones's Diary* (2001), for example, the two leading male characters are conspicuously associated with public forms of literacy: Daniel Cleaver (Hugh Grant), the successful but unscrupulous head of the pub-

The pragmatic and the sentimental 31

lishing firm where Bridget works, and Mark Darcy (Colin Firth), a human rights lawyer. Bridget Jones (Renee Zellweger) is shown pouring her private thoughts and emotions onto the pages of her diary, which in effect also provides the structure of the film itself. Bridget is also shown at work in the publishing firm, and later as a television interviewer, but in these public domains, her work is portrayed as comic and inept. At the publishing office, for example, we see her carrying on a flirtatious online repartee with her boss on the subject of her miniskirt. As for the television interviews, they work to reinforce her persona as an endearing and somewhat neurotic introvert, not to show her as a competent producer of public knowledge. In *You've Got Mail* (1998), to cite another popular film, Joe Fox (Tom Hanks) is an ambitious owner of a giant chain of retail bookstores. Kathleen Kelly (Meg Ryan) owns a very small, service-oriented bookstore that is put out of business when Fox's company builds a new store in the neighborhood. The two characters, who are enemies in public life, engage in an anonymous online romance, and in this arena the woman is "successful." As Kathleen and Joe communicate through instant messaging, the film visually quotes the computer screen, as is often the case when films represent computer-generated texts.

Diaries and journals figure again and again in association with female characters. In *Girl Interrupted* (1999) Susanna Kaysen (Winona Rider) uses the pages of her diary as a place to make sense of her life inside a mental hospital. In a pivotal scene, other inmates steal her diary and read it out loud. In the action film *Man on Fire* (2004), a little girl living in Mexico City (Dakota Fanning) is in danger of being kidnapped, and Creasy (Denzel Washington) is hired to be her bodyguard. She keeps a little pink diary. When the girl does get kidnapped, Creasy uses her diary to find a clue that sends him on a rampage of investigation and killing to retrieve her. In a final scene, Creasy arranges an exchange with the kidnappers. He meets the little girl on a bridge and returns the diary to her, as if to restore her life and innocence. Then she runs into the arms of her mother as he heads in the opposite direction, towards almost certain death.

It is rare, on the other hand, to see male characters in films keeping personal diaries, or for film narratives to exploit diaries to define male identity, as they do for female characters in the examples presented above. Occasionally, we may be shown a male character keeping a scientific log, like the naturalist (Paul Bettany) on board the ship in *Master and Commander: The Far Side of the World* (2003) who, Darwin-like, records his observations of the exotic specimens he has collected. Diaries in a male hand even get horribly pathologized in *Se7en* (1995), where they show up in the form of meticulous records kept by a demented serial killer (Kevin Spacey), who chooses his murder victims based on the ways they exemplify the seven deadly sins. The killer is never shown in the act of writing, but when the detectives stumble upon a wall of bookcases filled with row after row of

32   *Popular culture and representations of literacy*

cheap composition notebooks containing his minutely-observed thoughts, the scene thrills with a special kind of horror.

Even when male characters are playing out emotional dramas, films still tend to show them engaging with literacy not in private, but in public, sometimes ironic, ways. When Jonathan Trager (John Cusack) in *Serendipity* (2001) is trying to track down the woman he is sure he is in love with, for example, he is shown researching credit card receipts in a cavernous vault, and he employs the fact finding service of the *New York Times*. Jonathan's best friend (Jeremy Piven), who works as an obituary writer for the *Times*, supports him in a difficult decision not by telling him how he feels, or even by writing an earnest letter, but by writing a mock obituary praising Jonathan's character for the choices he "made" in his life.

When women play characters who are successful professional authors, films still often portray them engaging in literacy not as a form of public rhetoric but as a way of expressing emotion and working through problems in personal relationships. Sidda Walker (Sandra Bullock) in *The Divine Secrets of the YaYa Sisterhood* (2002), for example, is a professional playwright, but the plot focuses more on a private process of initiation that enables her to finally say "yes" to a proposal of marriage. Her career as a writer is represented as something of an interference with her personal life, and we are not shown her actually at work on her writing. More recently, and more dramatically, in *Something's Gotta Give* (2003), Erica Barry (Diane Keaton) is a successful, middle-aged playwright, who has an affair with an aging Lothario, Harry Sanborn (Jack Nicholson). When Harry jilts her, Erica is shown working through her private grief by writing a new play. Scenes of Erica at her computer show her sobbing uncontrollably as she writes, her desktop littered with crumpled tissues. And Carrie Bradshaw, the journalist who is the central character in the television series *Sex in the City*, appears in every episode writing her weekly column in her apartment, often sitting on her bed. The column she writes, of course, like the show itself, explores intimate relationships.

In the end, *As Good As It Gets* is most concerned with the tensions created by the antagonisms of the male protagonist. Melvin changes most in redefining his relationship with Simon, the gay man. Carol acts as a muse for to both Simon and Melvin, and in this sense, she continues to occupy a role that has traditionally been gendered female (a representation of women we discuss further in Chapter Seven). The muse has traditionally been defined as someone who can be both an object of sexual desire and a source of artistic inspiration for a male artist or creator. In Carol, the two muse functions are divided between Melvin, who feels physical desire for her, and Simon, who is inspired artistically by her. Even though Melvin is a writer, we are not given any evidence that his desire for Carol influences his work at all; he only says that Carol moves him to become a better *person*. Simon, as a gay man, is not moved by desire for Carol, but when he is unable to draw or paint after his attack, she inspires him to renewed artistic creativity. In relation to both male characters, Carol remains in the passive role, and does not break into a stronger form of agency.

It shouldn't surprise us as literacy educators to see popular portrayals of literacy as intimate, emotional, and private action for female characters, and as commodified, professional, and rational action for men, nor to see portrayals of literacy that reinforce the gendering of private and public domains. But it has been surprising to see how clearly these literacy events in the mainstream films we have studied both reflect and reinforce markers of power and gender.

CHALLENGING IMAGES OF GENDER AND LITERACY

In the previous section, we observe how popular films reflect and reproduce dominant conceptions of gender in relation to literacy. In this section, we consider a critique of gender and literacy in mainstream movies that appears in *In the Cut* (2003), a film directed by Jane Campion. In terms of literacy and gender, Campion's film is interesting because it presents a scathing critique, not in the form of an essay but in the medium of film itself. *In the Cut* links the silencing of women and violence towards women with many of the features that characterize popular romantic comedies, and it raises the question of how dominant ideas of gender and literacy can be altered within film representations themselves.

In the Cut centers on Frannie Avery (Meg Ryan), an English teacher at an urban campus in New York City. Frannie is working on a book about slang, and the walls of her dingy apartment are papered with notes on which she has collected bits of spoken language or poetry overheard on the street or found in her reading. When a serial murderer strikes in her neighborhood, a homicide detective, Giovanni Malloy (Mark Ruffalo), comes to Frannie's apartment to question her. Malloy later asks Frannie to go out with him, and they begin an affair. But when her own half-sister, Pauline (Jennifer Jason Leigh), is murdered by the serial killer, Frannie begins to suspect Malloy, and she is forced to decide whom to trust in the investigation. In an interview with the BBC, Campion says that the story, based on a novel by Susanna Moore, gave her "an opportunity" to comment on the fact that "women today are dealing with both their independence and also...satisfying the romantic models [they] grew up with," a circumstance that she says "creates enormous amounts of grief" (Applebaum 2003). "Women often postpone their lives," she says, "thinking that if they're not with a partner then it doesn't really count...And as much as we don't discuss that, because its too embarrassing and too sad, I think it really does exist" (Applebaum 2003). One dimension of Campion's treatment of *In the Cut* includes satirizing uncritical representations of relationships and marriage that appear in mainstream films, representations that promote the romantic models that Campion wants to question. *In the Cut* comments on

34 *Popular culture and representations of literacy*

gender roles in mainstream movies, and, through the lead female character, who is a writer and literacy teacher, the film also suggests that these gender roles can limit women's ability to "be articulate."

In the Cut specifically targets *Serendipity* (2001), a frothy romantic comedy that had appeared just a few years earlier, for satirical attack. *Serendipity* is driven by the conceit that encountering a perfect soul mate is a matter of chance, a stroke of luck that will arrive while one is vigorously searching for someone or something else. Jonathan (John Cusack) and Sarah (Kate Beckinsale) meet by accident in New York City, in a department store packed with last-minute holiday shoppers. They go out for coffee and go ice skating in Central Park. As they part, they decide to let fate determine if they will meet again by playing a game: they will write their names and phone numbers on something they release to circulate out in the world. If that information somehow finds its way to the other person, then they will know that they are meant to see each other again. He writes on a five-dollar bill that he uses to buy something at a news kiosk; she writes on the fly leaf of a novel that she sells to a used bookstore. Fate, as mediated by these literacy practices, will either bring them together or keep them apart forever. Nothing happens until five years later, when both of them have become engaged to somebody different, but decide to look for each other one last time before getting married. As events unfold, their engagements to the other people get broken off, the five dollar bill and the novel with the contact information turn up, and Jonathan and Sarah meet again and get married—to each other.

One critic calls *Serendipity* "rotten cotton candy" (Apello 2001), and *In the Cut* is similarly harsh in its condemnation of the roles, identities, and values the film projects. *In the Cut* references and responds to *Serendipity* in a number of ways. Casting Meg Ryan in the role of Frannie serves both to cite the heroines of the sunny, romantic comedies in which she has so often starred before (*When Harry Met Sally* (1989), *French Kiss* (1995), *You've Got Mail* (1998), *Sleepless in Seattle* (1993)) and to intervene in those earlier roles. Both films are set in New York, but the relentless grittiness of cramped apartments, seedy bars, and crowded streets in *In the Cut's* version of the city (described in the official studio synopsis as "the underbelly of lower Manhattan"), is opposed to the sunny, glittery world of Bloomingdale's, The Ritz Carlton, and the chic bistros, bookstores, and boutiques that provide the setting for *Serendipity*.

In the Cut's sharpest attack appears in the gruesome way in which the serial killer in *In the Cut* victimizes women. According to police detective Malloy, the murderer disarms his victims by offering them a diamond ring and proposing marriage, then kills and *disarticulates* them—a forensic term meaning that he severs their heads from their bodies. Frannie's love for language—for *articulation*—stands in juxtaposition to the *disarticulation* that Pauline and the other murder victims suffer. Frannie is fascinated with words, a fascination that keeps her from having the single-minded

The pragmatic and the sentimental 35

focus on marriage that other female characters exhibit. When Detective Malloy notices the scribbled notes on the walls of her apartment, he asks Frannie if studying language is "work or a hobby" for her. "It's a passion," she replies. Frannie appears at work with language in other scenes: teaching students in an English classroom, meeting a student in a café to discuss a paper, and reading students' essays. Through the character of Pauline, Frannie's half sister, *In the Cut* critiques images of women that show them with only one overarching drive: a desire to get married, a traditional narrative for women's characters that films adapted from novels and the theatre. In one scene of the two sisters together in Pauline's apartment, Pauline plays the theme song from *Serendipity* as she confides to Frannie, "I just want to get married." Pauline's yearning for marriage makes it difficult to have a stable life. She cannot control an obsession she feels for her doctor, and she is scheduled to appear in court for stalking him. (She has made eleven doctor appointments in one week and stolen his wife's clothes from the dry cleaner's.) Eventually, Pauline's obsession with marriage makes her vulnerable to the lures held out to her by the serial killer—a ring and a marriage proposal, and she becomes his next victim.

Campion also satirizes the ease with which the lovers in *Serendipity* "know" they are meant for each other (after being together only for a few hours) and throw over their other, more long-standing relationships. "How long does a woman have to know someone before she gets engaged?" detective Malloy muses in *In the Cut* as he works to solve the murders. According to the plot of *Serendipity*, the answer to his question would be "a few hours." In *In the Cut*, Pauline tells Frannie that their father had been engaged to one woman, but instantaneously transferred both his affections and his offer of marriage to her mother after seeing her at an ice skating rink. (He left four years later, and her mother was devastated, Pauline says.) The story of Pauline's parents, filmed as a sepia-toned flashback, also makes fun of the glittering scenes set at the ice skating rink in Central Park that figure so prominently in *Serendipity*. In *Serendipity*, the lovers talk about the stars and have a good laugh together when Sarah falls down. But in the surreal skating scenes of *In the Cut*, things turn ugly; when the woman falls down, the sharp blades of the man's skates slice through her limbs.

Another important way that *In the Cut* responds to *Serendipity* is through the thematic role it gives to Virginia Woolf's (1927) novel *To the Lighthouse*. A scene of Frannie in her English classroom shows her leading a discussion of *To the Lighthouse*, and a drawing of a lighthouse on the blackboard visually emphasizes its importance. When Frannie asks the class what they think of the work, one student says that nothing really happens in the book; all that happens is that "one old lady dies," as he puts it.

> "How many ladies have to die to make it good?" Frannie asks acidly, and the student replies, without irony, "At least three."

36   *Popular culture and representations of literacy*

Later, when the killer wants to take Frannie to a place where they will not be discovered, he takes her to a secluded lighthouse. She kills him and escapes. In Campion's film, *To the Lighthouse* acts as a counterpart to a novel that plays a similar thematic role in *Serendipity*: Gabriel Garcia Marquez's *Love in the Time of Cholera* (1997). Both works deal with love and relationships, but approach the subject from very different, highly gendered perspectives. *Love in the Time of Cholera* centers on the male character of Forentino Ariza, and the structure of the novel can be characterized as "male" in the sense that it progresses, like the great nineteenth century European novels, forward through a singular, unidirectional time to its resolution. Virginia Woolf, on the other hand, labored in *To the Lighthouse* and other works to create a narrative structure—and even a sentence structure—that she felt could represent female consciousness. The novel centers on the character of Mrs. Ramsay, and devotes the greatest part of the narrative to a single, ordinary day in her life. It foregrounds individual consciousness, experience, and relationship, and only mentions events like the death of Mrs. Ramsay and two of her children in parenthetical asides of a single sentence. Woolf's novel questions the necessity of marriage, and in the unbalanced relationship of Mr. and Mrs. Ramsay, she "gives, gives, gives" and he "takes, takes, takes."

Love in the Time of Cholera is extravagantly romantic in its devotion to the idea that for the hero there is only one woman that he can truly love. The hero's devotion to one woman throughout his a lifetime, and the long postponement of the consummation of his love loosely inform the plot of *Serendipity*. The sumptuous passion and narrative opulence of the novel get watered down considerably in the film, however. *Love in the Time of Cholera* is pervaded by a sense that human emotions and relationships are much more mysterious and more spectacularly diverse than we imagine, and it rather shockingly challenges conventional views about the youthfulness of romantic feelings. While gesturing towards Garcia Marquez's work, *Serendipity* stays in safer, more conventional territory: the lovers do wait a few years, but they are still young when they get married. In the novel, the love the hero feels clearly arises out of his own capacity for passion; the object of his affection does not "cause" or "deserve" it because of her beauty or any other qualities. In *Serendipity*, on the contrary, the focus shifts to questions of whether the objects of desire are "real" or "fake" soul mates, questions that get echoed in plot devices like a mix-up between a real and an imitation Prada wallet.

In the Cut implies that males and females both need to create more balanced roles, and by presenting two sets of paired relationships, it suggests that male and female characters must negotiate a range of choices as they relate to each other. The range of choices for the female characters emerges through Frannie, who is able to escape the murderer, and her sister Pauline, who becomes a victim. The range of choices for male characters is represented in Detective Malloy, who wants to date Frannie, and his police

The pragmatic and the sentimental 37

partner, who wants to kill her. When Frannie borrows Pauline's clothes and becomes more sexually aggressive, she adopts some aspects of her sister's character, but not to the same unhealthy degree. Frannie is willing to enter into the relationship with Malloy, but it threatens her ability to keep her head and her body connected—literally and figuratively. Through a mistake in judgment, she does fall into the killer's hands, and is in danger of meeting the same fate as her sister. She had suspected Malloy, but finds out too late that it is his partner on the police force, not he, who is the killer. Ironically, when Frannie borrows Malloy's coat and gun and uses them to save herself from the murderer, she also adopts some aspects of the male character. Malloy, on the other hand, who can't protect her because he is locked in Frannie's apartment, says that he "Feels like a chick."

In the Cut failed rather spectacularly in the box office. Although it starred a famous Hollywood actress and was distributed in mainstream movie houses, *In the Cut* is really an art-house film, not a product of the Hollywood movie industry. The film is categorized as a thriller, but strays too far outside of genre expectations, making this movie very difficult to read as a piece of entertainment. The original backers, who expected that the film would be "like *Se7en* (1995)" (a stylish but gruesome thriller about a serial killer that garnered a great deal of attention when it was released) withdrew their support when they realized that Campion's vision differed from theirs. Campion explains: "I realized that for me the genre was of no value unless it was working for me rather than me working for it. So I kept saying, 'I want it to be a relationship-based story first,' and they didn't" (Applebaum).

Campion's anecdote discloses the real constraints that work to regulate film images and meanings, including representations of gender roles and of literacy. Countering representations within the dominant culture, as bell hooks (1994) argues in *Outlaw Culture: Resisting Representations*, demands learning "to do everything differently" (7). "Decolonizing our minds and imaginations, we learn to think differently, to see everything with 'the new eyes' Malcolm X told us we needed if we were to enter the struggle as subjects and not objects," hooks writes (6). She warns that it is easy to underestimate the difficulty of learning to do things differently, and easy to overestimate the transgressiveness of some works. Of the documentary film *Paris Is Burning* (1990), for example, she writes: "Even though the subject matter *appears* radical, it doesn't necessarily mean it's radical. Just to portray marginalized black gay subculture is not necessarily to be giving a portrait of subversion and oppositional life. One has to question more deeply what authentic terms of opposition might mean for any of us in our lives" (220). In *In the Cut*, Campion attempts a radical critique of conventional representations of gender and literacy, reworking them in the language of film itself. Because the makers of *Serendipity* focused on creating a fiction that would sell, the film doesn't violate received expectations, and their movie was, in financial terms, much more successful than *In the Cut*.

38 *Popular culture and representations of literacy*

USING LITERACY FOR CRITICAL ACTION

In this chapter, we have argued that in mainstream movies, the performance of literacy often serves as a marker for gender, and conventional gender roles also trump the possibilities for practicing literacy available to film characters. Male characters, for example, are shooed or shamed away from writing for personal or expressive ends, or even from writing and reading at all. Female characters are shooed or shamed away from writing for academic or other public purposes. The image on the cover of the DVD for *Ice Princess* (2005), a movie about a teenaged girl who becomes an ice skating champion, is divided into two halves: on one side is the image of a studious-looking girl carrying books and wearing glasses; on the other side is the sequin-spangled image of a figure skater—without glasses. The caption reads "From Scholastic...to Fantastic!" Even a film such as *Legally Blonde* (2001), which is funny because of its fluffy challenge to a masculine institution, does not transgress conventional gender expectations. The main character, Elle Woods (Reese Witherspoon), exploits her high-powered drive to master her image through clothes, workouts, and beauty treatments, but never questions conventional expectations or parameters of dominant ideas of what it means to be "female." In the end, she finds a newer, better boyfriend in graduate school and gets engaged to be married, affirming the dominant narrative.

But the vast world of the movies isn't entirely monolithic, and it isn't impossible to encounter images of female characters who use literacy for critical ends. We'll close this chapter with an example of a film character represented using literacy in a critical way. It appears near the end of *Million Dollar Baby,* the acclaimed 2004 picture directed by Clint Eastwood, when Maggie (Hillary Swank), a boxer who has been left paralyzed after a fight, refuses to sign a document that would cede control of her wealth to her mother and other members of her family. Unable to use her arms, Maggie holds the pen in her teeth as her family watches expectantly, and then drops the pen without using it. It is the only time we see her reading or writing, but in this brief, moving scene, literacy is summoned to enact a pivotal moment in the growth of Maggie's character and in the development of the story. Her action—or better said, her refusal to act according to expectations—is meaningful within the layered context in which it takes place, a context that includes the legal practices of composing and signing documents, as well as social relationships of family, class, and gender.

In a dirt-poor hard-scrabble life, boxing has given Maggie a way to accomplish something meaningful with the resources that she has available: heart and muscle. As stories dramatizing class or race struggle, (*On the Waterfront* (1954), *Ali* (2001), or *Cinderella Man* (2005)) boxing dramas are already a genre of their own. But in *Million Dollar Baby*, Maggie also fights against the confines of gender stereotypes. In the male-dominated world of boxing, it is very hard for her to persuade even a more or less

The pragmatic and the sentimental 39

washed-up trainer to work with "a girl." When Maggie does start to win fights and to make money in the ring, her first impulse is to buy her mother a house and to contribute support to her family. Her family's response, however, makes it clear that they don't value her or her work as a boxer, and her mother doesn't appreciate the gift. The person Maggie wants to be as a fighter creates a painful tension with the person she has always been as a poor, powerless woman in the eyes of others, including her own family.

Literacy is represented as a form of critical action in *Million Dollar Baby* in the moment when Maggie drops the pen. At issue is not whether Maggie knows how to read or write, how her level of literacy achievement may be measured, or even whether she is able to read or understand the poetry of Yeats that fascinates her trainer. What is important, rather, is that she is able to act critically within this very specific context. When she refuses to sign the document, Maggie is able to claim her own power as a person, ironically, as she lies immobilized in a nursing home, and do so even more completely than she could when she was bursting with physicality in the boxing ring.

3 Who's allowed to read and write? Literacy and social class

Since the Industrial Revolution, literacy has often been linked to economic development and prosperity. From childhood on, we are told by the social institutions that shape our culture that literacy is a key to the door that leads to a better job, economic comfort, and social mobility. Numerous reports from governments, school, and non-profit organizations echo the position of one literacy advocacy organization: "There are very few jobs available to those with poor reading, writing, and math skills" (ProLiteracy America 2003, 7). The same organization proclaims that "literacy education is a win-win situation for employees and employers. The programs help adults learn job skills, get jobs, and increase their earnings. They help employers gain more effective and more productive employees" (10). Such a definition is what Sylvia Scribner (1984) has called the metaphor of "literacy as adaptation" or a "functional literacy" necessary to undertake the tasks of daily life. As Scribner writes, "This concept has a strong commonsense appeal. The necessity for literacy skills in daily life is obvious; on the job, riding around town, shopping for groceries, we all encounter situations requiring us to read or produce written symbols" (37). Learn to read and write, and you can get a job. Learn to read and write well, and you can move up the professional and social ladder.

This model of literacy as a key for economic empowerment shows up in many films. From *Educating Rita* (1983) to *Stanley and Iris* (1990) to *Dangerous Minds* (1995) literacy is held out to characters as a lure and a promise of material gain. Implicit in this narrative of literacy is the promise that with a better job and more money will come social mobility. Economic status will translate into social class, and the people who read and write themselves into better jobs will be able to move up the class ladder, or at least move their children up. In early scenes in *Working Girl* (1988), for example, we see Tess (Melanie Griffith), though working as a secretary, is always carrying with her books about management or corporate finance as she tries to break into the executive class. We see her unpacking the books at her desk when she starts a new job, or reading late at night on the ferry from Manhattan to Staten Island. When one executive voices surprise at the extent of her knowledge, Tess replies, "I read a lot of things. You never know

42 *Popular culture and representations of literacy*

where the big ideas are going to come from." By the end of the film, Tess has used her literacy practices to gain a position as a corporate executive.

The opportunity for economic and social mobility is one of the most unshakeable and deeply ingrained myths of U.S. culture. Work hard enough, be smart and savvy enough, and nothing can stop you from making a fortune and becoming a person of substance. Economic success in the United States is considered to result from a person's embrace of such central ideological concepts as individualism, self-sufficiency, perseverance, and innovation. These words and the market capitalist ideology they reflect continue to resonate with people in the United States, as the speeches of any presidential candidate will quickly illustrate. There is just enough truth to this mythology, as illustrated in individual life stories from Andrew Carnegie to Bill Gates, to reinforce it in the culture.

Mainstream U.S. movies, as part of that culture, can be expected to reproduce this mythology and its familiar narratives decade after decade. Many films about working-class characters are dominated by the ideology of individual liberalism and narrative of success through hard work, including such recent favorites as *Erin Brokovitch* (2001). Though there are other films, rarer and usually less well known, that address class structures and identities in more systemic ways, such as *Matewan* (1987) and *Norma Rae* (1979), as John Bodnar (2003, xxii) notes, even in Hollywood films that deal in some way with issues of social class, the specific politics or ideological position of the films often take a back seat to stories of individual desire and relationships.

> In other words, the narrative form ruled rather than any one politicized version of reality. This would mean that you could have films in all decades that could take up or rearrange various political viewpoints; however seldom did they stray from the plight of the individual protagonist.

What is true for social class in film in general is true for representations of literacy and social class in particular. Though such representations are complex and occasionally critique existing social structures, in general the narratives and ideology reinforce concepts of individual liberalism and the narrative of success through hard work. Even those cultural positions are usually subsumed in the larger narratives of individual desires and personal relationships. (The representations in film of the "triumph of literacy" both in economic and personal terms will be the focus of Chapter Eight.) Yet even in films that focus on the individual and his or her plight, the representations of literacy practices often mark and reinforce existing notions and systems of social class.

If literacy can act as a key to the door of social and economic mobility, it can also act as the lock that reinforces class status and marks class distinctions. As Street (2001) and Barton and Hamilton (1998) have argued, literacy, as a function of culture and ideology, is always contextual and

Who's allowed to read and write? Literacy and social class   43

always inextricable from issues of history, hierarchies, and power. Simply learning to read and write will not guarantee a good job or social mobility any more than learning to drive a car or play a guitar. While government and institutional reports focus on "functional" literacies as a means of economic empowerment, social mobility and class status turn more often on the social contexts that shape literacy practices. Literacy practices, "straddle the distinction between individual and social worlds and literacy practices are more usefully understood as existing in the relations between people, within groups and communities, rather than as a set of properties residing in individuals" (Barton and Hamilton 1998, 7). Just as these social relations reproduce class distinctions and often reinforce class status, literacy practices and the qualities ascribed to the people enacting those literacy practices often work in the same way. What one reads or writes, in what context, and for what audience, is frequently a subtle way of revealing social bonds and affiliations.

Movies, as cultural texts, reflect and reproduce this capacity of literacy to act as a class marker. In many films, such markers are used as a brief cultural shorthand to establish the class status of a particular character. In the film *Vanilla Sky* (2001) for example, David Aames (Tom Cruise) is introduced to us at the start of the film as the head of an upscale publishing house. His position as a publisher is largely irrelevant to the plot or character development in the film, but gives the character a class status that is both financially and culturally elite, yet distinct from being say a stockbroker or investment banker.

Representations of literacy as a means of exclusion are perhaps less celebrated, but are just as, if not more, prevalent in films as representations of literacy as social mobility. As a brief example, in the romantic comedy *Serendipity* (2001), at an early point in the film, a character pulls a book from her bag on which to write a phone number. Though the character's posh English accent and stylish clothes have already given us ways to read her social class, the book that she produces—*Love in the Time of Cholera* by Gabriel Garcia Marquez, a well-known but still somewhat esoteric winner of the Nobel Prize in Literature—cements for us her class status as a member of an educated elite. We would read her character and social class quite differently if she were to have pulled a Danielle Steele or a Stephen King book or even a work of pop psychology or a cookbook from her bag.

This chapter will use as examples the films *Changing Lanes* (2002), *Catch Me if You Can* (2002), and *Office Space* (1999) to illustrate how literacy is represented as a marker of social class. In these movies, the way class is marked by literacy practices is either enforced by social institutions to frustrate character's aspirations, or used to attribute particular virtues and admirable qualities to characters that allow for blurring social class boundaries.

44 *Popular culture and representations of literacy*

LITERACY AND INSTITUTIONS OF POWER

The definition and display of literacy have been used as a means of establishing some claims to power, and excluding others, almost since the first cuneiform impressions were made in clay. From ancient Egypt through medieval Europe, priests often guarded access to literacy carefully to protect their authority and power. Those who could establish proof of literacy were often afforded special protections or privileges. In medieval England, for example, if a person being tried for murder in a civil court and facing possible execution could prove he was literate by reading a religious text in Latin, he could be turned over to the liturgical courts for more lenient treatment (Kendall 2005). With the rise of the nation-state government, authorities have often used "tests" of literacy as methods of denying access to power of non-elites. In the United States, for example, literacy tests were used in the twentieth century as processes for denying immigrants entry to the country and for denying African Americans the right to vote.

When discussing literacy and social class, it is necessary to think about how literacy operates within power and discourse. If, as Foucault (1972) would argue, discourse simultaneously represents our knowledge about a concept in a specific historical context and defines and produces our knowledge, it necessarily constructs how such concepts are practiced in the culture. Discourse and knowledge, and the way knowledge is both discussed and applied, are used to determine what is "normal" or "true," and to define others as abnormal, and regulate and marginalize their activities.

Conceptions of literacy are part of this system of power and knowledge. Like other elements of culture, literacy is defined and sustained within a culture's texts, artifacts, images, social practices, and institutions. Though the definition of literacy will vary across historical periods with shifts in forms and social practices of knowledge, each culture will define literacy in ways that sustain the power and authority of its moral, legal, educational, and economic discourses and institutions. Of course, this does not mean that there is a central controlling power defining literacy for the culture, but that discourse produces webs of knowledge and power that sustain such dominant definitions as reflecting a true and common perception of values and practices.

In the film *Changing Lanes* (2002), literacy is played out as a function of power and knowledge that is supported and enforced by some of the dominant institutions (legal, educational, and financial) in the culture. These institutional definitions of literacy act explicitly on the characters to reveal and reinforce their class status. At certain points in the film the two main characters encounter similar literacy events in legal, financial, or educational institutions, but their different class positions ensure different outcomes.

The plot of the movie is relatively simple (and farfetched). Gavin Banek (Ben Affleck), a Wall Street lawyer, must deliver in court a power of appointment, signed by a recently deceased philanthropist and giving the financial

Who's allowed to read and write? Literacy and social class 45

control of a charitable foundation to the senior partners in Banek's law firm. Doyle Gipson (Samuel L. Jackson) is a telephone service operator for an insurance company and a recovering alcoholic, who must testify in family court in a custody dispute with his ex-wife. Banek works in a modern, professionally decorated law office, while Gipson, reflecting the working conditions of many of the modern working class, works in a loud, large room full of people talking on telephones under the glare of fluorescent lights. As both characters drive toward the courthouse, each afraid he will be late for his court date, their cars collide, leaving Gipson's car disabled. In the ensuing confusion after the accident, Banek drops the file with the power of appointment out of his briefcase, and, in his haste to get to the courthouse, leaves the scene of the accident, leaving Gipson stranded on the highway, but in possession of the file. Banek reaches his court date without the crucial document, and Gipson eventually reaches the courthouse too late for his custody hearing. The rest of the film involves an escalating series of actions by each man to harass or punish the other, Banek in pursuit of the file, Gipson in revenge for losing his custody case. In true Hollywood fashion, however, each man sees the error of his ways by the end of the film; Gipson is reunited with his family and Banek ends the film vowing to use his power as a lawyer to do good in the world.

From our point of view, however, what is intriguing in this film is not the preposterous plot or ham-fisted dialogue, but the way literacy and class are represented. At several points in the movie, it becomes clear that what matters is not the papers either man has in his hand or his ability to read those papers. Instead what matters is who has the papers and how that person is read, in terms of class and power, by the institutions that support and define literacy. In this way the film offers a compelling example of Foucault's (1972) contention that the production of knowledge is always entwined with issues of power and the body, and the body is read and defined by institutions.

A striking example of this comes early in the film, after the accident, when both men arrive at the courthouse. We see Banek in his crisp, tailored gray suit, walk through the lobby, unhindered by authority, and enter a quiet probate courtroom with subdued lighting and light paneling on the walls. The courtroom is large and mostly empty, and the people in it are all some distance from each other, separated by tables and railings. Everyone in the room is well dressed in conventional suits, and all are speaking standardized, middle-class English. The scene is shot primarily in medium to long shots that emphasize a sense of detachment of the characters from each other, and of the audience from the characters. The judge, though concerned about Banek's tardiness, is solicitous of him when he mentions he has been in a car accident. Though Banek is flustered when he finds that he no longer has the file he needs, he explains to the court how he lost it in a voice and manner that make it clear he expects the judge to accept his explanation. The judge reminds Banek that his case hinges on the missing

46   *Popular culture and representations of literacy*

document, saying, "A piece of paper with an original signature on it still has great magical power," but gives him until the end of the day to retrieve the file.

By contrast, when Gipson finally arrives at the courthouse, having had to hitchhike from the accident scene in a suddenly inconvenient rainstorm, we see him working his way through a loud and chaotic lobby, delayed by X-ray machines and metal detectors. When he gets to the family court, the waiting area is filled with people we read as working class. Almost none of these people are in suits, and many are dressed in sweatshirts, jeans, flannel shirts, and other work or casual clothes. They are loud, and argue with each other; many of them are also minorities (as, of course, is Gipson), and a number are speaking languages other than English. The only people we see reading or writing, or even with papers in their hands, are officials such as lawyers or clerks.

(Though race also figures into some of the interactions in this film, the casting of an African American woman as the probate judge and a white man as the family court judge, along with Gipson's dress in a suit and tie, though a more worn version than Banek's, complicates issues of race and emphasizes the relationships focused on social class.)

Gipson is late for his court appointment, just as Banek was, but when he walks into the cramped courtroom the judge is unsympathetic, and awards custody to Gipson's ex-wife before Gipson can testify. The room is cramped, with bright fluorescent lighting, plain walls, and bland institutional furniture. People talk over one another, and the feel of the setting is chaotic and stressful. The scene is shot with a handheld camera in tight close-ups on the characters, emphasizing the claustrophobic nature of the setting and scene. Though Gipson has written his "plan" for getting his life back together on a legal pad, including the buying of a house, the judge is not interested, and is already moving on to his next case. Even as Gipson's ex-wife and attorney begin to leave the room and the people involved in the next case are entering the room, Gipson tries to present his case to the judge. He begins to read a prepared statement that is not about his financial situation, but a narrative about the need for young boys to be near their father. "The streets of this world are lonely for boys without their father," he reads. "I have grown and I have recognized my mistakes." The judge, however, is shuffling through official papers as Gipson reads his statement, and he looks up only long enough to interrupt Gipson to ask, "What kind of house?" But as Gipson begins to answer, the judge dismisses him, and calls the next case. Gipson leaves the courtroom in a frustrated, barely suppressed rage, and dumps all his papers in a trashcan.

Certainly, the two scenes are set up to emphasize the class differences between the two central characters. The literacy practices in each scene only emphasize these differences. Not only are the class readings of each man's body and social position crucial to how each is treated in different rooms of the same building, but the success of each man turns on his knowl-

Who's allowed to read and write? Literacy and social class   47

edge of the literacy practices accepted by the institution of the legal system. Banek clearly understands the specific literacy demands of the courtroom he has entered, and knows that the work he wants to accomplish cannot happen without the specific missing document. He understands what kinds of documents count as evidence and can produce cultural power in this institution as he points out to the judge that the documents he is presenting to the court have been signed, notarized, and witnessed. His class status assures that the judge, as well as the opposing attorney, will grant him the extra time he needs to find the file. Throughout the day, he quickly understands what producing the document will help him achieve, as well as recognizing the consequences of not recovering the document in time—a possible indictment for fraud. At the end of the day, after the senior partner, Stephen Delano (Sydney Pollack), has turned in a forged power of appointment without Banek's knowledge, and Gipson has finally returned the original file, Banek realizes a new meaning for the document. He then uses the power of appointment document to blackmail Delano into letting him do pro bono work for the firm.

Gipson, on the other hand, clearly does not understand the literacy demands of the courtroom he has entered. Even had he been on time for his appointment, his rambling document about the dangers for young urban boys growing up without paternal guidance would still be dismissed by the judge, as well as the audience, as inappropriate for this legal institution. The emotional, personal appeal Gipson is making does not count as evidence in the courtroom. The literacy practices that matter are the ones engaged in by the judge; the documents that matter are the ones the judge is shuffling through as he ignores Gipson's plea. But Gipson reinforces his class position in the eyes of the judge by producing an emotional, personal appeal instead of a document recognized by the legal system as valid. Because he is working class, and is without an attorney, in a working-class courtroom setting, his personal statement is of no value. By contrast, the personal statement on the missing power of appointment in Banek's courtroom will have decisive value, in part because it will be written in the conventions of the legal system, but even more, because it will be signed by a man of the elite, by a man of power. The "magical power" the judge in Banek's courtroom ascribes to a "piece of paper with an original signature on it" in fact is quite contextual. The magic is in fact dependent on the genre conventions of the document, the rhetorical situation in which it is produced, and the class and power status of the person producing it. Gipson, in the first courtroom, would fare no better than he does in the family court, while Banek would still understand the literacy and class demands of the family court, familiar as he is with the rhetorical and discursive demands of the legal system.

A similar example of the way social class and the institutions that reinforce class status are represented in literacy practices can be seen in the ways both men interact with the same loan officer in a bank. Early in the

48 *Popular culture and representations of literacy*

film we see Gipson sitting across the desk from the loan officer, Ron Cabot (Matt Malloy). The banker is looking through the forms on his desk and reading from a computer screen only he can see, while Gipson sits on the other side of the desk, unable to see any of the documents, with only his hat in his hand. Gipson, clearly anxious, asks the banker if he has signed all the forms properly, as the banker reassures him that his loan has been approved. Again, in this brief scene, we see Gipson's uncertainty of the literacy demands of the institutions that pattern his life.

Later in the film, when Gipson has refused to return the file to Banek in retribution for being left on the highway and missing his court appointment, Banek hires a private investigator to hack into the bank's computer and ruin Gipson's credit rating. The banker contacts Gipson, and when Gipson arrives, the banker tells him that the loan has now been denied, because the computer indicates that Gipson is bankrupt. As in most such situations, Cabot sits on one side of the desk, with the computer visible only to him. Gipson has to lean across the desk to look at the screen, but moves back quickly into the space where he cannot read what is on the computer screen.

Gipson tries to remain calm as he asks Cabot to help him. He says that Banek knew some kind of "computer voodoo" to change his records, and pleads with Cabot to help him, his voice getting louder until he ends in a shout: "I need this loan, Ron. I need it for my life. Now nothing has changed between yesterday and today. I'm still the same guy. I wasn't bankrupt yesterday and I'm not bankrupt today!" Cabot simply replies, "I'm sorry, Mr. Gibson. The computer says you are." At this, Gipson grabs the computer monitor, heaves it against the wall, and shouts, "Now it doesn't!"

The institutional power of the literacy practices again works against Gipson here. He is denied access to vital written information about himself, and when he tries to read from the computer monitor Cabot makes it clear with his body language that this is inappropriate. Gipson again does not have an awareness of the institutional literacy practices that could be used to change the situation. He first characterizes the problems as almost magical, a "computer voodoo" that neither man could understand. When that is not persuasive, Gipson, as he did in court, falls back on personal appeals, stressing both his situation and his relationship with Cabot to persuade the banker to help him. But Cabot's only power is through his control of the institutional literacies he understands. He uses his control as his response, and his shield, from Gipson when he replies that the "computer" says Gipson is bankrupt. Without the knowledge of how to access or discuss what literacy documents would be persuasive in this institutional setting, Gipson finally erupts in a rage and destroys the computer.

Again, the contrast of the class implications of literacy is clear when Banek, stricken by conscience, arrives later at the bank to rectify the situation. He introduces himself as "Doyle Gipson's attorney" and convinces the loan officer, even though it is closing time, to approve the loan. When the banker is initially reluctant, and Banek raises his voice, it serves to make

Who's allowed to read and write? Literacy and social class   49

the banker more intransigent. But the key to gaining the banker's cooperation is, again, Banek's knowledge of the institutional literacy practices. Banek does not call on personal appeals of his problems to persuade Cabot. Instead he says, "How can we get this whole thing straightened out?" When Cabot does not respond to this question Banek, instead of telling his personal story, sets up a hypothetical situation that examines how to correct a person's credit problems and approve a mortgage. Banek's language is more detached, and it recognizes the institutional literacies and knowledge structures that the two professionals can use together to fix the situation.

Changing Lanes illustrates how literacy operates through systems of discourse and power to order and discipline the lives of the characters, and in particular to oppress and disempower those who are not members of the elite classes. Even though Gavin Banek has his own frustrations, he moves through the culture's institutions with the confidence of a man who has a privileged position in the class system and who understands the discursive and literacy requirements of those institutions. His actions against Gipson are mostly conceived through literacy practices, such as ruining Gipson's credit rating. Gipson, by contrast, feels acted upon by the institutions, and bewildered and frustrated by literacy practices he does not understand and cannot adopt to achieve his social goals. His actions, both against Banek and against the institutions that order society, are physical, such as throwing a computer against a wall or loosening the lug nuts on Banek's car.

The representations of literacy practices in films such as *Changing Lanes* undercut the vision of literacy as a means of economic empowerment and social mobility. Indeed, by the end of the film the status quo has been restored: Banek is still a wealthy Wall Street attorney, for he has decided not to give up his salary and social status, even though he plans to do pro bono work. Gipson, though he has been taken back by his ex-wife and children, is still working a phone bank for an insurance company and buying a dingy house under a bridge.

J. Elspeth Stuckey (1990) argues that although literacy is often embraced as a key to economic and social mobility, in fact it may be just as likely to be used as an obstacle to deny economic empowerment to those who seek it. For Stuckey, the definition and control of literacy is inextricable from issues of the distribution of power and wealth. Literacy practices are always defined and distributed along lines of economic privilege. Those not privileged by economic class to gain access to the literacy practices that characterize the dominant cultural institutions will only be taught the literacy practices necessary to keep them in their economic place. Not learning the literacy practices of the elite is constructed as an individual failing, rather than the result of systematic forces that that continues to disenfranchise those without power.

We can see this in education where literacy for those in lower social classes is often approached as an instrumental, functional endeavor devoted to workplace needs and improved job skills, while literacy for the elite can

50   *Popular culture and representations of literacy*

engage the language, rhetoric, and literature of power and the imagination (Coles 2001). Literacy education and practices for the working class and poor are often discussed and approached as form of work, as a process of engaging in literacy simply to accomplish tasks. Literacy education for the elite, however, is just as likely to be defined in terms of activities that will enrich literacy learners' minds and feed their souls. In the U.S. context, one example of this is the discrepancy between required first-year university writing courses, which all students must take to prepare them for the world of academic work—though elite students often can bypass through placement tests and portfolios—and creative writing and honors writing courses, which are only available to the select and talented few, who must often get permission of instructors before they can write work that expresses their inner selves (Schweitzer 2004; Williams 2004b). In movies, this can be seen in the contrast between images in films such as *Office Space* (1999) and *Working Girl* (1988) showing rows of desks and cubicles filled with office drones engaged in literacy tasks that we are urged to regard as soul-stealing work, and images in films such as *Shakespeare in Love* (1998), *Finding Neverland* (2004), and *The Hours* (2002), in which the inspired artist writes alone and in romantic surroundings to express his or her genius and inner spirit.

GAINING THE UPPER HAND

It is worth noting that, occasionally, representations of working-class or poor characters' literacy practices show them as powerful in institutional contexts. Aside from the working-class character triumphing through the use of literacy that we will address in Chapter Eight, there are moments in film when working-class or poor characters successfully use literacy as a means of gaining the upper hand, usually only briefly. Like representations of working-class people in general, representations of such characters using literacy to wield power often draw on their comic or "pure" nature. In this way the characters are foils or catalysts for the more affluent central characters, and poor characters' use of literacy to gain power is usually both short-lived and tangential to the central narrative of the film.

In the film *Serendipity* (2001), for example, Jonathan (John Cusak) is searching for woman whose last name and address he does not know. He does know, however, that she bought a pair of gloves at a department store, and he has the receipt. His attempts to convince a clerk (Eugene Levy) at the store to search a computer database for the woman's name meet with comic frustration. The unnamed clerk turns this small moment of control of information to his advantage by pressuring Jonathan to buy a hideous, expensive suit that he clearly does not need in return for having his request for information addressed. Jonathan is a television producer, articulate, upper class, and attractive. He is the person we expect will get what he

Who's allowed to read and write? Literacy and social class 51

wants, when he wants it, and expect to understand the literacy practices that will meet the culture's institutional demands. The nameless clerk, on the other hand, is portrayed as funny looking, small-minded, and odd. We see the clerk's zealous and mercenary guarding of this shred of written information as petty and comic, even as we know that Jonathan will eventually get the information and end up with the beautiful British woman. When the clerk shows up again in the closing moments of the film, he is still a clerk, still small-minded, and still playing the comic relief.

Another example takes place in the movie *Love Actually* (2003), where it is the purity of the working-class character's spirit that momentarily gives her power in an institutional setting. In this film, the British Prime Minister (Hugh Grant) is infatuated with a member of his clerical staff, Natalie (Martine McCutcheon). When he finds that the visiting President of the United States (Billy Bob Thorton) has made an unwanted pass at Natalie, he is angry and also wary of the feelings he recognizes that he feels toward a young member of his staff. Prudently, he decides to have her reassigned from his office. Late in the film, we see the Prime Minister (he is never named), alone on Christmas Eve, sitting at 10 Downing Street with a pile of official papers in front of him. Weary of going through the dry documents, he begins to read the Christmas cards that have been sent to him. Most of the cards are from powerful people and organizations, and have pre-printed messages in them. Amidst all the pre-packaged and official cards, however, there is a handwritten card from Natalie that reads, "I'm very sorry about the thing that happened. It was an odd moment and I feel like a prize idiot. Particularly because (if you can't say it at Christmas when can you, eh?) I'm actually yours. With Love, your Natalie." At this point the music swells, and we see a look on the Prime Minister's face that tells us that he has just realized the true importance of love in his life. Of course he races off, finds Natalie, and ends up kissing her on stage at a school Christmas pageant, to the thunderous applause of all.

It is not Natalie's ability to negotiate the official literacies of the government that is powerful in this situation, but her position outside the conventions of the institution that makes her handwritten message stand out as honest and direct. In this instance, her lower-class status is portrayed as simple, pure, and uncorrupted by the cynicism of politics and dominant institutions. It is the equivalent of the child's hand-written and heart-rending note that is a trope in so many films. Such notes have emotional power, and, as we pointed out in Chapter Two, are often the province of women and children who are striving to make personal connections, while men's writing is more connected to power and commerce. Although the purity of spirit coded in Natalie's card does make her message stand out and persuade the Prime Minister to seek his true love, it is also worth noting that their class positions remain unchanged at the end of the film. He will remain Prime Minister, and if her class status changes at all it will only be through marriage.

52 *Popular culture and representations of literacy*

PERCEPTIONS OF IDENTITY AND CLASS

Though reports of government and educational institutions extol the virtues of Scribner's (1984) metaphor of the "literacy of adaptation" as the key to economic empowerment, and films such as *Changing Lanes* emphasize the social constructions of her metaphor of "literacy as power," genuine economic and social mobility as represented in movies is just as likely to turn on her metaphor of "literacy as a state of grace" (39–41). Literacy as a "state of grace" is the "tendency in many societies to endow the literate person with special virtues" such as a traditional liberal humanistic knowledge and wisdom accessible through reading and writing. As Scribner notes, "The term sounds elitist and archaic, but the notion that participation in a literate—that is bookish—tradition enlarges and develops a person's essential self is pervasive and still undergirds the concept of a liberal education" (41). Such a conception of literacy as enabling a richer, more worthy self through reading and writing great works continues to emerge in the work of cultural critics such as Allan Bloom, Neil Postman, and Sven Birkerts, particularly in their defenses of reading in what they see as the lamentable rise of popular culture. As Birkerts (1994, 80) writes:

> There is a metaphysics of reading that has to do with a good deal more than any simple broadening of the mind. Rather, it involves a change of state and inner orientation, and if we contemplate the reading process in this light we can hardly get away from introducing the word *soul* (or something very like it) into the conversation.

But Birkerts' perception of what literacy does for the individual is less about actually reading or writing than it is about cultural and class attitudes about literacy practices. It is not a matter of a person's ability to read or write that is important in this view, but what such an ability reveals about the qualities of the reader and his or her intellect, taste, and connection to the culture of the elite. Certain literacy practices—reading Proust as opposed to reading a tabloid, for example—place one in a particular social class and allow those around the reader, be they tabloid or literature readers, to ascribe a specific set of identity characteristics to the reader. Literacy practices, from this perspective, are connected to Bourdieu's (1984) concept of "cultural capital," or the knowledge and attitudes that shape ideas of taste and class that are different from economic and social capital. Bourdieu argues that even though people have the opportunity to make individual choices about cultural expressions such as art or music or clothing, their choices usually reflect the "tastes" of their social class. The way such preferences of "taste" are read by the rest of the culture determines their cultural capital. Such cultural capital can be particularly crucial in terms of social and economic mobility, from such overt aspects as wearing the "right" clothes to making the "right" jokes to fit in with business

Who's allowed to read and write? Literacy and social class   53

executives as opposed to auto mechanics. Movies often reflect this fish-out-of-water moment in films such as *Working Girl* (1988), when Tess realizes she must change her hairstyle and wardrobe to go from being perceived as a secretary to being perceived as an executive. Literacy practices are often an important component of cultural capital. The person who uses standardized conventions of grammar and spelling, for example, will be more able to operate in dominant class settings.

The accumulation and display of cultural capital, however, is not simply a matter of individual choices. Bourdieu points out that a central mechanism for the reproduction of class status and positions is the way that cultural habits and economic realities are transformed into a cultural capital that has meaning and seems to reflect naturalized tastes. People who have more money can afford to treat necessities such as food and clothing as displays of aesthetic sensibilities. The consequence is that those with economic privilege can and do emphasize form over function in everything from food and clothing and housing to literacy practices. "Upscale" newspapers, magazines, literary novels or collections of poems spend money on explicit considerations of form, both in their visual and material presentations as well as their content, in a way not present in tabloids, owners' manuals, and romance novels. As the systems of culture reproduce themselves, they are accepted by those at every class level as being natural and legitimate. In this way the social classes, especially those with power and privilege, reproduce themselves, even though there is an illusion that social mobility is possible with simple hard work and good individual choices. Taste becomes an individual quality, a matter of "just who I am," rather than part of a system of power and class.

The traditional perception of literacy as an autonomous set of skills plays into Bourdieu's framework. From this perspective literacy skills are available to all and those who use them in ways that illustrate particular conceptions of class—reading *The Economist*, for example—would seem to have personal qualities of taste and intellect that lead them to that publication. The working-class person using the same autonomous skills to read *The Sun* would reflect his personal qualities in the same way. The move away from an autonomous conception of literacy to a sense of situated literacy practices, however, allows us to see these same set of reading events as reflecting systems of culture that reproduce systems of class and economic privilege by making them seem products of natural qualities and individual choices. As Bourdieu (1994, 68) notes, such an ideology "naturalizes real differences, converting differences in the mode of acquisition of culture into difference of nature; it only recognizes as legitimate the relation to culture (or language) which least bears the visible marks of its genesis." In other words, while any person could learn to read or write, the perception of the "literate" person is one who seems to possess the innate ability, even perhaps genius, to make abstract and aesthetic judgments and connections about texts. Teachers who praise a student for truly being a

54 *Popular culture and representations of literacy*

"reader" are often referring to such abilities more than the decoding of words. The implication is often that the abilities are personal qualities and consequently the class status and experiences that constructed those abilities is not often discussed (Williams 2004a). Again, this split in the origin of reading and writing abilities and how they should be responded to is reinforced in educational systems that teach all students "functional" literacies but leave instruction in creative and abstract work to the chosen few. Literacy practices that seem to reveal personal virtues, then, are actually illustrating class status and social connections available to the individual.

PERFORMANCE AND LITERACY

The film *Catch Me If You Can* (2002) provides an intriguing illustration of how perceptions of literacy and the personal virtues it is believed to bestow on an individual establish class status and allow or deny social mobility. Based on the life of Frank Abdegnale, the film follows Abdegnale's (Leonardo DiCaprio) life as a teenager, who for several years succeeds both in forging checks and in impersonating everything from an airline pilot to a physician to a lawyer. Shaken by his parents' divorce and father's financial failure, he roams across the United States and Europe, forging documents and creating identities with enthusiasm and youthful panache. He is pursued by FBI agent Carl Hanratty (Tom Hanks), a humorless, plodding Javert who, often by following the literacy trail, relentlessly tracks Abegnale and eventually catches him.

The astonishing curiosity that drives our interest in Abegnale's story is the success a mere teenager has in passing in the adult world of some of our most respected and highest social status positions. What is of particular interest to us in this project is how intertwined perceptions of literacy and class status are essential to these successes. Abegnale succeeds because his documents attest to a class status his personal qualities seem to confirm.

Abegnale's story is framed in the experiences of his father, Frank, Sr. (Christopher Walken). We're introduced to Frank, Sr. at the beginning of the film as a man who uses language and charm on his wife and son and anyone else who crosses his path. As far as he can use his wit and charm he succeeds, but like Doyle Gipson in *Changing Lanes*, Frank, Sr. does not understand the literacy demands of the institutions that govern his life and thwart his desires. He is the owner of a stationery store, and the film begins with a scene of him being given an award from the local Rotary Club and being lauded as a "friend who keeps our pencils sharp and our pens in ink." Even as this award seems to connect Frank, Sr. to the world of literacy, it also underlines his position as a person who provides materials for the literacy practices of those in power without being able to engage in the same practices himself.

Who's allowed to read and write? Literacy and social class   55

Early in the film Frank, Sr. pulls his son out of school, dresses him as a chauffeur and has him pull up in front of the Chase Manhattan Bank. When Frank, Jr. asks his father what they are doing, he is told his father's theory of interpersonal relations.

Frank, Sr.: You know why the Yankees always win, Frank?
Frank, Jr: Because they have Mickey Mantle?
Frank, Sr: No. It's because those other teams can't stop staring at those damn pinstripes. Watch this. The manager of Chase Manhattan Bank is about to open the door for your father.

Once inside the bank, however, we see Frank, Sr. seated across the desk from a bank officer in a familiar movie shot that is immediately read as a scene of bad financial news. In this shot, the banker sits behind the desk, perusing official papers (or, in more contemporary films, a computer screen), while the customer on the other side of the desk leans nervously forward and pleads for mercy or special consideration, calling on the banker to move beyond the official documents to rediscover a common humanity. In *Catch Me If You Can*, as in so many other films, the scene ends in frustration and rejection for the customer. Frank, Sr. tries to charm the banker, but the banker simply looks at the forms, notes that Frank, Sr. is the target of an income tax audit, and tells him that the denial of his loan request is "not a question of winning or losing, it's a question of risk." This interaction sets a pattern for the father throughout the film, as we witness his charms slowly fading in the face of the relentless pursuit by the Internal Revenue Service. Although we never see Frank, Sr. talking with government auditors, we do see him reading letters from the agency or talking about his latest communication from them. Each time, he talks in bewildered anger about the audits, lamenting that "Those people want blood." Though Frank, Sr. may exhibit cultural capital through the dress and demeanor of a middle-class businessman, he has not adopted the literacy practices that communicate that cultural capital to institutions such as banks or government agencies. He understands there is a cultural code, and when he opens a checking account for his teenage son he gives him the book of newly printed checks and tells him, "From this day on you're in their little club." Even as he realizes that there is a "club" and that literacy plays a part in membership and social mobility, however, he never understands how to employ literacy practices and personal cultural capital in the pursuit of social mobility as his son will.

Frank Abegnale, Jr. demonstrates his understanding of the symbiotic relationship of literacy practices and the performance of cultural capital just after his family has had to move because of its financial difficulties. He arrives at his new school wearing a blazer and shirt and tie and carrying his books in a briefcase. This places him in contrast to the other students

56 *Popular culture and representations of literacy*

in sweaters and athletic jackets, and these students taunt him for looking like an encyclopedia salesman, and push him against the wall. It is at this point, he turns, walks to the front of the room, authoritatively writes his name, "Mr. Abegnale," on the chalkboard and opens his textbook and begins to lead the French class through a lesson. The class immediately falls to order and follows his lead as their teacher. Frank establishes his authority through the literacy event of writing his name on the board and asking the students where they left off in the textbook, two quickly recognizable actions of a teacher, and he performs them decisively. Yet writing his name on the board and opening a book, by themselves, would not have convinced the students; the actions had to be performed by someone in a coat and tie, speaking middle-class, conventional English. He is so convincing to the students that he continues the charade for a week, meeting with parents and planning field trips, before he is caught.

In this scene, and throughout the film, Frank understands that literacy practices are not just about producing or decoding texts, but about the situated nature of how those texts are presented and delivered, about the attitudes connected with that moment. Even as the principal is talking to his parents about his French class charade, Frank is sitting in the outer office, giving a fellow student advice about how to make the note she has forged to excuse herself from class look more believable. Looking at the pristine piece of paper in the girl's hand, he says, "When your mom hands you a note to miss school the first thing you do is fold it and put it in your pocket." The girl quickly and surreptitiously makes the document credible with a simple crease.

Frank has learned how literacy practices and cultural capital are performed in the institution of school, but after he runs away from home to escape his parents' divorce, he has to learn it in the culture of the everyday adult work. He fails miserably in his first foray into check forging. Even after changing his drivers' license to make him ten years older, his attempt to cash checks are rebuffed. We see him try a series of sob stories, relying on his personal charm to get tellers to cash checks for his grandmother's birthday or to buy books for school, only to be told by a stern teller that "We're not allowed to take checks from people we don't know." The real issue, however, is not that the bank does not know him, but that, dressed as a youth needing money for youth-connected items, such as school books, he lacks the cultural capital to support the forged checks and driver's license. It is the opposite of the problem that haunted his father in the bank at the start of the movie.

Life changes for Frank when he sees an airline pilot in a hotel treated like royalty. The power of the uniform and the performance of the man in the uniform as a person of substance and upper-class cultural capital makes clear to Frank what he has been lacking. Drawing on his youthfulness, he poses as a student reporter and interviews officials from Pan Am airlines on how pilots obtain uniforms, identification, and their air of entitlement.

Who's allowed to read and write? Literacy and social class   57

Once he has used this information to get a uniform and forge an airline identification card, he forges new checks and sets to work. We next see him behind the teller's counter at a bank, being treated with deference as he cashes his checks. The symbiotic relationship of literacy and performance of self is suddenly working seamlessly. His uniform and presence confirm confidence in the forged identification and checks, which in turn confirm confidence in his presence as a pilot in uniform. Literacy is reinforced by personal qualities.

Unlike his father, Frank understands that there are institutional literacy demands as well as ways that "literacy as a state of grace" results in the attribution of upper-class virtues to the person displaying the appropriate literacy practices. Consequently, Frank continues to learn how literacy practices work in the cultural settings in which he wants to live. He learns from observation or television how to perform as a pilot or doctor or lawyer should, from his dress to his language to his confidence. From bank tellers to airline clerks to hospital nurses, he engages people with his charm, and asks questions that allow him inside the literacy practices of the institutions that shape and rule the culture. When a teller shows him how a check routing machine works, he purchases his own at an auction and his forgeries get more sophisticated. Throughout the film people comment on how young he looks. As at the bank, if he only had forged checks without the proper dress or the uniform without good forgeries, his fraud would be quickly uncovered. But the combination of the appropriate dress, class manners and language, and good forgery—we seem him overtyping numbers on checks to make them look authentic—satisfies their concerns that he is who he claims to be.

This pattern is repeated throughout the film, such as in the scene when Frank decides he wants to work as a doctor (in order to be close to a cute young nurse). He creates a diploma from Harvard Medical School, using a fake seal of the university and letter press with the proper Gothic typeface. He understands the genre and rhetorical demands of the diploma as well as of the transcript he forges, and he is talented and meticulous in his work. Again, however, the documents by themselves are not enough. It is the combination of the transcript and diploma with Frank in a well-tailored suit and confident manner that convinces the chief of medicine at the hospital that the person he is talking to is a talented young doctor. The file says he is from Harvard, the suit and smile says he is an honest person with proper cultural capital. (Once Frank has the job at the hospital we see him studying medical books and novels and watching *Doctor Kildare* on television in order to learn the proper attitude and rhetoric to go with the job.) The proper institutional literacy practices are key to his identity performances, even as the documents themselves need to be delivered in the proper context to have the proper cultural capital.

Thus Frank's remarkable social mobility as a person who has not yet turned twenty would not be possible without a knowledge of literacy prac-

58   *Popular culture and representations of literacy*

tices that mark class status, the ability to reproduce them, and most of all, the personal qualities elite literacy practices supposedly endow upon the person enacting them.

Bordieu's (1984) concept of *habitus* is helpful in understanding Frank Abegnale's ability to pass himself off as people he is not, and the willingness of others to accept his presentation of self. Habitus is the "internalized form of class condition and of the conditionings it entails" (101). In other words, it is the way we all internalize and normalize the beliefs and values of the community and social class to which we tell ourselves we "belong." It gives us a framework for understanding the social practices around us and a sense of ease with how we position ourselves and respond to those practices. It shapes our perception and interpretation of experience, as well as our conception of what actions are possible or desirable. There may be many choices available to us at any given moment, but our habitus may limit our way of seeing the world so that it limits our sense of which choices we actually can act on. Even more subtly, habitus may limit those we think we *want* to act on as a matter of our personal tastes or desires, tastes and desires that are social constructs but that we internalize as innate parts of our being.

Frank Abegnale's gift is that he can get glimpses beyond his habitus to perceive other choices not normally available to his class status, and he can perform those choices in terms of his presence and his literacy practices. He has an almost instinctive understanding that certain social practices matter in these performances and that how he internalizes those practices, his comfort with his new class status, will determine how well he pulls off his impersonations. He succeeds in his deceptions because those he encounters, from pilots to doctors to district attorneys, are so comfortable in their habitus that the idea of someone from a different social class engaging in such deception on a grand scale is inconceivable. Though they may have momentary doubts about Frank Abegnale's youth or the quality of his forgeries, they imagine that his choices, desires, and values are part of the same social construction as their own, so they give him the benefit of the doubt.

Frank illustrates that it is possible to see beyond and move beyond one's habitus. Yet as one moves from one social habitus to another, the social practices have to be learned anew, and often conflict with former values and tastes. The sense of ease one had in negotiating class is shaken and tested. More distressing often is the alienation from people in the former social class such moves can cause. In movies about literacy and social mobility, such as *Erin Brokovitch* (2001) or *Educating Rita* (1983), there are often such poignant scenes. *Catch Me If You Can* portrays such a moment late in the film. Frank, now wealthy from his forgeries and having lived a life of well-tailored suits, fancy cars, and fine restaurants, goes to visit his father. He finds his father in a bar, holding yet another letter from the Internal Revenue Service, crumpled from multiple readings. The father's first words

Who's allowed to read and write? Literacy and social class 59

to his son are another complaint about his incomprehension at what the government wants, "Look at this letter. The IRS wants more. I had a deal with them. Two penalties. They ate the cake, now they want the crumbs." Frank tries to give his father, who is now working as a postal worker, plane tickets for a vacation and money to pay off the tax bills. But Frank, Sr. refuses, looking at the printed plane tickets on the table between them with a mixture of confusion and resentment. The conversation is strained and painful. Frank has moved into a different social class that his father does not fully understand, even as Frank can no longer move comfortably in his father's world.

When the FBI in the person of Carl Handratty finally catches up with Frank in a print shop in France, Frank is wearing only an undershirt and pants. Though we can see Frank's joy in the artistry of his forgeries as he marvels over the quality of the presses he's been using, we also see him as vulnerable and childlike. Without a pilot's uniform or a doctor's lab coat, he is again a teenager, his cultural capital gone. As he starts to run, he gathers the documents and checks he has been forging to himself like a blanket and shield. But it is not enough to protect him and, stripped of the protection of his documents, we see him stripped of his identity and sent to prison.

The irony in the film is that even as Frank's forged documents and social performances fool doctors, lawyers, bankers, pilots, socialites, they do not fool Carl Handratty. Handratty is played by Tom Hanks as humorless, dumpy, obsessed FBI bureaucrat. Handratty's interpersonal skills are questionable; he is divorced and seems to have no life beyond his job. But he is a master of both detecting forgeries and of understanding the social implications of literacy practices. While Frank succeeds in his impersonations, because he combines his forgeries with performances of appropriate cultural capital, Hanratty is able to track him down eventually, in large part because he encounters the documents on their own. Through close readings of the forged documents, he is able to engage in a systematic analysis of the literacy practices and, without being distracted by the personal performances, he can detect the inconsistencies.

It is only when Carl gets close to Frank, and personal performance enters into the equation, that Frank continues to succeed in eluding his nemesis. The first time we see this happen is when Carl finds the hotel room in Florida where Frank has been living. The room is filled with forged documents and printing equipment. Frank, who comes out of the bathroom in a suit and tie, quickly tells Carl that he is a Treasury Department Agent, handing Carl a wallet that supposedly has identification in it, which Carl does not open. Frank talks his way out of the room, leaving Carl holding a wallet he only then opens to find stuffed with scraps of waste paper. In a later phone conversation, Handratty asks Frank how he knew the agent wouldn't open the wallet. Frank repeats his father's philosophy:

60 *Popular culture and representations of literacy*

Frank: The same reason the Yankees always win. Nobody can keep their eyes off the pinstripes.

Hanratty: The Yankees win because they have Mickey Mantle. No one ever bets on the uniform.

Frank: You sure about that, Carl?

Even as Frank escapes their first encounter, it is only Handratty who understands the interrelationship between individual performance and literacy practices that allows Frank to succeed in his impersonations. When Handratty discovers that the pseudonym Frank gave him in Florida is also the name of the alter ego of the comic book hero The Flash, he puts that together with the reference to the Yankees to conclude that Frank is actually younger than he seems and from the New York area. A search for reports of runaway teens in that region soon leads Handratty to Frank's mother and Frank's yearbook photo, a performance of self on the page that betrays Frank's real identity. Later, when Handratty realizes Frank is getting married, he knows that Frank won't be able to change his name again without losing his love, so he can look for wedding announcements with the same name the Frank has been using for a while.

Handratty, though an adept interpreter of Frank's literacy practices, is disdained by his co-workers. His kind of detective work, requiring close and meticulous reading of documents, is derided, and we are shown his world as one of clerks, drab fluorescent offices, and low status. This drab and grinding world is always placed in contrast with Frank's adventures, in which the colors and soundtrack pulsate with vitality. There is no doubt which world we in the audience would rather inhabit, no doubt about whom we would rather know. After Frank has been arrested and imprisoned, Handratty finally arranges for Frank's release to help the FBI track forgers. But when we see Handratty take Frank into the FBI offices for the first time, Frank's anguish at the bureaucratic, mundane reality of institutional furniture and endless files is palpable. Frank asks, "How long do I have to work here?" and Hanratty replies, "Every day. Every day, Frank, until we let you go." Hell, for Frank, is endless bureaucracy, and he contemplates running away once again, but does not, and returns to work. The last shot of the film is of Frank and Carl reading files in the drab office with wall of file cabinets hemming them in. After the glamour of Frank's previous world, it seems still like a prison, unchanged by even the final words on the screen that attest to Frank's subsequent success with the FBI. We want him to run again.

INFORMATION AND CONFORMITY

The representations of literacy in terms of social class in films such as *Changing Lanes* and *Catch Me If You Can* remind us again that "literacy

Who's allowed to read and write? Literacy and social class   61

practices are patterned by social institutions and power relationships, and some literacies become more dominant, visible, and influential than others" (Barton and Hamilton 1998, 7). The situated nature of all literacies and the role of ideology and power in determining which literacies are valued and rewarded stand in stark contrast to the cheerful and positivist rhetoric of literacy skills as the key to economic empowerment.

A final ironic reading of literacy practices as economically empowering can be seen in the film *Office Space* (1999). A low-budget unheralded comedy when it was released, it has since become a cult hit because of its cynical representation of the life of office workers in the current "information economy" and has served as a precursor to popular television series such as *The Office*. *Office Space*, which is set in a nameless, placeless suburban office park, chronicles the lives of low-level workers in a high-tech company called Initech. Though we know Initech is a high-tech company, we don't know exactly what the company does, and it really doesn't matter. What does matter is the gray, grinding drudgery of the employees in their gray cubicles, and how literacy, far from being empowering, is an oppressive force throughout the movie. In the first scene in the office, early in the movie, Peter (Ron Livingston) is criticized by his supervisor (Gary Cole) for not having his paperwork in order.

Lumbergh: We have sort of a problem here. Yeah, you apparently didn't put one of the new cover sheets on your TPS reports.
Peter: Yeah, I'm sorry about that. I forgot.
Lumbergh: Um, Yeah. You see we're putting the cover sheet on all TPS reports now before they go out. Did you see the memo about this?

Within minutes two other supervisors similarly castigate Peter for not including the proper cover sheets. As this scene sets up, literacy throughout the film is represented as a set of meaningless exercises imposed upon employees by an inept and uncaring management. From an obsession with cover sheets to slightly menacing inspirational banners on the office walls (Is This Good For The Company?) to office equipment that instead of working, lights up with a "Paper Jam" messages, the literacy practices in *Office Space* are portrayed as relentlessly mundane and enervating.

When Peter finally has had enough, he encapsulates the message of the movie when he rants, "Human beings are not meant to sit in little cubicles, staring at computer screens all day, filling out useless forms, and listening to eight different bosses drone on about mission statements!" From this point on, the rebellion of Peter and two of his colleagues to this dehumanizing system is encapsulated in acts that destroy the machines and products of literacy. Peter is seen cleaning fish on the "TPS Reports" he is criticized for at the beginning of the film. Peter and his friends take the balky copy

62   *Popular culture and representations of literacy*

machine out to a field and bash it to bits. Finally, at the end of the film, the entire office building goes up in flames as the camera lingers on burning computers, files, and inspirational banners.

In the film's coda, we see Peter, standing amidst the charred remains of the office building, hard-hat on his head and shovel in his hand. He has rejected the white-collar world of meaningless forms and drab cubicles for a job as a laborer, "This isn't so bad," he says. "Making bucks. Getting exercise. Working outside." And soon after, we leave him in the sunshine, away from oppressive literacy practices of the corporate world, and the credits roll to the tune of "Take This Job And Shove It."

4 Writing others
Images of race and literacy

Racialized images of literacy can emerge in any popular film, even one that does not pretend to address either race or literacy. Consider, for example, a minor scene in *Hollywood Homicide* (2003), a cop buddy movie. Joe Gavilan (Harrison Ford) is showing a $7 million mansion to a prospective buyer—a young African American rap musician (Master P) whose recording sales have suddenly taken off and rocketed him into wealth overnight. Gavilan, a homicide detective on the Los Angeles police force, moonlights as a real estate agent to make ends meet, and the boundary between his two jobs blurs, inevitably. He has met both the seller, a fading movie producer (Martin Landau), and the prospective buyer during the course of a murder investigation. The movie producer's mansion is redolent of old Hollywood glamour. When the cop/real estate agent suggests that his client take a moment to look around the library, the rapper, lolling regally on a sofa, replies, "I don't need no *library*. What I need to know about is *the pool*."

In the blink of an eye, this scene draws a distinction between literate and illiterate along a line of racial difference. The wealth of the black musician appears as an anomaly, not least because he is represented as being less literate than the white cop. The hard-boiled Gavilan is hardly a literary sort, as other scenes in the movie make clear. His partner on the police (Josh Hartnett) force aspires to become an actor, and ropes Gavilan into helping him learn his lines for a part in *A Streetcar Named Desire*. Gavilan has apparently never heard of Tennessee Williams, and reads his lines with wooden ineptitude. Nevertheless, Gavilan does appear to value the *idea* of a library, and, unlike his client, he recognizes having a personal library as a sign of class status. In this film, the Williams play and the private library represent "culture," while the black music is portrayed as comic, violent, and lucrative, but not a literate form of culture.

This scene illustrates one dimension of the representation of literacy and race: how "others" are depicted. We are presented with a stereotype in the character of the black musician, and the scene is built on a stereotyped assumption that a person of color is probably less literate than a white person. The musician fits one of the stock characters—the comic entertainer—that Stuart Hall (1995) lists in "The Whites of their Eyes: Racist

64 Popular culture and representations of literacy

Ideologies and the Media," an essay about stereotypes and racialized narratives that perpetuate racist perceptions and concepts in the media, including film. The entrance of directors, writers, and celebrated film stars of color into the movie industry within the last few decades has not meant that such tenacious stereotypes have disappeared. In *Bamboozled* (2000), the story of a black television producer who makes it big with a TV show that reincarnates the minstrel show, Spike Lee, the African American film director, responds scathingly to the expectations imposed on him by large studio production and by critics, expectations that he felt pushed him back into narratives and characters dominated by old racist stereotypes (Benshoff 2004, 93).

Critical theories of race that we draw on for this chapter, however, emphasize that it is not only those who are marked as racialized—persons of color—who are defined by race; all modern subjects have a racial identity, including those who are *not* marked as racialized—white persons. Leslie G. Roman (1993) also points out that white people tend to "[treat] the concept of 'race' as a reified synonym for racially subordinate groups" (73), and to consider themselves as "raceless," when, according to critical race theories, they are not. It is most often the case that "'race' simply inscribes another othering discourse," Keith Gilyard (1999, 48) writes. "It is an unproblematized marker of the nonwhite, the other." In *Racist Culture*, David Theo Goldberg (1993) argues that the modern European state has been racialized from its inception. The primary purpose of race, according to Goldberg and others, is to establish a system of white dominance that functions on many different levels: juridico-politically, economically, spatially, culturally, epistemologically, and even somatically (Mills 2003, 42).

Insisting that all modern subjects are identified according to race is important for studying film, since it means that film, as a visual medium, has never been able to avoid representing race, an identity that is tied so closely to (though not limited to) bodily appearance and skin color. In other words, the scene in *Hollywood Homicide* also works to represent whiteness through the character of Joe Gavilan. This scene was chosen as an illustration for our discussion because it contains an exchange between a white character and a black one, but even scenes that feature only white characters reflect and construct images of race. As the lens of critical race theories reveals, *all* film representations of literacy could bear to be interpreted in terms of race, strictly speaking.

Critical theories of race were developed in response to concerns about some of the ways that discussions of race actually play out in current scholarship in any number of fields. In "On the Theoretical Status of the Concept of Race," Michael Omi and Howard Winant (1993, 3) note that for centuries—until the Second World War, more or less, race was considered to be a biologically-determined characteristic, and to be "an essence...whose meaning was fixed." By the last decades of the twentieth century, that idea had been generally discredited, at least by theorists, and race, like other

Writing others   65

modern identities, had come to be conceived as a social construction. Conceiving of race as socially constructed means understanding it to function as a system of categories that are defined not by inherent characteristics but only in their relationship to each other. It assumes that meanings of race constantly change over time and in different locations. Just as important, it emphasizes that both white and non-white identities are constructed through cultural processes of representation and identification—film, in this case. If we also accept that literacy practices are constructed and situated by cultural processes, then there is an obvious value in paying attention to ways in which representations of race and literacy intersect in films.

The presence of race is as complex and pervasive in the movies as it is in society itself. The two films we have chosen as examples for this chapter touch upon issues of race and literacy in two very different ways. First we analyze film images that both address and perpetuate the idea of "black underachievement" in literacy, centering our discussion on the popular Disney movie *Holes* (2003). In the second part of the chapter, we turn to a summer blockbuster of 1998, *The Mummy*, to consider the surprisingly prominent place that literacy receives in this film, which revives a number of racialized tropes and narratives.

RACE AS COLLECTIVE AND EMBODIED

One problem that Omi and Winant (1993) observe is that despite the fact that theorists no longer think of race in terms of biological essence, they can still "creep" into objectifying it in various ways, especially by assuming that "one just *is* one's race" (6). When this happens, they objectify race by failing to "grasp the process-oriented and relational character of racial identity and racial meaning"—to grasp in other words that there are not fixed categories of race (6).

A second problem Omi and Winant observe is that conceiving of race as a constructed reality has led some people to treat race as an illusion. Theorists that recognize race as a social construct, they write, are in danger of arguing or implying that in today's world race no longer has real ideological force—to imagine that discussions of race are left over from the past. One way of minimizing the real power of race in society, according to Omi and Winant, has been to consider the root of racial inequality to lie in individual or group prejudice (5). According to this idea, the best way to fight racism would be to confront and dismantle personal beliefs about the differences or inferiorities of others. *Crash* (2004) is an example of a recent film that focuses on individual prejudice. Through the events that unfold in the film, the lives of many members of a racially complex California community intersect with each other; events push the characters to confront their own misconceptions and distrust of people of other races. *Crash* presents a bold and sometimes moving challenge to racist attitudes,

66 *Popular culture and representations of literacy*

and at the same time stops short of acknowledging the system of power differences that creates the unequal realities of the characters lives. The emotional insights of the all of the characters, white and non-white alike are represented as similar, as something that shows their common humanity, despite prejudices and difference.

The assumption underlying this approach is that underneath "we are all alike." The problem with this "color blind" approach, Omi and Winant point out, is that it takes a naïve view of social constructs, which develop over centuries and are "enforced" pervasively, albeit usually tacitly; even if it is constructed, race is not illusory, but creates powerful social and experiential realities that don't simply go away if people "don't see" them (5). The philosopher Charles Mills (1997) sums up the dilemma that faces race theorists in these words:

> If race was previously thought of as in the body, it is now too often thought of as merely in the head: claims of nonreality have replaced claims of physical reality. But race is best conceived of not primarily as ideational but as embedded in material structures, sociopolitical institutions, and everyday social practices that so shape the world...as to constitute an "objective"...though socially constructed reality. (1997, 48)

A critical concept of race, Omi and Winant argue, would "steer between the Scylla of 'race as illusionary' and the Charybdis of 'racial objectivism'" (6). It would understand race as constructed and at the same time also acknowledge it as a powerful system that creates deep inequalities in the world. For the characters in *Crash*, confronting their own feelings in relation to racial others is an important shift in political and social awareness, but new individual consciousness is not enough to alter the substantial inequalities among them that race has constructed.

Identifying whiteness as a category of identity opens the way for considering how white identities get constructed and questioning the process through which individuals, even well-meaning individuals, can become willing participants in a system of domination that causes a great deal of suffering. Like other theories that explore the effects on consciousness of dominating or being dominated, race theory argues that achieving a racially dominant, white identity entails what Charles Mills calls an "agreement to *mis*interpret the world" (1997, 18). Mills explains that the system of race imposes an epistemology of its own on white subjects, a structure of knowing that he sometimes calls "an epistemology of ignorance" (93) and at other times refers to as a "schedule of structured blindnesses and opacities" (19). The effect of this "epistemology of ignorance" is to render white domination virtually invisible to those who perpetuate it. Peggy MacIntosh (1992) and Ruth Frankenburg (1993) have used self reflection and sociological research to chronicle the difficulty white persons have in perceiving their identities in terms of race, or in recognizing the privileges

Writing others 67

to which being white entitles them. As a consequence, when obviously racist incidents occur, they appear to be exceptional to the white majority. But, as Mills argues in *The Racial Contract* "racism and racially structured discrimination have not been *deviations* from the norm; they have *been* the norm" (1997, 93).

The "schedule of structured blindnesses and opacities" imposed by the system of race vitally affects the production and viewing of movies. In *White*, film scholar Richard Dyer (1997) has argued, for example, that the medium of film is shaped by race in fundamental ways not likely to be evident to white audiences and film producers. He contends that over the course of its development in the twentieth century, the medium has consistently glorified white bodies as ideals; the techniques of cinema production themselves—the methods of lighting, makeup and cinematography—have evolved specifically to showcase the bodies of white-skinned actors and actresses, like the "alabaster goddesses" of today's screens, such as Nicole Kidman and Kate Beckinsale, rather than dark-skinned actors. In another sense, race also influences the way that film genres are identified: Films with predominantly white actors dealing with topics of interest to white audiences, seen from a white perspective, are simply called "movies," but films with casts of predominantly African American actors and addressing themes of interest to black audiences get categorized as "black films" (Benshoff and Griffin 2004, 54). The assumption is that the film with white actors and themes is simply "mainstream" and could appeal to anyone, but the film with black actors and themes will appeal to a narrower, predominantly African American audience.

The most immediate association between race and literacy in the minds of U.S. educators and the general public alike may be the phenomenon of "underachievement" among black students and other students of color in schools. It is not uncommon to encounter movie images of literacy learning inside or outside of classrooms that show students of color left out or struggling. These movies do address a real and important issue: the clear and seemingly intractable differences in rates of literacy between whites and people of color in the United States. "A statistical correlation between high literacy achievement and high socioeconomic, majority-race status routinely shows up in results of national tests of reading and writing performance," notes Deborah Brandt (1998, 559). Lower scores are correlated with students of color, despite longstanding efforts to change this situation (Powell 1997; Richardson 2003). But literacy and composition scholars have questioned the assumptions about race and literacy presented in many of these movie scenes and narratives (Gilyard 1999; Giroux 1997).

One well-known example of a struggling learner can be found in Alan Parker's 1980 film, *Fame*, which follows the lives of several students as they make their way through the New York High School for the Performing Arts. The enthusiastic reception this film received led to a short-lived television series and to touring productions of a theatrical version which, according to

68 *Popular culture and representations of literacy*

a *Fame* Web site, are still performing on stages around the world. In *Fame*, each of the main characters must confront a personal obstacle that stands in his or her way of succeeding in the demanding program. For Leroy (Gene Anthony Ray), a black student, the issue is literacy. He is a phenomenally talented dancer, but consistently fails to do his work for English class. The high school English teacher, a middle-aged white woman, is not a "touchy feely" sort, but is tart-spoken and tough. In a classroom scene, the English teacher, Mrs. Sherwood (Anne Meara) lays it on the line for Leroy: if he fails her class, he's out of the program entirely. In a subsequent scene, which takes place outside of the classroom, it is nighttime, and the silhouetted figure of a man drifts through a smoky and wasted urban landscape. The figure is distant, and is hard to identify in the dark. He listlessly picks up a scrap of paper from the ground and slowly sounds out the words to himself: "B-u-y buy M-a-y-tag washing machines." It is Leroy, and the root of his academic problem is revealed here: Leroy doesn't do his work for English class because he is barely able to read.

The night scene contrasts sharply with the images of daily life in the school, which are colorful and brightly lit, crowded with people, and roiling with the students' ambitions and desires. The threatening darkness and loneliness in the night scene convey a sense of awful deprivation, as if this inhospitable place represents where Leroy is from, a place that hardly fosters anything beyond survival, and certainly not reading and writing. The scene, with the darkness carrying connotations of things secret and suppressed, also conveys a lurking sense of shame in his inability to read, a shame that Leroy masks with resistance and bravado in the classroom. And unlike the literature, poetry, and music that surround the students in the school, the scrap of text that Leroy reads is commercial and mundane. The night scene shows the private moment when—having discovered that his dancing brings him respect (at least in some circles) and the possibility of a career—Leroy chooses to apply himself to the hard work of learning "the basics" so that he can stay in the program.

Variations of Leroy's story show up in other films. In *Dangerous Minds* (1995), Louanne Johnson (Michelle Pfeiffer), a young white woman just out of the Marines, takes a job teaching high school in a poor urban neighborhood. She challenges a classroom full of poor, mostly Black and Latino "underachievers" to *choose* to study English literature. When her students ask her, not unreasonably, if reading poetry will help them deal with the harsh realities of their lives outside of the classroom, she hesitates a moment but firmly assures them that it will. "The mind is like a muscle," she says. The mind needs to be exercised, she tells them, and reading poetry can do that. Her students resist her at first, but decide to participate when she wins their trust—mostly by showing them that she genuinely cares about how well they succeed in school. She toughs out a first year in which one of her students is shot, two are withdrawn from the class by a guardian who sees the coursework as nonsensical and harmful to her boys, and one of the brightest students leaves when she gets pregnant. When Louanne

Writing others   69

announces to the class that she is quitting, her students convince her that she is needed, and that she should stay.

In each of these films, the student's commitment to schooling represents choosing a better life, or choosing to get out of a life assumed by everyone, including the characters themselves, apparently, to be a dead end. The better life is also represented by the white teachers in the dominant white culture's school. Critical theories of race and new theories of literacy both suggest, however, that the relationships between race, literacy, and representation are more complex than the emotional dynamics of these movie scenes would suggest. The images are meant to be inspiring: the white teacher, whether that is a formal teacher in a school, or an informal teacher outside of the school system, cares enough to challenge students, and the students care enough to drop their self defeating behavior and get to work. When the students succeed, they feel good about themselves, and seem to be on the road to material success. The teacher reaps the emotional benefit of helping along the way, often finding personal redemption in helping the disadvantaged students. But as Elaine Richardson (2003) points out, when images of literacy get framed purely in individual terms, they fail to show the broad, systemic ways in which literacy has been and still is tied to racist exclusions. Richardson and other literacy researchers have been working to articulate broader social dynamics that, in Deborah Brandt's (1998, 559) words, "[set] the terms for individuals' encounters with literacy." As Brandt observes, "the field of writing studies has had much to say about individual literacy development" but less to say about larger contexts (556).

Shifts and variations in ways of thinking about literacy have reflected the shifts and variations in concepts of race that Omi and Winant have mapped out. Ideas that objectified race, which perceived it to be "in the body" or to be an essence, led to the idea that capacities for literacy were inherent in race. African Americans were portrayed at one time as incapable of attaining high levels of literacy. More recently, with the development of basic writing as a field, error is described not as a sign of mere incompetence but as logical, often rule driven. Basic writing theorists explain that students of color can fail to become facile in use of academic literacy because they have not had the same training or home language as mainstream students. But Richardson and Geneva Smitherman (Richardson 2003, ix) point out that even these welcome developments in literacy theory still do not recognize African American literacies as powerful discourses in their own right, and thus continue to perpetuate problematic assumptions about black "underachievement" (Richardson 2003,12–13). Richardson grounds her own critique in a printed advertisement directed to recent college graduates, offering to forgive their college loans in return for two years of teaching with a literacy program for underserved school districts (7). The advertisement uses a young black student in its illustration, and taps into sentiments like those expressed in the two movies we have discussed. Like the film images, the advertisement conveys the idea that well-meaning, highly educated, but completely inexperienced people can make a difference, feel

70 *Popular culture and representations of literacy*

good about their contribution, and have their school loans forgiven into the bargain. Richardson comments that the literacy program the ad is for may help a few individual students, but can never make a significant difference, however well meaning its intentions, because the program fails to take note of or to question the dominant nature of the literacy that the students are being asked to learn (6–14).

Richardson's critique of the advertisement for the literacy program can also be applied to the film images we have discussed, in which dominant versions of literacy are represented as the only form of literacy that is important, the students are represented in terms of the skills they lack (ignoring the nondominant discourses that they are conversant with), and underachievement is represented as caused by a deficiency of individual motivation, whether on the part of the students or the teachers. In *Dangerous Minds,* for example, the poetry the students are studying is by traditional white, mainstream British and American writers. The teacher interests the students in poetry by creating a "Dylan/Dylan" contest—a contest to see which of Bob Dylan's lyrics is most like a poem written by Dylan Thomas. The winner of the contest is then treated to a fancy dinner with the English teacher at a French restaurant, complete with a supercilious waiter, menu offerings that the student has never heard of and can't read, and a dress code that is beyond his means. Within these cultural traditions and spaces, the black and Hispanic students enter as "strangers in the village": while they are expected to learn the mainstream language and poetry, there is no acknowledgement of the students' own languages, or any indication that their ancestors made contributions to the literature or culture that is being privileged in the classroom. Even when students succeed, they are vulnerable to accusations of plagiarism, as happens to Jamal, a talented black high school student in *Finding Forrester* (2000), and to Malik, a college athlete in *Higher Learning* (1995) (Gilyard 1999, 46). Linda C. Powell (1997) observes in "The Achievement (K)not: Whiteness and 'Black Underachievement'" that research into "black underachievement" has tended in the past to focus only on the experiences and needs of the black students. The research literature looks "either at the stresses and conditions of individual black students in a racist society...or at the ways in which schools could be more effective for these students" (3). Powell argues, though, that the "(k)not" of black underachievement does not lie solely within the black community, but is intertwined with whiteness (5–6). The phenomenon would be better understood, she argues, if it were to be seen as a phenomenon constructed by both blacks and whites.

IMAGES OF RACE AND LITERACY LEARNING: *HOLES*

Holes (2003), a Disney film based on a popular book by Louis Sachar, moves slightly closer to the kind of representation Powell suggests. *Holes* puts literacy at the center of a somewhat fantastic tale that frames the char-

Writing others   71

acters and their experiences in terms beyond individual desires and capacities, linking their fates to each other in ways that the characters themselves recognize only gradually, if at all. The action is set in a reform camp for boys, Camp Green Lake. The place is neither green nor anywhere near a lake; in fact, it is built on a flat, dry desert where it never rains. A white boy named Stanley Yelnats IV (Shia LaBeouf) gets sent to the camp when he is mistakenly accused of stealing a pair of basketball shoes. Isolated in the barren landscape, far away from the rest of society, each of the boys at the camp is made to dig a hole five feet deep and five feet in diameter every day. A camp administrator (Jon Voight) explains that this apparently meaningless task is designed to build character: "You take a bad boy, make him dig holes all day in the hot sun, and it turns him into a good boy. That's our philosophy." He vaguely instructs Stanley to report "anything interesting" he might find in the process of digging.

Stanley becomes friends with a black boy in his tent nicknamed "Zero" (Khleo Thomas) by the others, because, as the camp counselor, Dr. Pendanski (Tim Blake Nelson) explains, "nothing is going on" in his "stupid little head." As part of his approach to rehabilitation, Dr. Pendanski elaborately insists on calling the boys by the names that their parents gave them and by which society knows them. The boys just as zealously insist on being called by the nicknames that they invent for each other in camp. Before coming to the camp, Zero had lived alone on the street; his mother simply failed to return one day. He keeps to himself, refusing to talk to anyone. He is fascinated to see Stanley writing home and receiving letters in return, and this makes Zero understand that literacy could be a tool for finding his mother. He asks Stanley to teach him how to read, and at first, Stanley refuses, claiming to be too busy and too tired to do more work. But eventually they work out an arrangement by which Zero, the fastest hole digger, helps Stanley finish digging his required hole every day, and Stanley, in return, gives Zero reading and writing lessons. Stanley begins the first lesson by writing "Zero" on a piece of paper, when his friend informs him that his name isn't really Zero, but Hector Zeroni.

Hector's growing literacy disrupts the dynamics of power in the insular community of the camp. Observing Hector help Stanley dig holes leads the other boys to taunt Stanley for "having a personal slave." Tensions culminate in a fight between Stanley and one of the other boys. When the camp administrators investigate the fight, they learn about the reading and writing lessons, and forbid Stanley to continue teaching Hector. "You might as well teach this shovel to read," the counselor remarks. He gives Hector an impromptu test: "What does C-A-T spell?" When Hector refuses to respond, the counselor hands him a shovel, saying "Go ahead. Take it! It's all you'll ever be good for: D-I-G." Hector responds by knocking the counselor in the head with the shovel and running away into the desert. Without food or water, he faces becoming, in the boys' words, "buzzard food." Not long afterwards, Stanley, facing punishment for a different misdemeanor, runs away into the desert, too. He finds Hector, miraculously still alive,

72   *Popular culture and representations of literacy*

taking shelter under the hull of an old boat. He has survived by eating a syrupy concoction that tastes like peaches he has found in some old jars stashed inside the boat. When the two boys run out of food and water, they decide to trek to the top of a nearby mountain in search of water. Hector collapses while they are climbing, so Stanley carries him up the final slope to the mountain top. There they discover a spring and some vegetation—big, sweet onions that they eat until they can't eat any more.

In *Holes*, the dynamics of literacy learning between Hector and Stanley differ in some respects from the dynamics in *Fame* or *Dangerous Minds*. First, Hector is motivated to learn when he recognizes a direct purpose for literacy that is meaningful for him—communicating with his mother—not for any purpose that could be described as educational or institutional. Hector's motivation for learning contrasts with Leroy's in *Fame*: Leroy decides to learn not because of some personal desire for literacy but because of a school requirement that he must satisfy in order to continue doing what he loves—dancing. The students in *Dangerous Minds* are motivated by an abstract determination to "finish school"; the diploma represents a promise for an improvement in their lives, but the promise is not specific. Like the activity of digging holes in *Holes*, which is framed at first as an activity for the good of the boys and is later revealed to be much more for the good of the camp director, schoolwork in *Dangerous Minds* is represented by the teachers and sometimes by the students as mind-building and character-building. The teacher's energies are devoted to helping students realize that they are indeed capable of doing the requirements and keeping the students from dropping out, but the curriculum responds to what the dominant society prescribes. In *Holes*, a sign on the shed where the shovels are kept labels it, ironically, the "Library"—a comment on the dearth of reading and writing in the camp, and, also perhaps, on visions of education that impose uniform tasks for all. Like the shovels, reading and writing are tools that can benefit the "diggers," but this is by no means always the case.

The scenes of literacy learning in *Holes* are situated within a complex of broader events and relationships, including historical events. When the boys taunt Hector for being Stanley's "slave," and the camp counselor forbids Stanley to teach him any more, *Holes* evokes the actual days of slavery, when literacy practices were enlisted to enforce racial oppression. African Americans were generally considered by whites to be incapable of learning, and slaves were forbidden to acquire literacy, since it was viewed as a threat to the slave owners' mastery over their human property. Today, the accounts by Linda Brent and Frederick Douglass of learning how to read and write in slavery are among the most excerpted passages in their autobiographical narratives. Even after Emancipation, literacy tests were used as a way to prevent black citizens from voting. When Hector is asked to spell "cat" by the counselor in the camp there is an unmistakable echo of these historically punitive uses of literacy tests.

Writing others 73

Furthermore, the existence of Camp Green Lake and the camp director's obsession with digging holes is linked to another story of race and literacy from generations ago. The barren land around the camp had actually been covered by a lake at one time, and a thriving town had stood on the shore of the lake. The white schoolteacher in charge of the town's one-room schoolhouse, Miss Kathryn (Patricia Arquette), had spurned the advances of the son of the richest man in town, and fallen in love with a black farmer, Sam the Onion Man (Dulé Hill). When the spurned suitor had seen Miss Kathryn and Sam kissing, he incited the townspeople to shoot Sam (for having kissed a white woman, which was against the law) and to burn the schoolhouse down. After Sam was killed, the schoolteacher fled town to live outside the law as Kissin' Kate Barlow, the bandit famous for planting a red-lipsticked kiss on her victims before killing them. Then the rains had stopped, the lake dried up, and the town shriveled away. The rich man responsible for Sam's death had lost all of his wealth and developed an obsession with finding a chest full of stolen riches that Kissin' Kate was said to have buried in the desert, an obsession for digging holes that was passed on to his offspring, including his granddaughter, the Warden of Camp Green Lake, Warden Walker (Sigourney Weaver). She disguises the family mania for hole-digging as a rehabilitation program for young offenders.

While he is at the camp, Stanley develops a more critical awareness about his situation by using his literacy skills to piece information from his own family history together with observations and bits of information he reads at the camp. When he first arrives, he is naïve and suffers at the mercy of administrators and other boys alike. At first he acquiesces to the tyrannies inflicted on him and the other the boys, but puzzles over inconsistencies that he observes. He figures out, for example, that the Warden is searching for something specific, not just "anything interesting" that the boys might turn up while they are digging. Stanley finds a fossil, and one of the other boys finds a dial of some sort, but both of these artifacts are rejected with disgust by the camp counselor overseeing them. When Stanley finds a slim gold tube with the initials "K.B." engraved on it, however, the Warden is extremely interested. Stanley understands why when he reads a framed newspaper article about a train robbery carried out by Kissin' Kate Barlow and sees a framed "Wanted" poster for her in the Warden's cabin. Stanley realizes that the initials on the object he had found must have stood for Kate Barlow, and he identifies it as a lipstick tube, not a bullet, as he had at first thought. Stanley is able to understand that the narratives of history can be constructed from a set of literacy artifacts, when he can connect those to his own experience. This narrative would not yet be available to Hector, however, who does not have the literacy skills of the dominant culture.

Stanley knows about the legend of Kissin' Kate from his own family history, since his great grandfather, the first Stanley Yelnats, had made his fortune in the stock market, but was robbed of it all by Kissin' Kate in a

74   *Popular culture and representations of literacy*

stage coach hold-up, a calamity viewed in the Yelnats family as evidence of a curse passed from generation to generation of the Yelnats men. The curse had originated long before, in Lithuania, when Stanley's great-great- grandfather (Damien Luvara) had sought the advice of a fortune teller, Madame Zeroni (Eartha Kitt). She had told him to go to America, where he could make his fortune, and she also described how he could win the love of a local girl. In return, he was to carry Madame Zeroni up a mountain and sing a certain song while she drank from a spring there, so that she could "grow strong too." If he were to forget to do this, he would incur her curse upon himself and his family. The original Yelnats had gone to America, but forgot to carry out Madame Zeroni's request, and every man in the Yelnats family had, indeed, been unlucky ever since. As Stanley's grandfather put it, "It isn't enough to be smart—you have to be lucky, too!"

So Stanley and Hector, unbeknownst to them, have a relationship fatefully shaped by family histories. When Stanley Yelnats IV carries Madame Zeroni's great-grandson, Hector, up the mountain, he unwittingly fulfills Madame Zeroni's request at last, and counteracts the curse on the men in his family by helping Hector "grow strong too." The fortunes of Stanley, his family, and Hector consequently take a turn for the better. Stanley's father, an inventor who has been unsuccessful all of his life, suddenly finds the formula against foot odor he has been seeking for years: a combination of peaches and onions does the trick. Deciding that they "feel lucky," Stanley and Hector secretly return to the camp together, dig one more hole, and uncover the chest containing Kissin' Kate's buried fortune. When Warden Walker sees that they have found the chest that her family has been trying to dig up for decades, she threatens to seize it. But she is prevented by a mass of poisonous lizards—endemic to the area and feared by all—that appear and crawl on the two boys, but surprisingly do not bite them. The peaches and onions that the two boys have survived upon in the desert combine to produce a special smell that appeals to the lizards and keeps them from biting the boys. The chest, stolen, as it turns out, from Stanley's great-grandfather, bears his name, and Stanley is allowed to keep it. Inside the family finds not just the gold and jewels that they might have expected, but an unassuming packet of papers worth infinitely more: AT&T stocks purchased in 1905, worth millions of dollars each. Their fortunes turn on literacy artifacts, valuable only to those who can decode them. Stanley divides the wealth in the chest equally between his own family and Hector, who uses his money to hire private detectives to find his mother.

The development of Stanley's critical awareness, in which literacy events play crucial roles, allows him to resist the authority in the camp, which operates by repeatedly forcing inmates to deny their own perceptions and feelings. Anyone who voices a perception that is out of line with the Warden's views is frightened into retracting or restating their own idea and endorsing things that fly in the face of logic. When the Warden scratches the face of

Writing others 75

one of the administrators with her fingernails that have been painted with rattlesnake venom, causing his face to become horribly infected and swollen, the boys are intimidated into ignoring his obvious disfigurement, and to say that he looks just fine. When the Warden grandly orders all of the boys' water jugs to be filled as a reward, even though the counselor has just filled them, she rejects any implication that her order doesn't make sense. These and similarly bizarre incidents are everyday events in Camp Green Lake. But unlike the other boys, who, if they resist it in practice, accept character-building as an explanation for what goes on in the camp, Stanley's literacy helps him to uncover the corruption of the camp administrators, and emboldens him to fight back for himself and, even more, to protect Zero. When his parents hire a lawyer to bring him home, Stanley won't leave unless Hector comes with him.

Unlike *Fame* and *Dangerous Minds*, *Holes* clearly attributes Hector's marginal status and his inability to read and write to factors beyond his individual behavior. It is others who imagine that he is stupid, nickname him Zero, and prohibit him from learning. When Hector runs away, the camp administrators are afraid that state authorities will find out about his disappearance and bring legal proceedings against them. To conceal their misdeeds, the administrators decide to destroy Hector's file and obliterate any trace of his presence at the camp, reassuring themselves by saying, "He had nobody. He was nobody....Nobody cares about Hector Zeroni!" Though we know Hector's worth, the institutional power of literacy in the hands of the white administrators and culture can determine his "official" existence. Hector is only truly able to challenge the dominant culture's power structure when he and Stanley have discovered the stock certificates, documents that are acknowledged as having value and power of their own. Ironically, it is the fact that Hector's file has been destroyed that allows the lawyer to remove him from the camp. Through Hector's character, *Holes* acknowledges individuals and whole groups of people whose lives have similarly been obliterated from the historical record as if they don't count. Hector's reading and writing lessons are important not so that he can fit in with the dominant culture but so he can assert himself against the way others represent him, and so he can maintain his connection with his own past, especially with his mother.

The stories in *Holes* also insist that individual lives are inevitably connected to past lives in powerful ways. Stanley's misfortune is related to a broken promise made long before he was born, and the camp director is driven by the same greed for Kate Barlow's fortune that had motivated her grandfather. The stories also suggest that individuals, like literacy itself, are not autonomous and self-determined but connected and interdependent. For example, Stanley helps Hector learn to read and write because it is useful to both of them, not out of a sense of altruism. The schoolteacher in Old Green Lake gives the farmer jars of her canned peaches in exchange for the onions that he grows, and it is the combination of these

76   Popular culture and representations of literacy

two flavors—peaches and onions—that protects the boys from being bitten by poisonous lizards and that provides the chemical formula for Stanley's father's successful new product. Stanley's great-great-grandfather benefits from the advice of Madame Zeroni, but fails to acknowledge her advice or to help her "become strong too" (a failure that mirrors Western economies that have been built on the labor of slavery and exploitation, but fail to acknowledge that debt, and fail to include the descendants of slaves in the wealth of those same economies). Stanley acknowledges his interdependency with Hector by refusing to leave him at the camp after his own departure and sharing the contents of the treasure chest with him.

These film images of people who have not acquired literacy or who are "underachievers" in *Fame*, *Dangerous Minds*, and *Holes* reveal assumptions about literacy itself. Definitions of literacy usually do not make explicit reference to race, but can have implications, nonetheless, for how race is perceived. The autonomous models of literacy, as Brian Street (1984) refers to them, make broad universal claims for the cognitive and cultural developments that the technology of writing makes possible. Writing, the autonomous theories suggest, isolates ideas from the thinker and places them onto the paper, and makes the ideas thus more self-contained and complete. Claims for the effects of being able to isolate and contain meaning in writing, according to autonomous models, can include a shift in cognitive abilities (suggesting that being able to write allows literate individuals to think more abstractly, for example), and advances in economic and social development. As Street (1993) points out, we must question claims put forward by the autonomous concepts of literacy because through them "literacy...has come to be associated with crude and often ethnocentric stereotypes...and represents a way of perpetuating the notion of a 'great divide'" between the literate and the non literate (7). When autonomous models of literacy are embraced by educators, researchers, or policy makers, the danger is that those who do not possess literacy—or that do not possess a version of literacy favored by researchers—can all too easily be characterized as cognitively or socially deficient, a characterization that can map over onto racial difference. Even very sympathetic portraits, such as the images of Leroy in *Fame* or the images of the students in *Dangerous Minds* can perpetuate characterizations like these. *Fame* and *Dangerous Minds* both represent themselves as films that take up literacy education as an explicit theme, and are consequently more likely to influence public ideas about literacy achievement. The representations of literacy, illiteracy, and race in *Holes*, on the other hand, come closer to countering the implications of autonomous theories of literacy. Zero says, after being complimented on his math abilities, "I can't read, but I'm not stupid." Compared to what we see in most movies, the messages about literacy in *Holes* are unusual, and may not even be readily recognized as such, embedded as they are in an adventure story intended for children.

OTHERING LITERACIES: *THE MUMMY*

Set in Egypt after the First World War, *The Mummy* (1998) tells the story of Evie (Rachel Weisz), a young half-British, half-Egyptian antiquities librarian who undertakes an expedition into the desert to search for the fabled city of Hamunaptra. A huge treasure is rumored to be buried there, but, more important for Evie, the lost city is also the place where a powerful book is said to have been hidden—the Book of Amon Ra, which "contains all the secret incantations of ancient Egypt." Evie enlists an American mercenary, Rick O'Connell (Brendan Fraser), as a guide, because he has stumbled on the site by accident during the course of his own somewhat disreputable adventures. At the same time, another expedition, led by an unscholarly and unscrupulous group of Americans, is competing with Evie's team to reach Hamunaptra and find the treasure first.

The two teams race to locate the trove hidden under the shifting sands. A secret society that includes tribe of desert nomads descended from the pharaoh's bodyguard, as well as the chief librarian from the antiquities library where Evie works, has protected the ancient city from discovery for millenia, in the belief that disturbing the site will result in terrible catastrophes. The city contains the mummy of Imhotep (Arnold Vosloo), a high priest punished for treason and being buried alive; if his sarcophagus is ever opened, like opening Pandora's box, it will release a series of plagues and other evils into the world. The predictions prove true when the treasure hunters discover the tombs, disregard all of the warnings inscribed there, and plunder them of their precious objects, including an enormous book. As soon as Evie opens the book and reads some of the text out loud, Imhotep is awakened from his millennia-long incarceration and begins an indomitable rampage, seeking first to regenerate his own body by absorbing the life force of people he kills, and then to resuscitate the mummified body of his lover. Imhotep's strength surges with every victim that he takes. Meanwhile, Evie's team battles to find a way to stop the increase in the mummy's power, especially when it becomes apparent that he intends to use Evie as a human sacrifice in a rite to raise his dead lover. Stopping Imhotep entails both scholarly detective work and monumental fighting. Evie learns that reading from another ancient book can undo the spell that released the mummy from its sarcophagus, but before they can find the book and read it, hordes of mummy soldiers must be fought and kept at bay.

The Mummy signals its concern with race in studio publicity, which proclaims that the film combines "the thrills of a rousing adventure" with the suspense of a 1932 horror classic (also titled *The Mummy*), two narrative genres that theorists have linked to anxieties about race. The category of "adventure" evolved in nineteenth century literature, during the height of British imperialism, as Stuart Hall (1996, 21) points out, citing the work of literary scholars. "The very idea of adventure became synonymous with the demonstration of the moral, social, and physical mastery of the colonizers

78 Popular culture and representations of literacy

over the colonized," he explains (21). Hall's claim is further supported by the work of Hernán Vera and Andrew M. Gordon (2003) in "The Beautiful American: Sincere Fictions of the White Messiah in Hollywood Movies," in which they claim that "Hollywood fictions of the white self did much to legitimate white privilege" (125). Vera and Gordon argue that "the white American self-concept is a sincere fiction that is maintained with intense symbolic labor (such as movies) so that people fail to recognize the brutal reality of American race relations" (113). They identify a figure they call the "white messiah," which has appeared over and over in films of the twentieth century, from the very early *The Birth of a Nation* (1915) to more recent productions like *Stargate* (1994), *Three Kings* (1999), *Indiana Jones and the Temple of Doom* (1984), *Die Hard* (1988), *Terminator* (1984), *Alien* (1979), and *Men in Black* (1997). White messiahs are usually (but not always) men, and they tend to be altruistic people who find themselves through acting to liberate oppressed "others." The white messiah is often a misfit in his or her own society, and usually represents a lone individual pitted against highly organized, megalomaniacal evildoers. In this respect, "the white action messiah reaffirms the fantasy of an autonomous individual" rather than showing larger forces at work in society (116). The natives the white messiahs encounter "seem helpless to liberate themselves" (120). In films that Vera and Gordon discuss, images of Indians, Arabs, or Vietnamese, for example, are largely projections or fantasies of the filmmakers: "The white messiah movies tell us little about those other races but much about the desire of the white self to avoid guilt and to see itself as charismatic and minorities as needing white leadership and rescue" (125).

Scott Trafton (2004) also links American anxieties about race to a characteristic trope of horror films about mummies—the "uncontrollable awakening," in which the desiccated body of an Other, long believed to be dead, returns to life and introduces chaos, disrupting a previously ordered situation. Trafton describes how, because it was distinguished by an inherent in-between-ness, Ancient Egypt came to represent racial instability in the American imagination: chronologically, as the oldest civilization, Egypt stood between barbarism and civilization; in racial terms, it could be perceived as a civilization either of whites or of blacks (130). American representations of Egyptian mummies altered during the nineteenth century: First exhibited as inert artifacts alongside such objects as dinosaur bones, mummies later came to be "the century's preeminent sign of the ultimately unmanageable terms of ... unstable relationships [such as the relationship between black and white]-and thus the agent of their destructive consequences" (125–130). The trope of "the uncontrollable awakening" became the principle characteristic of mummies in literary and other representations (125); it has persisted until today, and is reiterated in the 1998 version of *The Mummy*.

Evie's relationship to Imhotep is especially revealing of the underlying meanings of race in the film. She is thrust into becoming the guardian of white racial boundaries—a role that is not unusual for women in a racial-ized culture. Unlike the other characters in *The Mummy*, who face threats from the mummy hordes such as death by desiccation, death by swarming scarab beetles, or death by leaping mummy soldiers, the dangers Evie faces are highly eroticized. At one point, the newly- awakened Imhotep steals into Evie's room and kisses her as she lies sleeping, pressing his grotesque, only partly-revivified face to hers before her friends burst in and save her. In another, more telling scene, Evie is captured by Imhotep and his minions and taken back into the tombs of Hamunaptra for the ritual in which her life will be sacrificed to infuse life into the mummy's ancient lover.

From the perspective of literacy, what is most striking about *The Mummy* is the way it foregrounds texts and reading. Although this is not what people initially associate with action-adventure films, the power of texts is often a prevalent theme in such films, as we will discuss in more detail in Chapters Five and Six. In *The Mummy* the object that first excites Evie's interest in Hamunaptra is a small, intricately-made metal box that is a key for opening both the sarcophagus of the mummy and the fabled book buried in his tomb. When the box springs open, Evie finds a map show-ing the location of Hamunaptra. The adventurers who find the first book are looking for loot, not books. "Who cares about a book," they exclaim. "Where's the treasure?" They don't recognize that the texts themselves are priceless, powerful and incantatory—the language in them is performative, so that reading from the books out loud will cast a curse or lift a spell. The Egyptologist working for the other team of tomb raiders warns her not to read from the book, but Evie dismisses the warning: "It's just a book. No harm ever came from reading a book."

Evie's racialized role in *The Mummy* is also intersected by literacy. Like Indiana Jones, the sometime professor, sometime adventurer hero of the series of popular films starring Harrison Ford, Evie is associated with the world of academic scholarship. In a moment of tipsy intimacy with Rick, Evie casts about for the best way to define her own identity, finally announcing proudly: "I am a *librarian*!" Vera and Gordon point out that literacy—the ability to read, translate, decipher or compose texts that oth-ers cannot—can be an important feature in the character of the "white messiah" figure (117) The "white messiah's" ability to decipher unusual documents or inscriptions gives her power and often a position of authority among the population of surrounding "others," as seen in other adventure films of the same kind such as *King Solomon's Mines* (1937) and *King Kong* (1933) as well as their subsequent remakes. Evie's half-British half-Egyptian identity makes her a bit of a misfit in the social world, though it is always clear in the movie that she is identified as being part of the white European civilization and not part of the Egyptian "others," but helps her become an excellent translator. She is the only one who is knowledgeable enough about ancient hieroglyphics and hieratic to read and translate the script that can defeat the mummies.

80 *Popular culture and representations of literacy*

Reading figures centrally in the climactic scene at the end of *The Mummy*, which takes place inside the tombs of Hamunaptra. Imhotep has made all of the preparations for performing the sacrificial rite to raise his lover from the dead. Evie is bound to the top of a sarcophagus alongside the female mummy, and they are circled by mummy priests that Imhotep has resuscitated. Imhotep begins to read from the huge black book unearthed from his tomb—the same book that Evie had read from when she reawakened him. Earlier, Evie has discerned that this text is not the Book of Amon Ra that she had been seeking, but a different book. She realizes that they can stop the mummy by finding the golden book of Amon Ra, and learns by studying an inscription in the museum exactly where this second book must be concealed. Rick and Evie's brother, Jonathan (John Hannah) race to find the book before Evie is killed. They finally unearth it and fight their way against mummy hordes to bring it to the scene of the sacrifice. Jonathan's ability to read hieroglyphics is much weaker than his sister's, but by describing what confusing parts of the script look like to Evie, who tells him what the symbols mean, he is able to sound out enough of what is written on the book's cover to interrupt the ritual and summon more mummy soldiers—except these are obedient to him. In the battle that ensues, Rick is able to release Evie from her bonds, and they are able to take the key for opening the book away from Imhotep. Evie opens the Book of Amon Ra and reads a spell that strips Imhotep of his immortality. Until this moment, he had been able to simply regenerate his body to recover from any wounds that could be inflicted on him. But this time, when he lunges for Rick, Rick kills him. Physical combat is crucial throughout this scene, but, ultimately, the outcome of the battle is determined by control of the two ancient texts. Evie and her companions defeat the mummy by gaining access to the secret incantations in the Book of Amon Ra; without them they didn't have a chance.

In *The Mummy*, the exotic texts at the center of the adventure serve to normalize the literacies and texts of the academic library where Evie is a librarian. The books and spaces of the academic library stand in stark contrast to the legendary ancient books and inscriptions that entice the researchers and adventurers into the desert to find them. In the scene in which we first meet Evie, she is standing on a tall ladder in the library, reshelving books in alphabetical order. Ceiling-high bookshelves filled with orderly rows of books march in ranks across the cavernous room. Leaning to place a book in its proper spot, Evie loses her balance, and the ladder she is standing on falls against a neighboring bookcase, tipping it over. This sets off a domino effect, and one by one, all of the other bookcases topple, spilling all of the books into piles on the floor. In this scene, the artifacts of academic literacies are represented as mere physical objects on the most literal level—they seem like nothing more than blocks of paper and cardboard, subject to the laws of gravity like any other object. The books do not get opened, and the ideas in the books are not mentioned. Rather it is the alphabetical ordering and the iconic status of the names that Evie murmurs as she keeps the books in order that seem important: "'sacred stones,'

Writing others 81

'sculpture and aesthetics,' 'Socrates'..." The texts that are the object of archeological interest, on the other hand, figure much more prominently in *The Mummy*. They are exotic, colorful, and precious. The two books at the center of the film action—the Book of Life and the Book of the Dead as they are called—are hidden within an elaborate, symbolic network of tombs, and each one is buried deep under the statue of a god. The ancient books themselves, when they are disinterred, turn out to be magnificently crafted metal artifacts. The covers are fitted with special locks, and the pages of one of the books are thick sheets of gold stamped with esoteric script that only a few experts are able to read. Such books are the domain of specially trained priests, not of illiterate masses. As is so often the case with magical books, only those who have special knowledge, such as priests and wizards, should read from them or risk unleashing horrible powers. It is intriguing that in *The Mummy* Evie, as a scholar from the white imperialist culture, first sets lose the peril through her rationalist hubris, but then is also able to vanquish it in the end through her superior literacy skills.

In *The Mummy*, the ancient texts and languages are othered, the way the Orient itself has been othered in modernity, as Edward Said (1978) has famously claimed. In *Orientalism* Said broadly argues that the idea of the "Orient" came to be constructed through a wide range of Western discourses, such as anthropology, biology, geography, and art history, over the course of several centuries of scholarship and travel. The Orient, in Said's view, is not a reflection of any entity that exists in reality, but is an invention, a projection devised by the West that serves to affirm its own identity as Western, European, "civilized." The idea of the Orient is not extraneous, but is essential—by negation—to Europe's sense of itself. Similarly, the exotic, "othered" texts of Hamunaptra serve to render the books and practices of the antiquities library where Evie works—seemingly so innocuous by contrast—as the dominant form of literacy, in the end. The Book of Life and Book of the Dead belong to the mummy's ancient culture, but it is the white explorers who appropriate them and read them. The adventures of Rick, Evie, and the other treasure-seekers do not contribute as much to the knowledge of the ancient texts or their writers and users as they contribute to the self-definition of the adventurers themselves. The characters marked as racialized (ancient and modern alike) are either liberated or defeated by the "raceless" white adventurers. In the chaos of battle, Hamunaptra is reduced to a pile of rubble, and both of the fabulous books are lost.

WRITING OTHERS AND OTHERING LITERACIES

Theories and practices of literacy have been and still are extensively intertwined with race. Often the connections are not explicit or even conscious. Reading representations of literacy in films has proven to be instructive for us to understand more about the varied relations between race and literacy. One of the ways that studies of literacy and literacy teaching can

82 *Popular culture and representations of literacy*

be implicated with race is by valorizing European and European-derived cultures differently, ignoring the accomplishments of other civilizations, or failing to recognize the extent to which European culture has benefited from the contributions of others, "hence...bleaching of the multicolored roots of human civilization" (Mills 2003, 45).

In the films we have studied, this point emerges in the nature of the English lessons in *Dangerous Minds*, for example, which appear to focus on a narrow range of authors and texts. This form of othering also, perhaps, informs the radical split between the "exotic" and difficult-to-learn literacies of ancient Egypt and the "ordinary" literacies of the antiquities library in *The Mummy*. The split expresses a fascination for the ancient, and at the same time appears to negate any possibility that there might be a connection between the ancient past and the present, or even that the modern forms of writing and the texts could be indebted to the ancient forms. As Goody (2004) argues, the idea of antiquity in European history has until only recently represented Greece and Rome as having produced a radical shift in culture that became the basis of Western civilization. This shift, which was considered to have been produced in part by writing and by the political institution of democracy (to name just two important factors), occludes insights into the accomplishments of other cultures and the contributions they made to Western progress. Goody (2005) illustrated this point by noting that paper and printing, both of which were developed outside of Europe, were essential for the growth of literacy inside early modern Europe, but this fact is rarely acknowledged.

Another, more obvious way that literacy is intertwined with race appears in patterns of access to literacy, and in assumptions about how these patterns are shaped. *Holes* depicts the most blatant form of the racialization of literacy, which occurs when people of one race are forbidden to acquire literacy. When this happens, literacy becomes conscripted to act as a marker of racial difference—even within the same race. When people of one race are excluded from literacy—or from a dominant form of literacy, this also reinforces inequalities between races, and prevents those who are excluded from using literacy as a tool. In *Holes*, again, Stanley's ability to read allows him to figure out that the camp warden is not simply interested in the activity of digging holes for its own sake, but is searching for buried treasure, a connection that allows him to find the treasure himself. If he were not able to read, Stanley would not have been able to make these connections. Less obvious, but equally powerful, are the situations in which, although access to literacy is not forbidden outright, some persons still do not acquire it, or do not acquire dominant forms of literacy, as is the case with Leroy in *Fame*.

Like literacy practices, race is a social phenomenon we often watch in movies without really seeing. Yet, as a visual medium, film offers a compelling place for studying the narratives and images of race and literacy that all too often operate invisibly in our daily lives.

Part II
Literacy and social contexts

Emma Watson in Harry Potter and the Chamber of Secrets (2002). ©Warner Bros/Photofest.

5 Control and action
Literacy as power

It is fascinating to wonder who taught James Bond how to read. Though all we know about his education is that he may have gone to Cambridge, you have to be impressed with the quality of his literacy education. The most famous superspy in popular culture, like most contemporary action heroes, displays an astonishing range of literacy abilities. He can read anything, in any language, in any medium, in any context, and, often, while the fate of the world hangs in the balance. Like most of his skills, James Bond's literacy practices seem effortless. We never see him working on them, we rarely see him stumble, either in comprehension or interpretation. What's more, he is often able to employ his literacy practices to outwit his enemies and save himself, the damsel in distress, and the day in general.

Although Bond displays a particular grace and élan in his activities, his uses of literacy are, in fact, quite similar to those by action heroes in some of the most popular films in the genre, ranging from *Mission Impossible* (1996), *The Bourne Supremacy* (2004), *Indiana Jones and the Last Crusade* (1989), *The Peacemaker* (1997), *Clear and Present Danger* (1994), and *The Fugitive* (1993). In all of these films, the action hero's literacy skills are part of his power, part of what allow him (and it is almost always a man) to control those with less power or to outwit others in power. In addition, the action hero's literacy practices, while prodigious and effortless, often stand in opposition to the conventional literacy practices of his superiors, bureaucrats, scientists—and, of course, the villain. Routine and conventional literacy practices, like anything else routine and conventional, are disdained by the action hero who must work outside the system to be effective. The system itself, including its literacy practices, proves impotent against the danger, and that's why the action hero must save the day.

Of course, the use of literacy in the action movie genre is limited. It is important for the action hero to have omnipotent literacy skills and to be able to employ them instantly as part of his powers. In the end, however, literacy itself cannot save the day. He may be able to read a newspaper or book or computer screen at the crucial moment, but that literacy event will

86 *Popular culture and representations of literacy*

not provide the narrative climax. In the end he will have to shoot someone. The book by itself is not enough.

The villains, bureaucrats, scientists, and, often, women, however, are often highly literate and dependent on conventional and institutional literacies for their identities and power. Such dependence, in fact, eventually puts them at a disadvantage in relation to the action hero, who can match their literacy skills, but is also a man of action who can move beyond reading and writing. Too much dependence on conventional literacy is unmasculine, unheroic. Literacy is power, but only to a point.

In this chapter we look at how literacy functions as power in the hugely popular genre of action films. Rather than focus only on one or two films, in this chapter we are choosing to look at action films as a genre in order to demonstrate how representations of literacy practices can fulfill similar, and expected, narrative conventions in one action film after another. The scenes of reading and writing in action films, whether in a popular series such as the James Bond movies or a single film such as *The Peacemaker*, get repeated as set pieces that not only fulfill genre conventions, but also act as particular markers of the character of the action hero and his relationship with society.

ACTION, HEROES, AND GENRE

With the beginning of film, as with other narrative forms, there soon developed recognizable genres that helped describe the characteristics of different films. As with other popular culture forms, film genres are important for producers and the audiences because they help define expectations on both sides of the text. Meeting such expectations is a crucial part of the capitalist exchange that makes mass popular culture possible. Making a film meet certain genre expectations often means that a large audience can attend the film, confident in what it will encounter on the screen. At the same time, the producers of the film realize that to reach such an audience, they must fulfill genre expectations. These shared expectations are what make genre films both widely popular, as well as widely predictable. Not only can the narrative often be predicted before the first reel is over; audiences can, in fact, often predict the narrative arc of a genre film before walking into the theatre from the film's posters, trailers, or simply its cast list.

In fact, in many ways what happens in the actual narrative of a genre film often begins to matter less than the film's fulfillment of the necessary genre expectations. Genre films begin to depend less on the development of characters or specific narratives than they do "on the cumulative effect of the film's often repeated situations, themes, and icons" (Altman 1999, 25). In other words, it doesn't matter really what happens to the gangster/cowboy/alien/ingénue/action hero in the end of the movie, as long as the genre conventions, image, and themes are satisfied throughout the film.

Control and action 87

At the same time, as James Welsh (2000) notes, genre movies have to strike a balance between predictability and variety. If a movie is too formulaic, too predictable in its adherence to genre characteristics, it becomes either boring or ridiculous. On the other hand, "as filmmakers attempt to integrate new ideas and characters and dilemmas they risk the danger of tampering with the original formula, for if this is twisted too far and bent out of shape, the audience is also likely to be bent out of shape. Too much originality, then, can be risky and dangerous, once a successful formula has been established" (168).

The development of genres is not unique to film, of course. Yet the economic necessities of mass popular culture that require film producers to reach mass audiences mean that working within film genres that have proven popular with as many people as possible demands decisions of financial wisdom more than artistic design. Consequently, popular genres, such as action films, dominate film production year after year.

A common narrative of the development of film genres regards them as evolving through a three-stage process. First, there is the initial period of consolidation in which specific narratives, symbols, and visual conventions are shaped into configurations that begin to meet recurring audience expectations. This initial period is followed by the "golden age" of a genre, during which the genre is highly popular, and the narratives and features, while meeting audience expectations, also branch out into many different permutations of the central narrative. The final stage is marked by the wearing out of the genre as it declines either into parody or into revisionist, self-reflexive narratives (Collins 2002). As genres develop recognizable characteristics, they become less connected to the world outside the film and more dependent on intertextual references to other films in the same genres. In other words, spy films are more about other spy films than they are about real world political situations (Altman 1999). (Though some have questioned the simplicity and linearity of this model, it is useful in considering how certain scenes and symbols become part of the characteristics of a genre. Indeed, most films draw on more than one genre, and those genre characteristics operate discursively in multiple discursive sites. A single film, then, cannot be always neatly defined in one genre that is read the same way by all audiences.)

Still, though genre is not as easy to define as the categories at the local video store might lead one to believe, it is still an important means of understanding how films are both produced and interpreted. As Rick Altman (1999) notes, genre films maintain strong connections to the culture that produced them: "Whereas other films depend heavily on their referential qualities to establish ties to the real world, genre films typically depend on *symbolic* usage of key images, sounds, and situations" (26). For example, in a western, the actual location of a town in the film is less important than the iconic images of the saloon or the frontier farm. In action films, an example of such a symbolic moment might be the villain's high tech office

88   *Popular culture and representations of literacy*

or hideout, or the hero's offhand quip after dispatching an adversary. As we will demonstrate, literacy practices in action films fulfill similarly symbolic roles and expectations.

The contemporary action hero genre began with the James Bond movies of the 1960s. Action movies, though clearly connected in their approaches to character and narrative with such genres as westerns, war, and gangster films, developed through their initial stage with the James Bond films of the 1960s and early 1970s, went through a popular golden age in the 1980s and early 1990s, with film stars such as Mel Gibson, Arnold Schwarzenegger, Sylvester Stallone, and Bruce Willis defining the genre. Currently, the genre is in a period when it remains popular but is also often parodied in films such as *Undercover Brother* (2002), *Loaded Weapon* (1993), and the *Austin Powers* (1997) series. The stars of more recent action films (Tom Cruise, George Clooney, Nicolas Cage, Ewan McGregor), unlike the earlier action heroes such as Stallone and Schwarzenegger, have also become less identified with that particular genre as they move back and forth from action movie to "serious" dramatic roles.

Still, the action films of today are constructed around recognizable genre characteristics that are presented to fulfill audience expectations. James Welsh (2000) offers a summary of the genre that it would be possible to plug any movie into, from *Dr. No* (1962) to *Die Hard* (1988) to whatever opened at the local multiplex this most recent July:

> Clearly, then, viewers know and understand what action-adventure movies involve: a tough, potentially brutal, sometimes cynical, often laconic, preferably muscular, oversized hero, an action-packed spectacle involving car chases (or some equivalent—motorcycles, boats, buses, trains—speed and recklessness being necessary to quicken the pace), explosive devises and demolition, impending disaster caused by either natural causes (fires, floods, earthquakes, meteors, tornadoes, hurricanes, and the like) or the evil machinations of wicked villains, terrorists, mad bombers, anarchists, power-hungry despots, or crime lords. The task is always to avert the disaster, disarm the bomb, control the situation, thwart the villain, and save the day. (170)

In addition, the hero is usually aided by a sidekick, who is either a woman or a much less masculine man. Also, the hero is often a person either outside of the mainstream culture or at the very least extremely at odds with authority. He finds authority, particularly in the form of his superiors, stifling, inflexible, and dangerous to his plans to save the world. (In this respect, action heroes are often much like central characters in Hollywood comedies, who use the institutions of school, government, and business as their ridiculously rigid foils. In fact, action heroes have also often relied on moments of comic relief—such as the coy quip made after dispatching an adversary—as well as muscles and explosions.)

Control and action 89

BEYOND BUREAUCRACIES

Though not listed in the summary above, there are scenes of literacy practices that appear and reappear in action movies over the years, and fulfill similar narrative and character needs, and by extension, audience expectations, even as the genre has changed over time. We all expect an action film to have a chase scene or two (or three or more), and we are rarely disappointed. We can be equally confident of seeing certain scenes of literacy, if we pay attention to them. One measure of how familiar these scenes of literacy have become in action movies is the way they have shown up in action movie parodies in recent years as self-referential, recognizable gags. It is the repetition of these scenes of literacy in action films that draws us in this chapter to look at a number of movies across a genre, rather than singling out one or two.

One example of such a literacy event in action films is what we call the "file-on-the-desk moment." This scene often occurs early in many action films, including the Bond films, the *Lethal Weapon* (1987) films, the *Dirty Harry* (1973) films, *Beverly Hills Cop* (1984), *Behind Enemy Lines* (2002), *SWAT* (2004), *Rush Hour* (1998), and too many others to count. The hero has, often within the first few minutes of a film, been involved in a chase or shootout or fight that has saved the situation, but has somehow also violated either an institutional or a cultural rule. Very often, this violation is focused on the destruction of property (houses, buildings, cars, and so on). The file-on-the-desk scene is the moment when the hero is called into his supervisor's office and berated for his irresponsibility and inability to follow the rules. The supervisor has, either on his desk or in his hand, a file that we are told contains either a report of the hero's unconventional actions or complaints from those who define the culture, such as the mayor or the police chief or business leaders or many ordinary citizens. The supervisor uses this file as evidence that the hero is a threat to the community, even though he has just succeeded in vanquishing the foe, and uses it as the rationale for suspending or demoting the hero as well.

A specific example of this scene happens in the recent, loud, but inane action film, *SWAT* (2004). At the start of the film, two police officers, Jim Street (Colin Farrell) and Brian Gamble (Jeremy Renner), disobey orders in a hostage situation, killing the suspects, but wounding a woman hostage in the process. Soon after, we see them in the office of their superior officer, Captain Fuller (Larry Poindexter), who has several important looking files on his desk and one in his hand. As the officers defend their actions, arguing that the woman is still alive, Fuller waves the papers in his hand and berates them saying, "Yeah, alive and suing the city for millions. Chief says if he pays, somebody else does, too, and it sure as hell isn't going to be me."

The officers are asked where their "tactics" were, and Street answers, "Saving a woman from getting shot, that's where they were." Fuller replies,

90   *Popular culture and representations of literacy*

"You disobeyed a direct order. End of story. You're off SWAT." With that Fuller demotes Street to a clerical job.

All the common themes of the file-on-the-desk scene are present in this exchange. The bureaucrat, bowing to political pressure, with files in hand that support his case, castigates the action hero for disobeying orders or policies. When the action hero argues in response that his reliance on instinct and street smarts actually worked, he is sentenced to doing paperwork, the worst fate possible for a man of action and intuition.

In the Bond films, the obligatory opening action sequence is almost always followed by an obligatory scene at the headquarters of MI6, where Bond is surrounded by the literacy artifacts of bureaucracy. Both M, Bond's superior, and Moneypenny, M's secretary, have files on their desks, in their hands, and in cabinets near their desks. M is often reading a file as Bond enters the office, but Bond rarely touches paper in these scenes. Instead, M often asks him what he knows about a particular subject, and Bond is able to respond knowledgably, without having to consult notes or files. In *The Man with the Golden Gun* (1974), for example, Bond (Roger Moore) enters M's office, where M (Bernard Lee) is perusing files with two other older, graying, bureaucrats. The following exchange takes place:

M: What do you know about a man named Scaramanga?
Bond: Scaramanga? Oh yes, 'the man with the golden gun.' Born in the circus. Father a ringmaster, possibly Cuban. Mother English, a snakecharmer. He was a spectacular trick-shot artist by the time he was ten, and a local gunman at fifteen. The KGB recruited him there and trained him in Europe, where he became an overworked and underpaid assassin. He went independent in the late Fifties. Current price: One million dollars a hit. No photograph on file. But he does have one distinguishing feature, a superfluous papilla (M looks puzzled) a mammary gland, a third nipple, sir. He always uses a golden bullet, hence 'man with the golden gun.' Present domicile, unknown. I think that's all. Why sir?

Rather than needing to read the files, Bond instead offers expertise, quips, and a quick escape from the desk-bound environment back to the world of action and intrigue. As with many scenes of literacy in action films, the file-on-the-desk confrontation is so ritualistically repeated that it is also a staple of action film parodies such as *Undercover Brother* (2002).

Although in more conventional dramatic films, the person with the file on the desk is a person of power—an attorney, doctor, police officer, teacher, and the file is regarded as a threat, in action films, the relationship of literacy to power is not so straightforward. The supervisor may be a figure of authority with some power over the hero. Yet we are clearly meant to read his (again, it is usually a "he") fury as impotent and wrong-headed.

Control and action 91

The supervisor is rule-bound, unimaginative, and has lost touch with the grim realities the hero must confront. The hero, on the other hand, is the person actually in control of the situation. For we know, having seen this scene play out countless times, that the hero may be suspended or demoted, but will leave the office unchastened and still resolute in his determination to find and defeat any villain who crosses his path.

The file-on-the-desk scene, set early in the film, helps establish the hero as a rebel, as a charismatic loner not bound by institutional rules and traditions. The lone, anti-establishment hero not only connects the action hero to other Hollywood genres, such as the western or gangster film that preceded the action film, but also offers the audience "generic pleasure as an alternative to cultural norms. This pleasure derives from a perception that the activities producing it are free from the control exercised by the culture and felt by the spectator in the real world" (Altman 1999, 156). The lone hero gets to live outside the constraints of a culture of conformity and obedience that the audience inhabits, but wishes to forget, at least for a time. If the loner does not completely step outside of the apparatus of ideology, at least he offers some vicarious thrills of being able to flout authority and yet still remain the admirable hero of society. As Altman notes, action films always return to cultural norms as order is restored, and the hero often rejoins the mainstream culture or even the good graces of the institution from which he has earlier been estranged, but in the middle of the film, there is a pleasure offered in the hero's rejection of mainstream culture and its institutions.

One of the consistent rejections the hero makes in action films is that of institutional and bureaucratic literacy practices. Just as the hero rejects the concerns contained in the file on the desk, occasionally even physically tossing the file aside, he rejects any literacy practices that seem constrained by bureaucratic needs or rules. In a scene from *Die Another Day* (2002), Bond (Pierce Brosnan this time) is being supplied with his array of high-tech gadgets by the exasperated Q (John Cleese). Bond is presented with a new Aston-Martin equipped with, among other "modifications," guns on the front that automatically track and shoot objects in the air. After quickly explaining all the gadgets on the car, Q hands Bond a thick book:

Q: Why don't you acquaint yourself with the manual? You should be able to shoot through that in a couple of hours.
Bond: (Takes the book, gives it a disdainful glance, and tosses it in the air, at which point the guns on the car spin around and blow the book into confetti. Bond smirks): Just took a few seconds, Q.
Q: Wish I could make you vanish.

The audience can always count on Bond to find the literacy practices of bureaucrats to be both stultifying and unnecessary. Like most action heroes,

92 *Popular culture and representations of literacy*

he won't engage in literacies that are conventional or bureaucratic (such as reports, journals, or official letters), or respect the people who do engage in such reading and writing. He has no time for organizational literacy, in part because he is too busy saving the world. Bureaucrats, administrators, and teachers, with their institutional literacies and pedantic instruction, get in the way of real knowledge and action. We know that Bond will be able to use the car without reading the manual, and will do so later in the film. Certainly, the scene captures the feelings of many people toward technical manuals. Most of us would prefer to be able to simply start using the new software or cell phone or computer with ease and expertise, without having to wade through thick and possibly poorly written manual. The difference is that James Bond can always do so without bringing the whole system down.

The rejection of bureaucratic literacies also reinforces the common theme of action films of pitting institutional knowledge against "real world" knowledge or "street smarts." Bond doesn't need the manual or the files, not only because he is competent, but also because he knows that such institutional knowledge will not be useful to him on the street. Such scenes are even more pronounced in action films where the hero's class status, unlike the well-educated English Bond, also puts him at odds with dominant cultural institutions. In such scenes, the rough, roguish action hero, portrayed as being more connected to the working class, and also usually American, rejects the institutional knowledge of a bureaucrat or scientist because he knows that it is incompatible with what he knows of the "real world." Of course, this "street" knowledge invariably trumps the institutional knowledge and humiliates the so-called expert.

In *The Peacemaker* (1997), an early scene in the film provides an example of such an exchange. After a nuclear weapon explodes in Russia following a train collision, Dr. Julia Kelly (Nicole Kidman), an acting director of a federal nuclear weapons agency, is holding a briefing about the incident in a large amphitheatre-style room. She stands behind a podium with a series of high-tech screens behind her, while military and other officials sit in the audience with large briefing books in front of them. Kelly is discussing possible terrorist suspects for the explosion, and telling her audience that they can read about "other possibles on our terrorist list as outlined in Section Four of your packet," when Lt. Col. Thomas Devoe (George Clooney) walks in, late. Devoe has already been established, in an earlier scene, as a roguish but charming rule-breaker, who values street-smarts over regulations.

As Kelly is about to talk more about why some group might have set off the bomb, Devoe interrupts her and asks if the terrorists have made demands. She replies that they haven't, but that they may be forthcoming, and tries to continue her briefing. Devoe interrupts again, and, when she still tries to continue her briefing, he gets out of his chair, walks past her, and gestures to a satellite photo projected on the wall.

Control and action 93

Devoe: Excuse me, again, I'm sorry to keep interrupting. You see these blobs at one meter resolution, here and here? Those are people jumping off the passenger train before it crashes. Now take a look at the other train, that's the one with the nuke. Nobody's jumping off that. Why not?

Kelly: (Looking flustered but coming to a realization): They were already dead. Are you suggesting this was a robbery? ...

Devoe: I'm sorry ma'am, this was a hijacking. The detonation was a smoke screen, and whoever stole these things got off the bus a long way back.

Kelly: (Resentful as room buzzes with conversation): Well, we'll certainly consider your theory. Thank you. Thank you very much.

Devoe: (Smirking): Well, it's just an opinion.

Devoe's street smarts prove to be persuasive and more accurate than the extensive written documents Kelly has produced and distributed. She is forced to admit, in public, that her reliance on written words and analysis has led her to an incorrect interpretation of events that Devoe could ascertain almost instantly, like any good many of action. (The scene also sets up the dynamic between the action hero and his literate sidekick that indicates that she can help him, but that his ability to work on intuition and act decisively will in the end be more important, another common trope in such films that we will discuss later in the chapter.)

It is important in this scene that Kelly is well educated. For if the action hero rejects institutional literacies, one of the institutions often singled out for his scorn is education. Most often in action movies, as in the scene from *The Peacemaker*, the scenes that represent this rejection involve scientists, rather than directly involving literacy teachers or other educators. As in *The Peacemaker*, however, many films include a scene of the street-smart action hero rejecting the conventional and institutional knowledge and literacies of the scientist to produce a more unconventional but more accurate interpretation. The implications of such scenes are that academic or schooled literacies are worthless for solving real problems, and, instead, may lead people to conclusions or ideas that actually get in the way of solving problems properly. In addition, the scientist in such scenes, when not played by Nicole Kidman, is often portrayed as pedantic, arrogant, and disconnected from the "real world." When such scientists are men, they are portrayed as unmasculine; when women, if not being set up to be the hero's love interest (once she takes off her glasses), they are portrayed as asexual. For both sexes, scientists are unquestionably nerdy. Academic literacies are not only worthless, but they are the domain of bookworms and nerds who don't have a clue about how to solve genuine problems.

A similar stance toward masculinity and conventional literacy exists in films based on popular comic book heroes. Superman (Christopher Reeve) saves lives not by being a reporter, which is his mild-mannered alter ego,

94   *Popular culture and representations of literacy*

but by shedding his glasses (again, always the mark of a nerd) and acting, not writing. In the Spiderman movies, Peter Parker (Tobey Maguire) is forced to choose between being the powerful superhero or being a nerdy student who can succeed in school. In *Spiderman 2* (2004), we see that when Peter is being Spiderman, he is chastised by a professor (Dylan Baker) for failing in school, but when rejects his superpowers, we seem him reading, wearing his glasses, and getting high praise for his academic work. We understand that when he returns to being Spiderman, as we know he must to save the day, his studies and books will again have to take a back seat. Reading and writing would not be enough to defeat a supervillain. Superheroes may be literate in their daily lives, but then they are also impotent. It is only when they get away from institutionalized literacy that they become powerful. Even Indiana Jones (Harrison Ford), supposedly a university professor, has little time for institutional literacies. In *Indiana Jones and the Last Crusade* (1989) we see him, when confronted by students who wish to discuss coursework, escape through his office window so he can be off on a real adventure.

James Bond, Indiana Jones, Thomas Devoe, and most other action heroes have no need for school or for schooled literacies. They can dismiss institutional literacies, not only because such literacies are often superfluous to the actions they must take, but also because on those occasions when they need to read and write they are usually able to do so in ways that match the needs of any situation. If James Bond needs to read a computer screen, write a note, decipher a code, he can do so in any language he pleases. We never see him learn the literacy skills, they simply are available when the need arises. His literacy skills, unlike those of teachers, scientists, and bureaucrats, are always useful, always correct. Literacy is most powerful in action films when is seems effortless and spontaneous.

SOCIAL STATUS, DISCOURSE AND POWER

The effortless nature of the literacy practices of action heroes is also often evidence of their class and social status, just as literacy practices in real life often reveal class markers in the ritualistic way they allow for the proving of identity. (For more on this issue see Chapter Three). James Bond, for example, often gets away with dismissing institutional literacies because of class, race, and gender status. It is hard to imagine Moneypenny, in her position as a female secretary, for example, getting away with the same kind of disdain for bureaucratic literacies as Bond. The same can be said of the Devoe character in *The Peacemaker* in the way in which he uses his status as a white, male, military officer, or, similarly, of Ethan Hunt (Tom Cruise) in the *Mission Impossible* (1996) films, or of the character of Indiana Jones.

Not all action heroes are members of the elite classes. The pervasive cultural mythology in the U.S. that celebrates social mobility and yet fears the elite classes results in Hollywood action films that revolve around smart and resourceful working-class characters, such as John McClane (Bruce Willis) the off-duty police officer in the *Die Hard* films. Even though he is just a simple police officer (who just happens to be married to a beautiful high-powered corporate executive), McClane also has no trouble reading any text he encounters. His facility, along with the facility of his fellow action heroes, to read or write what they want on demand raises a question about literacy, learning, and acquisition.

James Gee, in his discussions of discourses over the years, has maintained that there is a distinction between the literacy skills we learn through direct instruction and the discourses we acquire through our immersion in a particular culture. Gee (1989) defines discourse as "a sort of 'identity kit' which comes complete with appropriate costume and instructions on how to act, talk, and often write, so as to take on a particular role that others will recognize" (526). Discourse, in Gee's definition, is not just the literacy skills one possesses, but the cultural knowledge of how and when to display such skills. James Bond is the classic example of a film character who is comfortable in every discourse. He always knows what to read or write in any situation, in any language, in any culture. He is as comfortable with a wine list as he is with a blueprint or a diplomatic document. This is particularly impressive, given Gee's argument that discourses cannot be learned through direct instruction, but are instead acquired through trial and error through meaningful activities in the midst of a culture. Though there are all manner of discourses, some we are reared in, and others that we acquire along the way, it is clear that some discourses are more privileged in any given culture. Gee calls these "dominant discourses" and describes them as the discourses of power, of cultural and economic capital in the dominant culture (527–528).

James Bond is obviously comfortable with the dominant discourse. Well-educated and well-read in the dominant culture, he not only can read or write in any circumstance, but he is unfailingly correct in understanding the appropriate cultural context for his literacy practices. No one ever questions Bond's presence at auctions, cabinet meetings, charity balls, or laboratories. In *Diamonds Are Forever* (1971), we see Bond (Sean Connery) handle literacy events in a laboratory, luxury penthouse, and casino with equal ease. He is the quintessential master of the dominant discourse, and that provides him access to the corridors of power, both good and villainous, access that is central to his power to save the day. Yet while Bond is the most polished of contemporary Hollywood action heroes, many of them (*The Bourne Identity* (2002), *Clear and Present Danger* (1994), *Air Force On* (1998), *The Peacemaker* (1997), *Executive Decision* (1995)) share with him the ability to adopt the dominant discourse, or at least understand it,

96 *Popular culture and representations of literacy*

when necessary. Again, working-class action heroes, like John McClane or Roger Murtaugh (Danny Glover) and Martin Riggs (Mel Gibson) in the *Lethal Weapon* movies, still seem to be able to step into the dominant discourse when it is necessary to thwart international terrorists or smugglers. As Gee notes, discourses are inherently ideological, and wielding literacy and power within a discourse requires an understanding of the values and assumptions of that discourse. Power, in terms of literacy, often comes from more than the skills of reading and writing, but rests on the ability of knowing how, when, and why to display their literacy practices.

Those who have not mastered a discourse lack the same power. For, unlike learning a language or a particular literacy skill, the cultural knowledge that accompanies a discourse must be complete if a person is not be marked as an imposter.

> Someone can speak English, but not fluently. However someone cannot engage in a Discourse in a less than fully fluent manner. You are either in it or you're not. Discourses are connected with displays of an identity; failing to fully display an identity is tantamount to announcing you don't have that identity, that at best you're a pretender or a beginner. (Gee 1989, 529)

As we noted in our discussion in of class in Chapter Three, part of the success of the imposter in *Catch Me if You Can* (2002) comes not from his knowledge of literacy practices, but from his understanding of the discourse of each culture he tries to inhabit. You can fake reading, but even if you can read and write, if you display it in the wrong way at the wrong time, you're an outsider.

In the famous example from *From Russia with Love* (1963), Red Grant (Robert Shaw), a Russian agent working for SPECTRE tries to pass as a British agent. Though his accent and demeanor seem flawless, he orders red wine with fish, raising Bond's (Sean Connery) suspicions (though not enough to avoid a rousing fight scene). A similar moment comes at the end of *Diamonds Are Forever* (1971), when a would-be assassin's (Bruce Glover) lack of understanding of a wine list tips Bond (Connery) off just in time dispatch his foe.

Bond: The wine is quite excellent. Although for such a grand meal I would have expected a claret.
Mr. Wint: But of course. Unfortunately, our cellar is poorly stocked with clarets.
Bond: Mouton Rothschild *is* a claret. And I've smelled that aftershave before, and both times—I've smelled a rat.

Real action heroes would never have the problem of endangering their lives through misreading. They have acquired the necessary literacy practices and the cultural knowledge to know how to employ them at a moment's notice.

LITERACY IN THE NICK OF TIME

How and when, then, does an action hero wield literacy as a tool of power?

First, of course, an action hero has to engage in literacy practices that support the expectations of the genre. Such expectations require that he usually act alone, be able to read or write what is necessary at a crucial moment without showing signs of struggle or previous education, and not rely on literacy to solve the final conflict when action is required.

Action heroes, like their film ancestors in westerns and gangster films, most often embody the mythology of the lone hero. As many scholars have pointed out (Stroud 2001; Zender and Calvert 2004; Sanchez-Escalonilla 2005), all these genres draw on the archetypal mythology of the lone hero, addressed at length by Joseph Campbell, who must turn his back on his past and embark on a quest that both allows him to discover his true nature as well as save society from grave danger. As we have already noted, this means that the action hero often must, early in the film, distance himself from institutional literacies the represent the dominant and conventional institutions of the culture. ("Buddy" action films tend to either use both characters as outcast heroes, as in the *Rush Hour* (1998) films or *I Spy* (2002), or, more conventionally, pair one lone hero with a character tied more closely to the dominant culture. Eventually, the latter is brought around to recognize the wisdom of the lone hero's approach to working outside of the institutional culture, such as in the *Lethal Weapon* films. The conventional partner in such films also often acts as the surrogate reader and writer for the lone hero, as we will discuss later in this chapter.)

Once such a distancing has been confirmed through a ritualistic "file-on-the-desk" type scene, the action hero's actions, including his literacy practices, are carried out individually. James Bond, for example, spends much of his time engaging in solitary literacy practices. Whether he is reading secret files, hacking in to an adversary's computer, throwing the right switch on a control panel, or reading the information on his top-secret gadgets, he takes literacy into his own hands and uses it for his own purposes. In a number of the Bond films, for example *Dr. No* (1962), *You Only Live Twice* (1967), *The Spy Who Loved Me* (1977), *Diamonds are Forever* (1971) and *Tomorrow Never Dies* (1997), there is a scene where Bond is faced with a massive control panel in the arch-villain's headquarters and has to act instantly to foil his enemy's plan. Bond can always read the panel quickly and throw the right switch or turn the right wheel to throw all into chaos. Bond, like most action heroes, is a loner who engages in most of his literacy practices by himself (except when being helped by a sidekick). Yet even as Bond's literacy practices are often solitary, he remains comfortable in the social world. Though he may be a loner, reading and writing often away from community, he is not a solitary nerd.

Indeed, unlike the nerd, the action hero rarely displays the work or the evidence of his literacy practices to others, unless it is to establish his power through a greater knowledge than those around him (bureaucrats,

98   Popular culture and representations of literacy

scientists, adversaries). Even then, the action hero rarely reads or writes in front of others. Instead he offers information he has gathered through literacy practices, often that have occurred off-screen, as in the Bond scene from *The Man With the Golden Gun* (1974) discussed earlier, where he displays his knowledge of an assassin, or in *Dr. No* (1962), where he discusses rocket technology, or in *Die Another Day* (2002), when the subject is "conflict diamonds." Bond is the embodiment of Scribner's (1984) metaphor of "literacy as grace." He exhibits all the characteristics of the person who is thought to be "literate" in the sense of being erudite and cultured, without having to exhibit a sense of learning or work in order to achieve such literacy. He simply has the education, literacy skills, and knowledge of discourse, and can use them to gain the advantage of any person, friend or foe, in any situation.

Though Bond is perhaps the most extreme illustration of such a character, he is by no means the only action hero to display such abilities. In films from *Indiana Jones and the Last Crusade* (1989) to *The Fugitive* (1993) to *The Peacemaker* (1997) to *Mission Impossible* (1996) to *The Bourne Identity* (2002), the action heroes are not only able to read or write anything on demand, but they rarely show any indication of having had to learn such skills or having to struggle with them. In *The Bourne Identity*, for example, Jason Bourne (Matt Damon) has amnesia; he has no sense at all of who he is. Yet he can read and write, in any language he encounters, with fluency and without hesitation. His sophisticated and multilingual literacy skills often allow him to elude his enemies, even when he doesn't know who his enemies are, and mark him as a person of importance and power. Perhaps the ultimate, and ultimately ludicrous, example of this characteristic of the action hero comes in *The Matrix* (1999), where Neo (Keanu Reeves) never has to learn to read, but simply has information downloaded into his brain in seconds that provides him with the skills he needs.

As we noted above, the action hero is, more often than not, a man. As a consequence, his literacy practices are influenced by the same cultural representations of male literacy practices as we discussed in Chapter Two. The action hero rarely if ever uses literacy to establish or nurture a social relationship or to explore his inner feelings. (One intriguing exception to this is Jason Bourne (Matt Damon) in *The Bourne Supremacy* (2004) who, along with reading codes and passports and other top secret information, is also seen keeping a journal that he uses to help piece together the fragments of his forgotten past.) Instead, for most action heroes, literacy is an instrumental practice, employed to accomplish a task in the same way that a car is employed in a chase scene. Literacy is a tool, nothing more. And though, unlike the characters in the romantic comedies discussed in Chapter Two, the action hero is not using literacy to try to make money, as a man of action he uses it simply to "get the job done."

If the "file-on-the-desk" scene is a common literacy scene that is recreated early in many action films, the action hero using literacy at a pivotal

Control and action 99

moment in the plot is also common. In some films literacy is used to summon help. In *Air Force One* (1998), for example, the president (Harrison Ford), captive on his hijacked airplane, is able to send a fax to the White House giving details of a plan to help the plane's passengers escape, while in *Con Air* (1998), Cameron Poe (Nicolas Cage), a "good" convict on a plane hijacked by other prisoners, writes a message on the body of a dead guard to send word to an agent on the ground that he is working for the good guys. In other films the literacy moment comes in the discovery of the nature or location of the real villain. In *Mission Impossible* (1996), Ethan Hunt (Tom Cruise) not only uses literacy to steal the list of secret agents that is at the center of the film's plot, but notices an inscription in a Bible that gives away the fact that his friend is a traitor. And in one Bond film after another, key moments pivot on literacy. In *Dr. No* (1962), Bond (Connery) looks through the library of an agent who has been murdered, and, amidst all the other papers and books, knows instantly that a receipt for work in a geology lab is a key leading him to his nemesis. Or, in *License to Kill* (1989), Bond (Timothy Dalton) finds a secret computer file with the name of a key CIA agent (Carey Lowell), who will help him find and defeat the villain. Or in *Die Another Day* (2002), Bond's (Brosnan) ability to read the mark on a diamond he has taken from an enemy during a fight reveals the initials of the film's archvillain, Gustav Graves (Toby Stephens), and sends Bond off on his trail.

Yet, while the action hero can call on whatever sophisticated literacy skills are necessary at crucial moments in a film, he only relies on literacy to a point. In the end he has to shoot someone (or impale, blow up, crush, drop, or otherwise kill the bad guy). Literacy may be part of the action hero's power, both instrumentally and culturally, but in the end an action hero has to triumph through action, not intellect. Literacy is both too cerebral and too potentially feminine to be the ultimate weapon. The action hero, for all his literacy skills, needs to triumph on instinct, street smarts, and the purity of his heart. (In rare action films, it is literacy that actually saves the day, as in *The Sum of All Fears* (2002), when Jack Ryan (Ben Affleck) gets the Russian Premier to engage in online chat that calms everyone's nerves and averts a nuclear war.)

In fact, literacy is rarely the deciding factor for the victory of good over evil in non-action dramas either. Though, again, it may provide important information at a pivotal point in a film, literacy is not usually present at the crucial, climactic moment. What is more common is a scene such as the climax of the film *The Majestic* (2001), a movie that leaves no sentimental cliché untouched. *The Majestic*'s climax comes during a hearing in the 1950s in front of the House UnAmerican Activities Committee, at which Peter Appleton (Jim Carrey) is ready to read a prepared statement naming names and getting him out of trouble with the committee. But as he goes to testify, his newfound love gives Appleton a copy of the Constitution, as well as a letter from her boyfriend, who died in the war. (The letter is

100   *Popular culture and representations of literacy*

shamelessly plagiarized from the letter of the U.S. Civil War soldier Sullivan Ballou, made famous in the Ken Burns' popular documentary on the war.) In the letter, Appleton reads the line "When bullies rise up, the rest of us have to beat them back down, whatever the cost." This inspires him to cast aside his prepared remarks when he faces the committee, and to speak from conviction, telling the committee how disappointed the dead war hero would be at the proceedings:

> He'd tell you the America represented in this room is not the America he died defending. I think he'd tell you your America is bitter and cruel and small. I know for a fact that his America was big. Bigger than you can imagine, with a wide-open heart. Where every person has a voice, even if you don't like what he has to say.

Of course, this impromptu speech carries the day, humiliates the committee, rallies the public to his side, and gets him back his girlfriend. In the movies, real heroes speak and act from the heart, not from words on a page.

LITERATE SIDEKICKS AND VILLAINS

Though the action hero can read or write on demand to track his enemy or get out of trouble, he is not the only character who regularly engages in literacy practices in action films. Just as common as the action hero's literacy practices are those by either his sidekick or by the chief villain. While the archetype of the action hero story often has the young hero mentored by someone wiser and older, in Hollywood films such relationships are usually reserved for fantasy or science fiction films (e.g., the *Star Wars* or *Lord of the Rings* films). Instead, the sidekick in most mainstream Hollywood films, including fantasy and science fiction films, is subordinate to the hero, either by rank or by implication. Yet the sidekick often acts as a literate surrogate for the action hero, doing the reading and research necessary to help the hero achieve his goals. This frees up the hero from having to do the more intellectual and less-action oriented work of reading and writing. Even action heroes, like James Bond, who can and will read or write when necessary, often have a literate sidekick to do reading and research for them. It is no surprise, then, to see that the literate sidekick is often decidedly less masculine than the hero. The sidekick is either a bookish and nerdy male (*Van Helsing* (2004), *Hellboy* (2004), *Sky Captain and the World of Tomorrow* (2004), *X-Men* (2000), *Independence Day* (1996)), or a woman, as in the case of a number of the Bond films (*Moonraker* (1979), *Goldeneye* (1995), *The World is Not Enough* (1999)) or other action films (*The Peacemaker* (1997), *Top Gun* (1986), *I, Robot* (2004), *Paycheck* (2003)). The films with more traditionally masculine literate side-

Control and action   101

kicks (*Mission Impossible* (1996), *The Matrix* (1999)) still put the sidekick in a clearly supporting role in relation to the hero.

In the same way that the action hero has to avoid institutional literacies and rely on his street smarts and intuition, the literate sidekick allows him to be able to avoid reading or writing at all. This way, the hero can focus on being in action, acting on instinct, and making things happen. By contrast, the literate sidekick can provide support and information, but, because his or her literacy is either connected to institutions or simply cannot cause the death of the villain, the literate sidekick can only be a supporting character, not the person who provides the ultimate triumph. The existence of a literate sidekick allows some action heroes—Arnold Schwarzenegger and Sylvester Stallone come to mind—to rarely read or write at all in their films.

In the film *Van Helsing* (2004), for example, the title character (Hugh Jackman) may be the dashing hero who dispatches vampires and other monsters, but he isn't the person who reads inscriptions, does research, or takes care of other literacy chores. Those duties fall to his sidekick, Carl (David Wenham), a quick-witted, comic, but not particularly action-oriented friar. Carl is instrumental is decoding a magic tapestry that gives Van Helsing access to the lair of Count Dracula, for example. Early in the film, when Carl is advising Van Helsing on what weapons he will need to fight the Count, Van Helsing questions him, "You've never been out of the abbey, how do you know about vampires?" to which Carl replies, "I *read*."

Throughout the film, there is no doubt who is the star of the film and will end up fighting all the special-effects laden fights, and who will be the literate comic-relief sidekick. The relationship is even more stark in *Hellboy* (2004), in which the title character (Ron Perlman), a hulking half-human, half-demon who fights even more evil creatures than Van Helsing, is assisted by his literate sidekick Abe Sapien (Doug Jones). While, again, Hellboy does all the fighting and gets the love interest, Sapien reads the books and summarizes the information Hellboy needs to defeat the monster. Sapien is a slender amphibian-like creature with a high-pitched, aristocratic voice, who doesn't need to even touch the books to read several of them at a time. He is, perhaps, the ultimate representation of a disembodied, unmasculine, intellectual literate sidekick. But it is the hulking Hellboy who is the hero.

Although the action hero often depends on a literate sidekick, he is called on at times to either correct the sidekick's misreading of information (as in the earlier example of the briefing room in *The Peacemaker* (1997)), or to in some other way establish his dominant cultural position. This is a particularly common trope in the Bond films. Sometimes Bond corrects or extends his female, literate sidekick's reading of information. The sidekick will offer one piece of information, and Bond will make the crucial connection to information he possesses that puts the information in the proper context. Or, given that Bond's literate sidekicks are usually beautiful women, in addition to being physicists, for example, he seduces

102 *Popular culture and representations of literacy*

them. In treating them as sexual conquests, Bond ignores or denigrates their intellectual and literate identities and re-establishes himself as the person in power in the relationship.

For example, in *The World is Not Enough* (1999), Denise Richards plays a nuclear weapons expert improbably named Christmas Jones. On the one hand, she is introduced as a scientist who can disarm the most dangerous weapons; on the other hand, the first time we see her in the film she is taking off her protective jumpsuit to reveal that she has come to work at a former Soviet military base in nothing more than a tank top and tight shorts. In the film, every time Jones demonstrates her expertise, Bond is there to either correct it or reinterpret it. For example, after a nuclear warhead has been stolen, there is an alert inside an oil pipeline. Jones looks at the readout on a computer screen and states, "There is no sign of the bomb." But Bond corrects her, saying that the bomb is inside the pipeline. She is right that the readout shows no sign of the bomb. Bond's more accurate interpretation comes from his superior intuition that goes beyond what can be read off a screen. By the end of the film, once the villain has been vanquished in the waters off Istanbul, however, there is the obligatory scene where Bond seduces the woman, as he would if she were a scientist or not, with the usual campy dialogue.

Bond: I've always wanted to have Christmas in Turkey.
Jones: Isn't it time you unwrapped your present?

The other obvious literacy practitioners in action films are the villains. Villains in action films are often highly literate. But, like literate sidekicks, the literacy of villains is often portrayed as standing in contrast to that of the action hero. In many of the Bond films, for example, highly literate villains—Dr. No (Joseph Wiseman), Ernst Stavro Blofeld (Donald Pleasance, Telly Savalas, Charles Gray), Hugo Drax (Michael Lonsdale), Elliot Carver (Jonathon Pryce)—are often portrayed as elitist, effete, and decidedly unmasculine. This is the case in other action films, such as *Raiders of the Lost Ark* (1981), *Indiana Jones and the Last Crusade* (1989), *Die Hard* (1988), *Lethal Weapon 2* (1989), and *Sky Captain and the World of Tomorrow* (2004), among others. Indeed the villain in such films often needs to be highly literate to be taken seriously as a "criminal master-mind." If the villain is not sufficiently intellectual he (and, again, it is almost invariably a "he") cannot be plausibly the head of a large organization with grand plots for world domination (as caricatured so thoroughly in the guise of Dr. Evil (Mike Myers) in the *Austin Powers'* films). But the highly literate villain is not usually a man of action. Instead, he relies on a series of henchmen and thugs to carry out physical tasks. An exception to the reliance on thugs comes in comic book movies, where the villain is often highly literate and intellectual—often a good scientist driven bad by accident or injustice—but has developed super powers, such as the Green Goblin (Willem Dafoe) or

Control and action 103

Dr. Octopus (Alfred Molina), in the *Spiderman* films, or Magneto (Ian McKellen), in the *X-Men* films.

The character of Elliot Carver (Jonathan Pryce) in the Bond film *Tomorrow Never Dies* (1997) is a particularly effective example of such a character. He is not only highly literate, but is, in fact, a news media and computer software tycoon. As such, his plots are complicated and intellectual. He is slightly built, wears glasses, and speaks with a coy and upper-class English accent. When he wants enemies eliminated or he needs protection, he has henchmen, assassins, and thugs at his command.

Early in the film, we see Carver in his headquarters, addressing his editors around the world as they are projected on a huge set of television screens: "Good morning, my golden retrievers. What kind of havoc shall the Carver Media Group create in the world today? News?"

When his editors report a variety of disasters, Carver responds with flamboyant glee, tapping out the day's headlines on a small, wireless keyboard. Pryce's performance is wildly campy and, as with many Bond villains, plays on homosexual stereotypes. As with other Bond villains, though he is involved with a beautiful woman (who will turn against him when seduced by Bond), his attentions and affections seem much more intense toward his chief henchman, often played by a younger, lean, and attractive actor. The homophobic portrayal of Bond villains has been discussed by other scholars (Jenkins 2005), but represents another intriguing way, along with feminine or nerdy literate sidekick, that literacy in action films is represented as decidedly unmasculine.

Later in the film there is the obligatory debate between Bond and the villain about the villain's plans. Carver is telling Bond about how he will fabricate the agent's obituary after he is killed.

Bond: I never believe what I read in the press anyway.
Carver: Therein lies your problem, Mr. Bond. We're both men of action, but your era and Ms. Lin's is passing. Words are the new weapons, and satellites the new artillery... Caesar had his legions, Napoleon had his armies; I have my divisions: TV, newspapers, and magazines.

For all the villain's intellect and sophisticated literacies, however, he will always be undone by the action hero. Sometimes there is a flaw in the literacy practices of the villain that contributes to this, such as a computer code the villain has built his plan around that the action hero is able to decode and disable. While the villain may be literate, he can never have skills superior to the action hero's. And while literacy may allow the villain to gain what power he has, it can ultimately contribute to his downfall. In *Tomorrow Never Dies* for example, Bond foils the technology of a "stealth" ship, making it vulnerable to attack.

104 *Popular culture and representations of literacy*

Whether the action hero can match the literacy skills of the villain is, in the end, usually immaterial. For the action hero's advantage over the villain is his capacity for physical action. The villain may devise ways for his henchmen to kill the hero, but the hero will not only elude such dangers, yet also be able to kill the villain. By the end of *Tomorrow Never Dies*, Carver has Bond at gunpoint, gloating over how the agent will die and the villain survive in glory. But Bond, standing against a ship's control panel, and able to read it instantly for the one thing that will save his life, pushes the control that activates a massive drill. As the drill bears down on his terrified enemy, Bond quips: "You forgot the first rule of mass media, Elliot: give the people what they want."

THE PEN AND THE SWORD

Educators and scholars may conceive of literacy as a path to power, but action films, perhaps the most popular genre of contemporary films, reveal a more complicated set of representations of literacy and power. The action hero, though not averse to reading or writing in the heat of the moment to achieve an instrumental end, does so with an effortlessness that undermines our understandings of how literacies are learned and practiced. In addition, the action hero can engage in any literacy he chooses, but invariably disdains both the people and institutions that represent conventional literacies and any more abstract intellectual literacy practices. Instead, the latter are consigned to acting as supporting, often comic, sidekicks and effete villains.

All of these representations of literacy have become ritualized and essential components of the action movie genre. The file-on-the-desk moment and the literate sidekick are as integral a part of the genre as the car chase and the action hero's quip after dispatching his foe. Film audiences are both prepared for these formulaic representations and to read such scenes and characters in conventional ways. Literacy is rigid, feminine, and not entirely to be trusted if it is intellectual or abstract. Heroism is masculine, physical, and effortless in its instrumental literacy practices.

In *Goldeneye* (1995), in the obligatory scene between Bond (Brosnan) and Q (Desmond Llewelyn), in which Q presents Bond with all his lethal gadgets, Q hands Bond a pen, explaining, "This is a Class Four grenade. Three clicks arms the four-second fuse, another three disarms it."

Bond (takes the pen and clicks it three times): How long did you say the fuse was?
Q (takes the pen back and disarms it): Oh, grow up, 007.
Bond: They always said the pen was mightier than the sword.
Q: Thanks to me, they were right!

In action films, the pen doesn't stand a chance against the sword.

6 The perils of misreading
Literacy as danger

For literacy researchers and teachers, the worst thing to imagine is illiteracy.

Illiteracy is what we strive to eliminate, in the fervent belief that literacy offers people an unalloyed good. Yet in contemporary movies, illiteracy itself is not usually portrayed as dangerous. People who are dangerous may also be illiterate, but it is rarely the cause of the threat. It's rarely even implied that the motivating force behind a serial killer in a slasher film is his frustration at his inability to read. No, in popular movies the greater threat is not illiteracy, it is incomplete literacy. Incomplete literacy—having the literacy skills to read and write but not the wisdom or education to correctly interpret and evaluate—is what often creates great danger for well-intentioned characters.

The misreading of texts, the misinterpretation of writing, the misplaced trust in the written word, are common paths to psychological and physical danger in the movies.

The misread or misinterpreted document is often a central plot component of suspense films. As just one example, Matt Whitlock (Denzel Washington), the local police chief in the film-noir inspired *Out of Time* (2003) misinterprets his wife's life insurance policy and medical report, and is subsequently implicated in the supposed murder of his lover and her husband. Whitlock then finds that other, previously innocuous documents, such as phone call records, become potentially incriminating. Such a misreading at a key moment is a plot device found in thrillers from *The Maltese Falcon* (1941) to *Body Heat* (1981) to *Minority Report* (2002). It reaches perhaps its most elaborate expression in the cult hit *Memento* (2000), in which the protagonist, Leonard Shelby (Guy Pearce), afflicted by a condition that causes him to lose his short-term memory every fifteen minutes, valiantly tries to make sense of his experiences by writing everything down, to the point of tattooing key phrases all over his body. He is desperate to find the person who murdered his wife. Unable to remember the context in which he wrote the cryptic phrases ("Never Answer the Phone" or "Do Not Believe His Lies"), Leonard misinterprets the messages and ends up murdering one of the few friends who is actually trying to help him. This compounds the irony when

106 *Popular culture and representations of literacy*

it appears that it was, in fact, Leonard who killed his wife, and it was the psychological trauma of that act that triggered his inability to remember.

Memento is a postmodern fairy tale told by a poststructuralist. In another genre, Leonard Shelby might be portrayed as a man under a spell, cursed by witches or the gods to not remember what matters most to him, and thus to move inexorably toward his ironic and fatal blunders. His inability to interpret texts correctly is connected with his inability to recognize good or evil. The texts, even the ones on his body, are free floating and disconnected from context, signifiers, and morality. It is in the misinterpretations and decontextualized readings of texts that the real danger of literacy in the movies emerges time and again.

Perhaps this display of literacy as danger is most pronounced and prevalent in the film genres of fantasy, horror, and science fiction. Time and again, in these genres, we see young people who are either brashly confident or naively innocent (or sometimes both), trust their own readings of mysterious or magical texts, and then must contend with the danger or evil their misreadings and misinterpretations unleash. A classic example of this is in *The Evil Dead* (1981), where five young friends, off to vacation at an isolated cabin, find a mysterious book, along with a tape recorder. On the tape is a translation of the book, the reading of which turns some of the friends into voracious zombies. As in *The Evil Dead,* the cause of dangerous misreadings in movies is often a problem with determining authorship of the text or an incomplete knowledge of context needed to come to a more accurate reading. The danger is compounded because the misreadings are often connected with a rejection of the wisdom of those in authority, often including school or other cultural institutions. Because the authorship of the texts is unknown or misleading, the "truth" of the texts becomes lies, and the power of literacy turns out to be ambiguous and dark. And when the impetuous youth (very often male) rejects schooled literacies and the protection of wise elders and cultural institutions, his subsequent misreadings cause suffering or peril for himself and those around him. Only the correct reading, or the intervention of a wise person to help guide the hero to the correct reading, can save the day.

In this chapter we focus on representations of literacy as a power that is dark, even overtly dangerous. As an illustration, we use the film *Harry Potter and the Chamber of Secrets* (2002) to show how, in some of the most popular films of recent years, fantasy and science fiction films, literacy is imbued with mystical and ambiguous power that echoes ancient and medieval perceptions. In this film and others like it, what is most dangerous is not illiteracy but unschooled literacy. Indeed the real literacies of power in such films are often represented in contrast to more ordinary school or scholarly literacy. The characters struggle with the literacies that pull them into a violent underworld paralleling the tame everyday. In these films, texts are often not to be trusted; those who can decode texts risk unleashing great dangers if they fail to properly interpret what they are reading.

TEXTS WITHOUT AUTHORS

In many ways, the critical theory that emerged in the late twentieth century to dominate literary and culture studies only explains what has been going on for years in the representations of literacy practices in fantasy and science fiction movies. Concepts such as the inability to establish authorial intent, the indeterminacy of meaning in a text, and the ambiguity of language are illustrated time and again in movies that stretch from *The Wizard of Oz* to *Blade Runner* to *The Lord of the Rings* trilogy. (It is worth noting here that there are many science fiction films, such as the films in the *Star Wars* series, that have very little reading or writing in them at all. It's as if literacy is too prosaic an activity to present in such a futuristic world where information is more often communicated through holograms.)

If triumph-of-literacy films and romantic comedies often portray texts as the product of clearly identified specific authors, fantasy and science films often shift the emphasis away from the identity of the author and focus only a mysterious text, whose author is unknown or unknowable. In one particularly enigmatic example, the black monoliths in *2001: A Space Odyssey* (1968) are clearly objects or even texts that have meaning, but that meaning as well as the creators of the objects remain a mystery to the characters in the film (and perhaps even to members of the audience). More contemporary examples can be seen in the films *Stargate* (1995), where a time portal is covered in Egyptian-like hieroglyphics, or *Signs* (2002), where crop circles occur in mysterious and ominous patterns. Even when we discover that the texts in both films are made by invading aliens, we never truly know the intent or the identity of the authors. But we know the texts have a significance that we, along with the main characters, can only speculate upon.

Even a general sense of authorial identity is often not useful in such films, in which the author may be long dead or far away. In the *Indiana Jones* and recent *Mummy* films, ancient texts are discovered whose authorship can be guessed at, but authorship is not considered instrumental for interpreting their meaning. As Roland Barthes, and, later, Michel Foucault argued, the contemporary notion of authorship is highly contextual. In fact, the concept of authorship as the attribution of a work to a single person is something that is by no means universal to all cultures or all times. As Foucault (1969) notes:

> The author-function does not affect all discourse in a universal and constant way, however...In our civilization, it has not always been the same types of texts which have required attribution to an author. There was a time when the texts that we today call "literary" (narratives, stories, epics, tragedies, comedies) were accepted, put into circulation, and valorized without any question about the identity of their author; their anonymity caused no difficulties since their ancientness, whether real or imagined, was regarded as a sufficient guarantee of their status. (347)

108 *Popular culture and representations of literacy*

We don't expect to know exactly who wrote the ancient texts in *The Mummy* films or *Stargate*; they have no byline or authors' biographies on them. Instead, they are mysterious works, taken literally out of context. The identities of the authors are meaningless, for many are long since dead, and all that can be focused on by the heroes is what they see before them in the text. As Barthes (1968) would describe it, "A text is not a line of words releasing a single 'theological' meaning (the 'message' of the Author-God) but a multidimensional space in which a variety of writings, none of them original, blend and clash. The text is a tissue of quotations drawn from the innumerable centres of culture" (146). Again, this is quite different from texts in contemporary realistic film genres such as romantic comedies where the text is often explicitly connected to the author.

Sometimes the result of this disconnection between authorship and text in fantasy or science fiction or horror is a misattribution of authorship, usually taking the form of assuming that a text was written by a good person, when it was actually written by a villain. A different result, sometimes connected to the first, is a misreading (often aloud in a long-dead language) of a mysterious text by a supporting character or villain, who thereby unleashes some terrifying power. It is then up to the hero (or the hero's female sidekick, as we noted in Chapter Five) to reread the text correctly and restore order and safety. In the remake of *The Mummy*, for example, it is the reading of the Book of the Dead that first unleashes the monster (Arnold Vosloo), and only the reading of another ancient text by the heroine (Rachel Weisz), in the nick of time no less, that returns him to the underworld.

It is not only the lack of a knowable author that creates problems in such films, however; the indeterminate meaning of a text, caused by its situated nature as well as by the ambiguity of language, can provoke difficulties, too. As poststructuralists of many stripes have pointed out over the years, there is no inherent meaning in any written text. In the teen horror film *I Know What You Did Last Summer* (1997), the seemingly innocuous title phrase has sinister implications for the main characters, who have been involved in covering up their killing of an old man. All interpretations of the phrase depend on the context in which it is read. Take a piece of writing out of its original interpretive community, move the signs even farther from what they signify, and the people who read it in its new cultural setting will have to try to make sense of it in terms of the references and assumptions that surround them. "These strategies exist prior to the act of reading and therefore determine the shape of what is read rather than, as is usually assumed, the other way around" (Fish 1980, 171). Because interpretive communities shift as culturally learned behaviors shift, the meaning of the text can be read quite counter to the way it would have been originally received, as occurs in films such as *Brazil* (1982), *The Matrix* (1999), and *Eternal Sunshine of the Spotless Mind* (2004).

The perils of misreading   109

Another source of the misinterpretation of texts in such films is the ambiguity of language itself. That written words are ambiguous is a complaint that has extended from Socrates to Saussure. Because signs are not signifiers, because words often have double if not multiple meanings, any text may be misread. In fantasy and science fiction, however, such misreadings often have more significant consequences. Sometimes this shifting feature of language is played for humor, as in *The Lord of the Rings: The Fellowship of the Ring* (2001), when the inscription over the door to the mines of Moria seems clear enough— "Speak friend and enter"—yet resists all of Gandalf's (Ian McKellan) incantations that attempt to prove he is a friend. In fact, the inscription simply needs to be read literally. The door opens when Gandalf—at Frodo's (Elijah Wood) suggestion—speaks the word "friend" in Elvish. More often, however, the effect of ambiguous language results in something more ominous, if not directly threatening. A famous example of this occurs in the television science fiction series *The Twilight Zone,* when a book brought by alien visitors, titled *To Serve Man,* ends up being a cookbook.

In fantasy and science fiction films, dangerous powers unleashed by literacy events are often the result of the actions of the young or impetuous or greedy, who will not heed the wisdom of their elders or the rules of their institutions. There is often a character who is aware of the power of the written text and warns against it. In *The Lord of the Rings: The Fellowship of the Ring*, for example, Gandalf is aware of the power of the ring, a power he confirms through his research and access to ancient books. Yet he knows better than to read the inscription on it in its original language, "the language is that of Mordor, which I will not utter here." Power, in fantasy, science fiction, and horror films is always ambiguous. And true power, like fire, is always just as dangerous as it is beneficent. In these films, those who can tap into such power realize it is both a blessing and a curse, or find that all hell can, literally, break loose in the power's wake.

Though critical theory may give us a way to think about the shifting nature of textual meaning, the portrayals of literacy practices in fantasy, science fiction, and horror films also contain a moral intent. Such magical representations of literacy can be read as metaphors and cautionary tales for the supposedly mystical power of literacy itself. Like literacy, the accessing and reading of magical or mysterious texts is portrayed as having the power to transform the individual or the situation. Reading such texts offers the character the possibility of great knowledge and power. Certainly, literacy has for years been regarded as a practice that can reward the individual with knowledge, power, and personal transformation. Such rhetoric continues to dominate public discussions of literacy policies from politicians, scholars, and teachers. Yet in these film genres, literacy is also dangerous, if not properly guided and controlled. In this metaphor, there are also resonances with perceptions of literacy across the ages. In times

110   *Popular culture and representations of literacy*

past, the potentially dangerous power of literacy was enough to keep it restricted to an elite or priestly class, or to scribes or scholars, and out of the hands of the masses, who could not be trusted to use such power judiciously without supervision. Such concerns continue in more contemporary debates about literacy, particularly in terms of which books and magazines are appropriate for school children to read. Many parents and teachers worry a great deal over the potentially damaging effects of letting children "read whatever they want" and possibly letting them encounter potentially dangerous ideas for which they have not been properly supervised or instructed. The result of these concerns is often protest or campaigns to ban certain texts that are deemed dangerous from schools and libraries. As in many films, the concern is that young people, reading on their own without the guidance of wise elders or institutions, may, in fact, release great dangers on themselves and on society.

LITERACY IN SCHOOL AND OUT

The *Harry Potter* series of films focus on the adventures of the titular hero as he faces the dual challenges of growing up and battling evil while he is a student at Hogwarts School of Witchcraft and Wizardry. Each film covers one year in the life of Harry (Daniel Radcliffe), orphaned in infancy, but somehow, even as a child, able to defeat his nemesis, the evil Lord Voldemort. The films take place in a world filled with literacy practices, where characters are constantly reading and writing. Such an emphasis on literacy can be attributed in part to the school setting of the films, though there are many films set in schools, including a myriad of teen romance films such as *She's All That* (1999) and *10 Things I Hate About You* (1999), where literacy is virtually invisible. It is also possible that the emphasis on literacy comes in part from the origin of the films in the set of astonishingly popular books by J.K. Rowling. Not only is it often easier to reflect reading and writing in print, and not have to worry about the uncinematic nature of watching a person read or write, but the British schoolboy adventure genre of the books is one in which literacy practices, including secret notes and puzzling codes, are common plot devices. As the Potter films have been faithful to the central narratives of the books (lest they incur the wrath of a large and devoted audience) so, then, do the plots of the films also have to turn on acts of reading and writing.

The literacy practices in the Harry Potter films reflect rather old-fashioned views of technologies and attitudes toward reading and writing. Invitations arrive in handwritten script on faded parchment, families and friends communicate by owl-delivered letters, books are thick, hardcover objects, and writing happens with quill and ink. Word processing, e-mail, paperback books, and other literacy forms of contemporary life are absent from the Harry Potter universe. As this is a world of wizards and

The perils of misreading 111

witches, literacy is routinely magical, such as book covers with life-like animated images of the authors upon them, but they are not technologically modern.

In these movies, there are countless scenes of children sitting in classrooms with books piled on the tables in front of them, or lounging in dormitories, studying for tests. Professors read announcements from scrolls of parchment or refer to books in the snatches of lectures that we hear. Of course, the focus of the scenes in the classrooms is rarely the reading or writing, but the portrayals indicate that the expectations in the school are that fairly conventional educational literacy practices take place. These conventional practices are clearly sanctioned, ordered and monitored by the teaching staff of the institution.

Yet though there are visible manifestations of sanctioned literacy practices in the school, what dominates the films, including *Harry Potter and the Chamber of Secrets* (2002), are the unsanctioned and unschooled literacy practices that happen outside the realm of institutional control. In their quest to solve the annual mystery at the center of each film, Harry, his intrepid friends, Ron (Rupert Grint) and Hermione (Emma Watson), make extensive use of texts they know to be forbidden to them by explicit prohibition or by general school rules. Yet it is the powerful magic in these forbidden texts, such as hidden books and magical maps, that threatens them, but also helps them triumph by the end of the film. Before the trio of friends can solve each mystery and keep Lord Voldemort at bay once again, they inevitably find that the ambiguity of the power of these magical literacy practices cannot be anticipated or controlled, and frequently is almost their undoing. The unschooled literacy practices are, just as often as not, dangerous. Like fire or gunpowder it seems, if there wasn't a risk in using them then the forbidden literacies wouldn't be powerful. In the world of Harry Potter, if you pick up the wrong book at the library, it may erupt in your hands into howls of fury, or try to take a bite out of you.

But the real danger in *Harry Potter and the Chamber of Secrets* comes not from voracious books, but from the slippery nature of any text's connection to the truth. For at key moments in the film, the trust that the main characters put in the truth represented in written texts turns out to be dangerously misplaced.

THE AUTHOR AS FRAUD

Two significant plotlines in *Harry Potter and the Chamber of Secrets* illustrate the ambiguous and often threatening nature of the written word. Though one plot line is played for more for comic relief, while the other is central to the danger in the narrative; both demonstrate how Harry and his friends are deceived by their trust in texts. More to the point, they learn that school-sanctioned literacies are often fraudulent and impotent, while

112   Popular culture and representations of literacy

the forbidden texts they must learn to use on their own are the repositories of both true power and peril.

The central plot of the film finds the Hogwarts community facing an unknown menace that is somehow paralyzing some of the students (and one of the cats) at the school. Next to the first victim, a message written in blood announces that the Chamber of Secrets has been opened, and that the enemies of the "heir" should beware. We find out later that the "heir" in question is the descendant of Salazar Slytherin, one of the founders of the school who later left after losing a battle to restrict the racial purity Hogwarts' students (he wanted students from wizard families only, no regular human "muggles"). The central problem in the narrative, then, is for Harry, Ron, and Hermione to find the monster before it kills a Hogwarts' student.

A connected subplot is thrust into this rather dark plot, meant to provide the film with a running sense of comic relief. There is a new professor at Hogwarts, Gilderoy Lockhart (Kenneth Branagh) who has been hired to teach "Defense Against the Dark Arts." In other words, Lockhart's charge is to teach the students how to defend themselves against monsters, demons, and evil wizards and witches. Lockhart is well-known throughout the wizarding world for his fame in vanquishing such threats. Lockhart is also fatuous, self-promoting, shallow, and self-centered. His exploits are well known primarily because he has written about them extensively in a series of best-selling books. Throughout the film he constantly reminds everyone around him of his literary output. For example, at one point in the film, before he is going to instruct students on how to protect themselves, he tells them he will be teaching them the methods he has used when he has "defended himself on countless occasions," quickly adding: "For full details see my published works." We also see scenes of Lockhart answering fan mail and autographing photos. He is a model of a modern author, never resting in his marketing of his books, and of his persona as an "author."

We see this relentless zeal for marketing, as well as how Lockhart constructs his persona as an author, in the first scene with him. The scene takes place in Flourish and Blotts, a magical bookstore in London that caters to wizards and witches. Harry and other Hogwarts students are in the bookstore to buy their textbooks for the coming school year. Their arrival happens to coincide with Lockhart's book signing of his latest bestselling memoir, *Magical Me*. The scene opens with an establishing shot of the bookstore, a narrow and cozy place with dark wood shelves and spiral staircases reaching high up to the ceilings and hardbound books stacked everywhere. It is the kind of dark and cramped, yet comfortable, space that is rare today in most bookstores, looking instead as most of us would now associate with used book stores. Certainly there is nothing about Flourish and Blotts that looks anything like the large chain book retailers that dominate the current marketplace. The bookstore set is one example of the nostalgic atmosphere surrounding literacy practices in Harry Potter films. Like the use of quill and ink or messages by scrolls, the antique

The perils of misreading 113

technologies and environments that surround literacy in the films serve several purposes. First, they connect the world of wizards and witches to a past when magic was believed in. As in so many renderings of the past, there is an implicit nostalgia for a purer, more honorable time. They also remove the narratives from the contemporary world of mass production and mass marketing. There is commerce in the world of Harry Potter but it takes place in small, owner-operated stores with cauldrons and wands that seem to have been crafted by individual artisans. Books and quills and parchment are represented as part of this culture of individual crafts-manship. Literacy is represented as an individualized practice, created by artisans and consumed by individuals with an appreciation and reverence for books. Conversely the only mass-produced items in the Harry Potter universe are popular-culture-like items, such as trading cards, candy, and sporting goods (catering to the unquenchable desire of the students for a faster broom with which to play Quidditch).

This is the kind of literate world that "discursive nostalgiacs" like Sven Birkerts (1994) and Neal Postman (1985) pine for in their rants against the rise of electronic popular culture. It is the kind of literate world that people envision when they speak with passion and touch of melancholy, about the deep delights and enrichment of the soul that comes through reading and writing. It is worth noting that Hogwarts is a boarding school isolated in what looks like the Scottish Highlands, without a single television, computer, or video game in sight. Again, this sets the stories in a time before technology, when magic seemed possible. It also helps explain in part the popularity of the Harry Potter stories with parents. While adults enjoy the narratives and the imaginative writing, the setting puts the children in the book in the kind of educational setting that most parents remember from their youth (or wish they had experienced) and would wish for their children to experience (minus the monsters, of course).

At the front of Flourish and Blotts there is a prominent display of *Magical Me*, with a moving image of a preening Lockhart on the cover. The bookstore is packed with people waiting for the book signing. Lockhart sweeps into the room, posing for photographs with the skill of someone well-practiced in front of the camera. When he spots Harry in the crowd he calls him forward, knowing that Harry is already a celebrity of sorts for his status as the person who helped defeat Vodelmort. Lockhart pulls Harry to his side saying "Nice big smile, Harry. Together, you and I rate the front page." The picture-taking is followed by Lockhart seizing the moment to make further headlines by piling books in Harry's arms and announcing to the crowd.

Ladies and gentlemen! What an extraordinary moment this is! When young Harry here stepped into Flourish and Blotts this morning to purchase my autobiography, *Magical Me*—which, incidentally is celebrating its twenty-seventh week atop *The Daily Prophet's* Bestseller

114 *Popular culture and representations of literacy*

List—he had no idea that he would, in fact, be leaving with my entire collected works! Free of charge!

The audience applauds in appreciation, even as Harry tries to make a quick escape from the bookstore. Harry, Ron, and Hermione are portrayed as being appalled at Lockhart's behavior and puzzled why others, such as Ron's mother, are so taken with the author.

The portrayal of Gilderoy Lockhart as a pompous, self-serving self-promoter stands in contrast to the romantic idea of the writer as an individual artisan interested in craft and meaning. We are meant to recognize that Lockhart is less an author to be respected than he is a shallow celebrity to be mocked. Lockhart's character is funny and fatuous, in part because we recognize him as a modern marketing machine in a nostalgic age of true artisanship. We are also meant to see through his opportunistic use of Harry to promote sales of his book, and to be suspicious of Lockhart's motives and his work. Even before we have seen Lockhart teach or cast a spell, we suspect in this scene that he is at best a slick salesman and at worst a charlatan and a fraud.

It does not take long for Lockhart's ineptitude to become clear. He continues to talk about his great skill and reputation, yet every bit of magic he tries to work somehow goes wrong. For example, when Harry's arm is broken in a game of Quidditch, Lockhart casts a spell to set the break but instead dissolves the bones in Harry's arm (which have to be regrown in hospital).

One particularly intriguing scene, meant to illustrate again Lockhart's lack of skill, takes place in his "Defense Against the Dark Arts" class. Yet the scene also represents the film's disdain for institutionalized literacy and foreshadows even more serious revelations about Lockhart's identity as an author. Lockhart, surrounded by pictures of himself, introduces himself to the class by telling them that he is, among other things, the "five times winner of *Witch Weekly's* Most-Charming-Smile Award." He then tells the class he plans to challenge them by unleashing a cage filled with Cornish pixies on the room and see how the students deal with them. The moment Lockhart opens the cage the little blue creatures proceed to tear about the room, terrorizing students, and destroying books. Lockhart flees in fear (as do the representations of him in the magical photographs), leaving the children to fend for themselves. Harry alertly picks up a thick textbook and begins to whack the pixies like a determined cricket batsman. The chaos only subsides when Hermione casts a spell to freeze the creatures in midair.

This scene definitively marks Lockhart as an incompetent fraud. The students and the audience now know that for all his authority as an "author," and all the cultural capital that provides him in the culture at large, particularly in educational institutions, he cannot, in fact, even deal with a roomful of cranky pixies. The implication of this scene in terms of literacy is that the authority and credibility that has been placed in Lockhart by the school and the students is misplaced. He has no power and, by extension,

The perils of misreading 115

neither do the books he writes. These are the books that are recognized by the school and the culture as authoritative and credible. But, as Harry demonstrates in the scene, these books lack real power, and perhaps the best use that can be made of such texts is to whack pixies with them.

The final substantial scene with Lockhart and his position as an author is both darker and more significant in its implications about the film's representations of literacy practices. Near the end of the film Ron's sister, Ginny, has been abducted by the monster and taken to the Chamber of Secrets, with another bloody message left behind reading, "Her skeleton will live in the Chamber forever." Harry and Ron, in hiding, hear the professors discussing the situation turn to Lockhart and tell him that his "moment has come at last" to prove his abilities as a wizard and defeat the creature. As Professor McGonigle (Maggie Smith) says to him, in voice lightly tinged with irony, "Your skills, after all, are legend."

Lockhart replies that he needs to return to his office to prepare. Harry and Ron follow him, not convinced of his abilities, but at least hoping he can show them the secret entrance to the Chamber. Yet on entering Lockhart's office, the boys find the professor furiously packing, and explaining that when he took the teaching position he hardly imagined he would have to battle monsters. It is at this point that the issue of authorship and truth becomes explicit.

Harry: After all the stuff you did in your books?
Lockhart: Books can be misleading!
Harry: You wrote them!
Lockhart: My dear boy, do use your common sense. My books wouldn't have sold half so well if people didn't think *I'd* done some of those things.
Harry: You're a fraud! You've just been taking credit for what other wizards have done.
Ron: Is there anything you *can* do?
Lockhart: Yes, now that you mention it, I'm rather gifted with memory charms. Otherwise, you see, all those wizards would have gone blabbing and I'd never have sold another book. In fact I'm going to have to do the same to you.
(Ron and Harry are faster draws on their wands than the professor and they haul him off to help them look for the entrance to the Chamber.)

Not only has Lockhart's position as an incompetent wizard been confirmed, but he has also been shown to be a plagiarist. His autobiographies are in fact anthologies of the deeds of others. The texts exist, but they do not represent his life or experiences. His identity as an author—his author-function—is nothing but an image, a marketing strategy that is not connected to the content of the text. In this case the critical theorist position—that the author does not produce a single meaning in a text but that a text is a com-

116 *Popular culture and representations of literacy*

pilation of multiple authors and meanings—is quite literally true. Gilderoy Lockhart may serve as comic relief in the film, but he is very postmodern and poststructuralist comic relief. The final ironic twist in the Lockhart plotline occurs on the way to the Chamber of Secrets. Lockhart steals Ron's wand, which, after being broken, has a tendency to backfire, and, trying to use his memory spell on the boys, he succeeds only in erasing his own. Now the texts are completely without an author who has any memory of the deeds inside them or of the writing of the words. The books are left on their own, to have whatever meaning readers might make of them.

Lockhart also is guilty of the most despised academic transgression—plagiarism. Taking credit for the work of others is a far worse scholarly sin than simple incompetence. It turns Lockhart from a buffoon to a thief. It also makes him a more threatening character than he has been up to this point. Not only has he taken credit for work that was not his, but he has attacked other wizards in the process, and wiped out their memories of their experiences. In this case, the literacy practices that gained Lockhart his celebrity do more than violate the implicit codes of honor, integrity, and ownership that are part of the academic system, including at Hogwarts; Lockhart's practices are threats to the identities of those he comes in contact with. Thus the cult of the celebrity author is built, both literally and figuratively in this case, on the unsung deeds of others. It is not a difficult stretch to see parallels in our culture among authors whose names go on the front of books largely researched and written by uncredited assistants. Certainly it is not difficult to find echoes of Gilderoy Lockhart in recent plagiarism scandals involving prominent popular historians such as Stephen Ambrose or Doris Kearns Goodwin. In the academic world, a similar pattern can involve senior scholars who exploit the research of junior colleagues and graduate students to put the senior scholar's name on a book or article. What Harry and Ron have discovered is similar to the realization some graduate students have when they see a senior scholar receive an award for an article for which the students did the primary share of the work. Writing can be a powerful way to transmit ideas, but such power is distributed unevenly and mediated by cultural forces such as status and class.

The paradox of the situation is that in some ways the disgust Harry and Ron feel toward Lockhart's plagiarism runs counter to a poststructuralist position that the identity of the author does not matter at all. Harry and Ron feel it matters deeply that an author take credit only for his or her own work. To do otherwise is, as Harry claims, to engage in fraud. The accusation of fraud is filled with anger and betrayal on the part of Harry and Ron, who realize that the institutionally sanctioned literacy Lockhart represents is not only impotent, but rests on lies and deceit. Lockhart has revealed for the boys that the literacy that is sold in bookstores and recognized as authoritative by the school is empty of power and honor, and they should have no reason to trust it. As in so many films about educational institutions in general, the knowledge that is presented in the classroom, as well

The perils of misreading 117

as the teacher who presents it, is represented as being rigid, irrelevant, and impotent. Certainly this is the portrayal of school-sanctioned literacy in the Harry Potter films.

DIFFICULT, FORBIDDEN, AND DANGEROUS

If the literacy approved of by the culture and school won't help Harry, Ron, and Hermione save the day, then they must turn to the forbidden but powerful literacies for help. The trio understands that they are not supposed to access and use such texts, but also that such texts are their only hope of vanquishing the evil they are confronting.

The first example of this understanding comes fairly early in the film when the initial attacks have taken place. Harry, Ron, and Hermione wonder if two of the resident bullies in the school, Crabbe (Jamie Waylett) and Goyle (Joshua Herdman), might be able to provide information about what is happening. As they realize that there is little chance of tricking the two rather dim students into telling them what they need to know Hermione drops her voice and says, "But there might be another way. Mind you, it might be difficult, not to mention that we'd be breaking about fifty school rules. And it'll be dangerous. *Very* dangerous." This is followed by a shot of Hermione taking a thick book titled *Moste Potente Potions* from the rich wood library shelves. She turns to a page with eighteenth-century style type and illustrations and explains to Ron and Harry that the "polyjuice potion" will allow them to transform themselves into Crab and Goyle long enough to get the answers they need. "But it's tricky," she warns. "I've never seen a more complicated potion."

In these brief two scenes, the themes are established for the ambiguous nature of the literacies of power in the fantasy world. First, such literacy practices must be "difficult" and "complicated." If just anyone could figure it out and use it, then the power wouldn't be special. Second, such literacy practices must be forbidden and the use of them somewhat subversive. Using forbidden texts usually require "breaking about fifty school rules" or otherwise circumventing or defying authority. This reinforces the pervasive sense in fantasy films that those in power are always hiding the literacies that provide access to real power and will not reveal them willingly. Finally, such literacy practices, to be truly powerful, must be "dangerous. *Very* dangerous."

Difficult, forbidden, and dangerous are not the words most teachers would want to ascribe to literacy. Instead teachers want to think of literacy as something inviting, something positive, and something that we can make easier for students to use. But, as we've already noted, in fantasy films powerful literacies are not to be found in the classrooms.

It turns out, of course, that the potion is trickier and more dangerous than Hermione had imagined. As often happens in such stories, it is the per-

118 *Popular culture and representations of literacy*

son who dares to attempt to use the most powerful literacies to access the most powerful magic who ends up the victim of unintended consequences, caused by forces beyond her control. In this case, for the polyjuice potion to work, it requires a piece of the person each student wants to change into. While Harry and Ron succeed in using hair from Crab and Goyle, Hermione mistakes a cat hair for the hair of her target, Millicent Bulstrode, and succeeds only in turning herself into a half-girl/half-cat hybrid. Implied in this turn of events is that a guiding, wise teacher or elder might have known all the risks involved and kept Hermione from making her embarrassing blunder. But, of course, a wise guiding teacher, understanding the dangers involved in Hermione's inability to fully contextualize the spell and to be aware of its potential ramifications, would have probably dissuaded the students from trying such a ploy in the first place. Despite Hermione's mistake, Harry and Ron, in the form of Crab and Goyle, do find out important information about the mystery. Real magical power succeeds, but, as often happens, it leaves victims in its wake.

The true and more lethal danger of powerful literacies is illustrated in the use of reading and writing in solving the central mystery of the plot. While trying to figure out who opened the Chamber of Secrets and released the monster years before, Harry and Ron come across a book in the girl's bathroom. (And there is certainly a sense of transgression for any twelve-year-old boy to go into the girl's bathroom.) The book has seemingly appeared from nowhere, so clearly it is magical. The boys just have to figure out how. Harry takes the book back to his room and studies it. The book is bound in black leather with blank, parchment-like pages. The only writing on the book is on the bottom of the back cover, where Harry finds the name "Tom Marvolo Riddle." Confronted with a book filled with blank pages, Harry takes the next logical step and prepares to write in it. But when he drips ink from his quill, the drop quickly disappears into the page. Fascinated, Harry writes "My name is Harry Potter," only to see the words vanish and be replaced with the sentence: "Hello Harry Potter, my name is Tom Riddle." Harry eagerly writes again, and the following exchange takes place:

Do you know anything about the Chamber of Secrets?
Yes.
Can you tell me?
No. But I can show you.

At which point Harry is literally sucked into the book, where he sees scenes from the last time the monster from the Chamber of Secrets struck. These scenes, which feature a young Tom Riddle (Christian Coulson), implicate Hagrid (Robbie Coltrane) as the person who unleashed the monster. Hagrid is the current groundskeeper at Hogwarts and a fast friend of the three students. The book then deposits Harry back in his room, where, excited by the new information at hand, he races off to tell Ron.

The perils of misreading 119

Like many adolescents, and many adults, Harry believes what he reads in books. He does not question the authenticity of what he finds out from the book, or the identity of the author who is imparting the information. He believes that the words and images he sees in a book must be honest representations of the identity and experiences of the author (for this scene happens before he understands the nature of Gilderoy Lockhart's work). Even as we are told that print culture is being replaced by electronic media, many still find an authority in words placed in print. Certainly this kind of naïve acceptance of the authority of the book and the identity of its author is powerful for many students, even those who don't spend that much time reading (Williams 2002). In our culture, and in representations of literacy on film, the book is still often a totemic object of truth. Print culture in more realist movies is often the repository of authority and revelation (such as in the secret files of action films we discussed in the Chapters One and Five). We don't find it unusual, then, that Harry finds the information from the book convincing.

Watching this scene of Harry dialogue with Tom Riddle in print is reminiscent for us today of instant messaging and chat rooms on the Internet. Like those forums, the written words get an immediate, real-time response so that a dialogue can take place. Like those forums, it is impossible to know precisely the identity of the person with whom one is having a conversation. Instead a writer has to take on faith that the person with whom she is corresponding is being honest about her identity. Like the famous cartoon maintaining that on the Internet, no one would know if the author was a dog, for Harry Potter and his magical book, no one would know if the author was an evil wizard. That, then, is the difference for the audience in how we regard this book and how we regard books in more realist films. For we know that in a fantasy film a magical book's power may very well be ambiguous and could be as dangerous as it is helpful. Appearances in fantasy are often deceiving and texts are often misleading or dangerous when read out of context. As Harry enters the magic book and takes from it the information he is eager to share with others, we watch the scene with wariness about what might really be the consequence of being sucked into a magic book whose author's identity we have to take on faith.

The true danger of placing such trust in literacy is revealed in the film's climax. After the magical book has been stolen from Harry, and Ginny Weasley (Bonnie Wright) has been abducted, Harry makes his way to the Chamber of Secrets to face the monster, now identified as a basilisk (or giant snake). There he finds Ginny, unconscious, clutching the magic diary. Standing next to her is Tom Riddle, in the same youthful form Harry saw when he was sucked into the diary. There seems something menacing about Tom Riddle as he begins to explain that it was Ginny who, under the power of the diary, wrote the bloody messages and opened the Chamber. But when the diary began to frighten her she tossed it away in the girls' bathroom where it was found by Harry, the person, Tom says, "I was most anxious

120 *Popular culture and representations of literacy*

to meet." He explains that the images implicating Hagrid, images Harry now knows to be false, were created to gain Harry's trust. When Harry expresses confusion at what is happening Tom explains: "I decided to leave behind a diary, preserving my 16-year-old self in its pages, so that one day I would be able to lead another to finish Salazar Slytherin's noble work."

Though Harry now realizes he has been duped by believing in the book and its author, the real nature of the threat does not become clear until Harry asks why Tom cares so much about Harry and how he vanquished Lord Voldemort, given that "Voldemort was after your time."

Tom replies, "Voldemort is my past, present, and future," and turns to write "Tom Marvolo Riddle" in fire in the air and then, with a wave of his hand, rearranges the letters to spell "I am Lord Voldemort." Harry, then, has not only been misled by his trust in literacy, his trust in the magic book, but has been deceived by not recognizing the author as his arch-enemy, the greatest evil in the Harry Potter universe. It is clear that Voldemort has literacy practices with great power, from his ability to converse with Harry through the magic book to his ability to manipulate fiery letters in midair.

Harry has been misled by his trust in books and authors. Like so many children, Harry believed that if a person wrote something in a book and said it was true, then it must be true. He made the mistake first with Gilderoy Lockhart, and now he made it again with potentially much more dangerous consequences. Like many students, and, in fact, many adults, Harry has believed in the direct correlation between the name on the cover of a book and the identity of the author. Not only must the person named on the book have written what was inside, but it must an honest reflection of the "truth" and the true nature of the author. We can see this today when readers become disenchanted with authors whose personalities or deeds do not live up to their writing or who bend and embellish the "truth" of memoirs and autobiographies. In realist films about writers, this is a common trope of betrayal between the idealistic reader and the author whose real identity ends up being a profound disappointment. You can see examples of this narrative in films such as *Bullets Over Broadway* (1994), *Wonder Boys* (2000), *Barton Fink* (1991), and, most disturbingly, *Misery* (1990).

The additional deception in the Harry Potter films, and in many fantasy films, is the deception of young readers by older writers. Part of the lesson young heroes must often learn in fantasy or science fiction films is that authority is not necessarily to be trusted. Indeed, there is often a wise adult figure who can help the young hero, but whose advice is either initially rejected or unheeded while the hero succumbs to the seductive counsel of the villain. Part of the hero's maturation is understanding how misguided he has been and recognizing which authority figure he should trust. In *Harry Potter and the Chamber of Secrets*, Albus Dumbledore (Richard Harris) the wise and good headmaster of Hogwarts asks Harry if there is anything he would like to talk about. But Harry does not reveal what he knows, even after finding the magical book. Of course Dumbledore, who

The perils of misreading 121

knew Tom Riddle as a student at Hogwarts and certainly as Lord Voldemort, would have been able to warn Harry about the dangers of believing
the book, and could have given Harry the necessary context to correct the
boy's naïve misreading. The real danger for Harry has come from his trust
in and use of literacy practices that are unschooled and unadvised.

Having revealed his true identity, Voldemort now explains that he will
become fully corporeal when Ginny dies and then sends the basilisk to kill
Harry. Harry, in a good piece of deus ex machina luck ends up with a magical sword and kills the basilisk, but not before with the beast has planted a
fang in his arm, which begins to slowly poison him. Voldemort, as any self-
respecting villain would, proceeds to gloat at Harry's weakening condition.
And, as with all villains, undoes himself with his gloating:

> So ends the famous Harry Potter. On his knees in the Chamber of Secrets.
> Defeated at last by the Dark Lord he so unwisely challenged…Funny,
> the damage a silly little book can do, especially in the hands of a silly
> little girl.

These final words cause Harry to look down at the book in Ginny's
hands and remember what Voldemort said about preserving himself in the
diary. Harry grabs the book and plunges the basilisk fang deep into its
pages. As ink flows from the pages like black blood, Voldemort screams in
pain and, in a nifty show of special effects, dissolves before our eyes.

Although this scene may give a more literal meaning to the concept of
the "death of the author," it points to an intriguing paradox in the way the
book and authorship are represented in the film. Even as the words in the
book may be misleading or untrue, they are still the embodiment—in this
case literally so—of the author who wrote them. This reflects a concept of
authorship as romantic individualism that we discuss in Chapter Seven. It
certainly is the view of the author as connected to the text that is adopted
with a deep fervor by many adolescents. When Voldemort says that leaving
behind a diary would be "preserving my 16-year-old self in its pages," he is
articulating the hope of many a teen diarist, poet, or writer to cling to the
intense, transient days of adolescence by writing down what seem to be the
most important and valuable thoughts and feelings in the world. As Harry
demonstrates, if you destroy those thoughts and feelings you can destroy
their author. Many adolescents might think death preferable to having a
diary read or destroyed. Consequently, though meaning can shift with context and though language can be slippery, fantasy films still reinforce the
concept that authorship is connected to an individual person. In the fantasy
world, however, an evil author will necessarily produce an evil book.

The other line in the final scene that deserves attention is Voldemort's
musing of "Funny, the damage a silly little book can do, especially in the
hands of a silly little girl." Though it may seem at first as if this is a dismis-
sive claim of girls' abilities to handle powerful literacies, given the context

122 *Popular culture and representations of literacy*

of the rest of the scene and the Harry Potter films overall, it has to be read as more ironic. First, the silly little book ends up undoing the great evil wizard who gives away the secret to his own demise. But more subtle and more pervasive is the connection of girls with literacy and power in the Harry Potter universe, most notably in the person of Hermione. On the one hand, Hermione reinforces a number of stereotypes about girls, literacy, and schools. She is relentlessly studious, always getting the highest marks in class and always answering the teacher's questions. As such she is indeed the "teacher's pet" and an irritant to many of her classmates. Yet in every Harry Potter narrative, Hermione's literacy practices, particularly her knowledge of books and her ability to read widely and apply her reading to the situation at hand, are central to helping save the day. In *Harry Potter and the Chamber of Secrets*, not only is her work with the polyjuice potion spell vital in helping gather information—at the cost of some comic relief—but she identifies the nature of the monster at a key moment in the film. Hermione is found paralyzed, but Harry and Ron notice she is holding a scrap of paper in her hand that has information about the basilisk on it, including that it can paralyze or kill with its gaze. Clearly Hermione was involved in research when she was attacked, but had the pluck and presence of mind to tear out the vital piece of paper. As in the roles of literate women in action films (see Chapter Five), her literacy practices never provide the ultimate salvation, for that must be left to the man (or boy) of action. Hermione's literacy skills give her power, but she will never have the power to be the central hero because, as a girl, her literacy is ultimately too disciplined and school bound. Still, it is clear in the film that a "silly little girl" with a book in hand can do great damage indeed.

A CHILDHOOD OF AMBIGUOUS LITERACY

Fantasy, science fiction, and horror have consistently been the most popular genres of film in recent years, particularly with young people. As this chapter makes clear, the representations of literacy in these films is often as powerful, yet potentially deadly. Literacy practices, particularly those that are outside of school or institutional authority, can be potent forces for the hero. But the very removal from the safeguards and wisdom of authority makes such literacy practices subject to dangerous misreading and misinterpretation. At the same time, institutionally sanctioned literacies are regarded as impotent. Students raised on such films receive conflicting messages about literacy. Literacy is powerful, but dangerous. Language is useful, but slippery. Books contain important information, but read out of context may lead to disaster. Elders may provide vital wisdom and guidance for reading and writing, but elders who are evil may lie and mislead with written words. Literacy outside of authority is vital, but rebellion may end in disaster.

The perils of misreading   123

Perhaps the ambivalent attitudes and representations of literacy practices in such films can offer fruitful possibilities for students to rethink the conventional, school-sanctioned approaches to literacy. Perhaps students can learn, along with Harry Potter, that texts cannot necessarily be trusted, that words can mislead, that reading depends on context, that language is slippery, and that literacy, unschooled and unadvised, can be powerful and dangerous. Perhaps then they will be ready to be truly critical readers.

But, in the words of Hermione Granger, it might also be dangerous. *Very* dangerous.

Part III
Literacy myths in the movies

Gwyneth Paltrow in Sylvia (2003). ©Focus Features/Everett Collection.

7 The passions of the romantic author
Literacy as individualism

The act of writing is not terribly cinematic. After all, what does it look like when most of us write? We sit at a desk or table and ponder, gaze out a window, fiddle with a pen or paper clip, write a few words, furrow the brow, write a lot of words, yawn and stretch and get a cup of coffee. Hardly the elements that constitute riveting films. That's why scenes of writing in many movies usually involve dramatic elements beyond the writing itself, such as a spy copying notes while in danger of being caught, or a woman writing a thank you letter while having an emotional confrontation with her mother. The lack of drama involved in the daily act of writing also helps explain why movies about writers often tend to be about everything but their writing—their loves, their families, their muses, their illnesses, their tortured souls.

As we've illustrated in previous chapters, there is a great deal of writing in many contemporary films. In these movies we see ordinary, and sometimes extraordinary, people writing for many different reasons, though almost none of them are writers by profession. Yet the irony in movies is that often there is more writing seen in these films that are not about writers than in movies about writers. Movies about authors—and in this chapter we use this word to describe writers of creative literary work to distinguish them in the popular imagination from other people who write in their daily lives, including journalists or writers of genre fiction—are about the creators of what would usually be considered "literature": serious fiction, poetry, and drama. The writing produced in these films is special, is high culture, and not the product of everyday individuals. Indeed, the films about the creators of literature tend to focus on three ideas. First, movies about authors portray them as unusual people. They can be quirky, neurotic, obsessed, inspired, gifted, but whatever the traits, they are quite simply not like the rest of us (*Fear and Loathing in Las Vegas* (1998), *Finding Neverland* (2004), *The Hours* (2002), *Sylvia* (2003), *Finding Forrester* (2000), *American Splendor* (2003), *Adaptation* (2002), *Deconstructing Harry* (1997), *Quills* (2000)). Also, in these films, authors suffer for their work. They may suffer with love or illness or in family relationships or with writer's block, but suffer they do. Often the author's suffering leads to tragedy, particularly

128 *Popular culture and representations of literacy*

for women, (*Sylvia* (2003), *The Hours* (2002), *Iris* (2001), *Mrs. Parker and the Vicious Circle* (1994)). For men, the suffering can lead to tragedy or at least unhappy endings (*Secret Window* (2004), *Misery* (1990), *Barton Fink* (1991), *The Shining* (1980), *The Door in the Floor* (2004), *Tom and Viv* (1994), *A Soldier's Daughter Never Cries* (1998)). Yet in the movies, male authors are often offered the possibility of having their suffering allevi-ated through a sustaining or revelatory relationship with another person, usually a woman (*Wonder Boys* (2000), *Nora* (2000), *Finding Neverland* (2004), *Shakespeare in Love* (1998), *Possession* (2002)) but not always (*Field of Dreams* (1989), *Finding Forrester* (2000)).

Finally, movies about authors show us, time and again, that when writ-ing does happen, it comes from deep in the soul in explosions of creative expression. Writing for these authors is a gift, a talent that makes them distinctive from ordinary people. We see this symbolized, in part, by the very materials they use to write. Unlike most of us, who use ballpoint pens or pencils or computers for writing, authors in the movies work not with latest or most expensive technology, but with pens with inkwells or ancient manual typewriters. They write not to be efficient or to get a message done quickly, but to create art, which is slow and laborious work requiring slow and laborious tools. Perhaps even more telling, however, is that the author's gift of writing is solitary, available to them alone and a mark of their dis-tinctive individuality.

The representation of writing as a solitary activity, born of genius and available only to the select, is quite different from the ways writing is por-trayed as a daily event of common people in other films. As we have shown in previous chapters, writing and reading in other films is often a public act, or a social or collaborative one, that is conducted for fairly instrumen-tal reasons. Writing connects characters, even in conflict. These films may be filled with people writing letters or emails or orders or notes or codes or school assignments, but they are engaged in these literacy practices to accomplish other tasks. There is no sense that this writing, except for jour-nal entries, happens for its own sake or is intended to produce art. In this chapter, however, we will focus our discussion on films about how, for authors, literacy practices separate them from most people. Their writing, rather than connecting them to others, tends to set them apart. The act of writing, rather than a social act drawn from and driven by social contact, is instead an interior and unique activity, driven by the inner desires (and often demons) of the author. An author might be inspired by a muse, but the writing itself is represented or discussed in such films as emerging from interior genius, in the tradition of Romantic individualism. Consequently what such films portray is that creative writing itself is mysterious and unavailable to the average person. Instead, the best we can do is see the behavior and character of an author. The focus is not on the writing, but on acting like a quirky, individualistic, and troubled "writer." When audiences

The passions of the romantic author 129

are shown these repeated representations of writing as an elite activity that comes at a high personal cost or as the creation of genius not craft, or as an individual not a social activity, it is perhaps easier to understand some of the conceptions of writing, and teaching writing, that continue to dominate the culture and students in the classroom.

THE IDENTITY OF THE "AUTHOR"

It is worth noting at this point that most films about authors, either historical or fictional characters, are presented as "art" or "serious" films (*Finding Neverland* (2004), *American Splendor, Shakespeare in Love* (2003), *Wonder Boys* (2000), *The Hours* (2002), *Sylvia* (2003), *Iris* (2001)). In other words such films are dialogue-rich, often employ complex narrative and cinemagraphic techniques, have a more deliberate pacing, period sets and costumes, and so on. Though some of these films are considered critical successes, garnering nominations and awards, and others make modest profits, none of them would be considered mainstream, highly popular films when compared with the action and comedy blockbusters that dominate local cinemas. Such a narrative and cinematic approach to movies about authors serves to reinforce the artistic and non-mainstream nature of the central characters. Movies about authors as "artists" have to reflect their "artistic" disposition in the way the films are made. Approaching films in this way reinforces the representation of the authors as being out of the mainstream by also placing the films themselves out of the mainstream. Art films give studios prestige, win awards, and are considered to be "good for you" in an enlightening uplifting kind of way, and so go unseen by most of the movie-going public.

The exceptions to the art-film portrayal of authors are thrillers that either focus on the mental instability of the author (*The Shining* (1980), *Secret Window* (2004)) or on the observational and deductive powers of a genre writer such as mystery novelist who, as a character, is really just a different kind of detective. There is also a common portrayal of authors as oddball comic relief in comedies (*You've Got Mail* (1998), *The Producers* (1968)). Even these films, however, often emphasize the oddness and unconventionality of the author.

Almost all films about authors are predicated on a common assumption: Authors are not like us. Whether tortured or eccentric or brooding or passionate, the distinctive individuality of the author is a given in such films. It is almost as if filmmakers use as their template for portrayals of authors in films the description of the "poet" from Wordsworth's famous "Preface" as "a man, it is true, endowed with more lively sensibility, more enthusiasm and tenderness, who has a greater knowledge of human nature, and a more comprehensive soul, than are supposed to be common among

130 *Popular culture and representations of literacy*

mankind" (1993, 147). This view, developed by the Romantic movement and writers of the nineteenth century, of the author as a unique, gifted, and passionate artist, remains a powerful and pervasive model of the nature of the author in contemporary culture. The author, in the Romantic tradition, is connected to humanity in his interest in issues of life, love, and loss, but, at the same time, alone in his ability to perceive the deeper truths of such matters and then draw on his passions to render these truths in language. As Wordsworth puts it:

> For all good poetry is the spontaneous overflow of powerful feelings: and though this be true, Poems to which any value can be attached were never produced on any variety of subjects but by a man who, being possessed of more than usual organic sensibility, had also thought long and deeply. (143)

Romantic ideals of unusual sensibilities, passions, and deep thoughts are the defining characteristics of authors in contemporary films. Whether they are productive or blocked, long-suffering of fast-living, authors are represented as both unconventional and gifted. Films portrayals of real authors tend to focus on the tragic or the eccentric such as Plath, Oscar Wilde, Virginia Woolf, James Joyce, J.M. Barrie, Lewis Carroll, the Marquis de Sade, George Elliot, Iris Murdoch, or Hunter S. Thompson. Authors who simply go about their lives, have families, hold down jobs, sleep well at night, and produce their writing without fanfare are not characters we find in films. We are unlikely to see films any time soon about authors such as Wallace Stevens or Ted Kooser, the recent poet laureate of the United States, who wrote fine poetry while holding down jobs as insurance company executives. Such writers, no matter the quality of their work, are not portrayed on film because their lives do not fit the profile of the Romantic author. Even if such an author had a conflict in his or her life that might drive the plot of a film, it would be unusual to see a movie focused on such a person. The writing is not important, the Romantic character is. Fictional authors in film are similarly cast as Romantic artists different in sensibility and passion from the rest of us whether they are recluses (*Finding Forrester* (2000)) misunderstood eccentrics (*Barton Fink* (1991)) or dangerously obsessive killers (*The Shining* (1980), *Secret Window* (2004)).

It is possible in these representations to see the playing out of what Foucault (1969) defined as the "author-function." For Foucault the "author-function" is not the individual who wrote a novel or poem, but is the way the author's name and the idea of the author operates within the discourse to create a special status that is denied the writers of less "literary" works.

> There are a certain number of discourses that are endowed with the "author-function" while others are deprived of it. A private letter may

The passions of the romantic author 131

well have a signer—it does not have an author; a contract may well have a guarantor—it does not have an author. An anonymous text posted on a wall probably has a writer – but not an author. The author function is therefore characteristic of the mode of existence, circulation, and functioning of certain discourses within a society. (346)

The author-function shapes our perception of what an author is, both as a producer of texts and as a person. It is not simply that one writes a novel or a poem that would make one considered to be an "author," but that one's work is recognized as worthy of recognition as a kind of literary work that would come from an "author." (Writing a book about literacy and popular culture, like most scholarship, is simply not exalted enough.)

Foucault argues that the concept of the author-function for literary works emerged in the Enlightenment and grew through the Romantic period with the emphasis on the inherent genius of the individual artists. Increasingly, then, the connection of a text with the author-function matters more than the writing itself. As Foucault points out, "if we proved that Shakespeare did not write those sonnets which pass for his, that would constitute a significant change and affect the manner in which the author's name functions" (345). As long as we believe that Shakespeare was the author, however, we will find everything he wrote to have some significance because we hope that it will lend us a glimpse into the genius of the authorial mind. Finding Shakespeare's grocery list would be considered fascinating; finding ours would not. It is noteworthy that in *Shakespeare in Love* (1998) the character of William Shakespeare (Joseph Fiennes) is written, with great irony, to fulfill all the characteristics of the Romantic author even as the matter of who Shakespeare really was, and what his role was in authoring the works attributed to him, remains an issue of often heated debate.

Consequently, movies that are considered to be about authors are not about the writers of technical manuals or school textbooks or even grocery lists. The films instead focus on those persons who seem to fulfill the cultural expectations of the "author-function." It matters less in these films what the author writes then how she or he fits the persona of the author as shaped by the Romantic conception of the artist. Is the author detached in some way from the rest of society? Is the author suffering for literature? Is the author writing in magical bursts of inspiration? If all that is happening, if the character is enacting all the expected traits of an "author" then that is what matters most in these films, not the writing or the texts themselves. Our guess is that many of the people who have watched and enjoyed films such as *Sylvia* (2003), *Iris* (2001), *Finding Neverland* (2004), or *Shakespeare in Love* (1998), have never read a word of the work of Sylvia Plath, Iris Murdoch, J.M. Barrie, or even William Shakespeare. But they could enjoy the films just the same because they understand what a film about an author is supposed to look like.

132 *Popular culture and representations of literacy*

THE AUTHOR AS TRAGIC GENIUS

The inspired suffering of the author is the central character trait of so many creative writers in films, as well as often the engine that drives the central conflict of the plot. In *Sylvia* (2003), for example, the films opens with a shot of Sylvia Plath (Gwyneth Paltrow), laid out in deathly pallor, presumably after her famous suicide, as her voice quotes from one of her poems, "Lady Lazarus" (Plath 1961, 7):

> Dying
> Is an art, like everything else.
> I do it exceptionally well.
>
> I do it so it feels like hell.
> I do it so it feels real.
> I guess you could say I've a call.

If this isn't enough to focus our attention on Plath's turbulent life, within ten minutes of the start of the film, Plath has met Ted Hughes (Daniel Craig) and shared with him her passion for poetry, and in particular his poetry. For she, as a fellow Romantic artist, is capable of perceiving in Hughes' poetry more than other more common readers. She tells him she admires his work for its "Great big crashing poems, not blubbering baby stuff like the others. Colossal. Magnificent. Great blowing winds on steel girders." Hughes, in turn, recognizes in Plath a fellow artist apart from the masses. He can talk seriously about poetry with her and they have the following exchange about poetry at a party, oblivious to those around them:

Hughes: It's magic! It's not about magic, it's not like magic, it *is* magic. It's real magic, it's not conjured tricks or pulling rabbits out of hats. Incantations. Spells, sermons, rituals. What are they? They're poems. So what's a poet? He's a shaman, that's what he is.
Plath: What is she?
Hughes: A fucking good poem is a weapon, not like a pop gun. It's like a bomb. A bloody, big bomb.
Plath: That's why they make children learn them in school. They don't want them messing about with them on their own. I mean, just imagine if a sonnet went off accidentally. Boom.

But poetry is not the real subject of the film, and the above dialogue serves in part as a quick way to establish Plath and Hughes as bona fide Romantic artists. The greater purpose of the dialogue is its role as the verbal foreplay. Soon the two are in bed together and, as they lie in bed after making love, Plath tells Hughes of one of her suicide attempts. Though it is not a surprise for those familiar with Plath's biography, or the subsequent

The passions of the romantic author   133

debates over her legacy and relationship with Hughes, the opening of the film makes it clear that its focus will be on Plath's passion for Hughes as well as her struggles with depression. That these two elements of her life are shown to inspire her poetry is also portrayed, but the writing is secondary to the anguish of her emotional life. It is clear from the beginning of the film, however, that no one truly understands the depths and torments of Plath's soul.

Although we know Plath is the poetic genius at the core of the film, we also know that we will have to see her suffer before she can get her gifts onto the page. Her suffering is primarily illustrated through her frustrations in her marriage to Hughes. Either he is basking in critical accolades, while she is dismissed (a critic at a book publishing party looks at Hughes surrounded by adoring women readers and says, within earshot of Plath, "Poor thing, can't be easy for her, being married to that."), or he is flirting with other women. The result of this is that Plath finds herself unable to write. Though she has arranged the ideal author's setting, a table furnished with typewriter and flowers with a view of the ocean, she instead spends her time baking. Just to remind us of what is coming, she also makes occasional cryptic comments about suicide. "I tried to drown myself once," she says, while gazing at the waves. "I guess it didn't want me."

There is brief contentment after Hughes and Plath have two children and she is able to publish her first book of poems. But soon that crumbles as Plath's work does not receive the attention of Hughes' and she then discovers that he is having an affair. After he finally leaves, she burns his papers. But then, in the depth of her despair and suffering as she again contemplates suicide, just where we would not be surprised to find it in an author, she finds her greatest inspiration as a writer and her strongest voice. We know this because we see scenes of her bent over a desk scribbling furiously, tears streaming down her cheeks, while her voiceover intones lines of her poetry backed up by dramatic, lyrical piano and violin music. Though this kind of inspired frenetic writing is not what most working writers report, certainly not with voiceovers and a moody soundtrack, this kind of scene is a common signal in film of an author's moment of inspiration. In *The Hours* (2002), as another example, Virginia Woolf (Nicole Kidman) is shown in several scenes in her room, in an overstuffed chair with a lap desk and inkwell as she gazes significantly into space. Her fingers are smudged with ink and the floor around her is covered with books and pages of handwritten manuscript. Then, with her brow furrowed and the lyrical music rising in the background, she puts pen to page and we hear her thoughts in the familiar author's voiceover, "A woman's whole life in a single day. Just one day. And in that day, her whole life." Again, the voiceover and the music are our cues that authorial inspiration is taking place.

In *Sylvia*, just in case we missed that the scenes of her writing with voiceovers and music are evidence of authorial inspiration, a scene is inserted where Plath explicitly describes her artistic epiphany to her friend

134 *Popular culture and representations of literacy*

Al Alvarez (Jarred Harris), "I've never written more. Now he's gone, I'm free. I can finally write. I wake up between three and four, because that's the worst time, and I write till dawn. I really feel like God is speaking through me." Plath now has tapped into her inner genius and, though she suffers more, it is also made clear that she understands more than the rest of us who are not authors. Like Wordsworth's Romantic poet she is writing "with storm and sunshine, with the revolutions of the seasons, with cold and heat, with loss of friends and kindred, with injuries and resentments, gratitude and hope, with fear and sorrow" (1993, 151). Yet even as she has done her finest writing, we see that she is hopelessly spinning into the depression that will lead to her suicide. When Hughes sees her dead body on the bed, he finds beside it her manuscript for *Ariel* (1961).

Sylvia is an example not only of the common representation of inspired suffering in films about authors, but also the theme of artistic genius as inextricable from illness. In such films as *The Hours* (2002) or *Finding Forrester* (2000), the source of inspiration is also the source of torment, often in the form of mental illness. The illness serves both as real affliction and source of insight as well as a metaphor for the gifted but tortured nature of the artist. Even authors who are not represented as geniuses, are often shown in films as suffering from mental illnesses of various kinds (*As Good As It Gets* (1997), *Secret Window* (2004)).

In *The Hours* (2002), for example, both the characters of Virginia Woolf (Nicole Kidman) and Richard Brown (Ed Harris) are gifted authors who are also ill and eventually commit suicide. We realize quite quickly that, though they suffer different illnesses, it is impossible to separate our sense of them as authors from our sense of them as individuals in psychological pain. In their illnesses, as in their genius, they are not like the ordinary people around them. They are gifted and diseased, inspiring and dangerous. They fit the image of the brilliant, diseased artist as one who burns too bright with genius and, though creating great works, dies too soon. This is a theme found not only in films about authors, but about other creative artists as well such as *Vincent and Theo* (1990), *Amadeus* (1984), and *Pollock* (2000). Just as others around them often cannot understand their mental anguish, so that is a metaphor for the inability to truly comprehend the source of their talent.

Yet ordinary people are drawn to these troubled authors because of their genius. In *The Hours*, Leonard Woolf (Stephen Dillane) is portrayed as caring and solid, but unimaginative in his perception of Virginia Woolf's illness and art. We see him editing, setting type, talking about copyediting errors and page proofs. At one point, as he looks at proofs he is printing, Virginia walks into the room, telling him she is going for a walk, and he replies, "If I could walk mid-morning I'd be a happy man." He is business-like and professional, working with words but not authoring them. We soon see, however, that she is doing more than going for a walk, she is engaging her artistic soul. Though she is in the park, surrounded by people,

The passions of the romantic author   135

we see her looking pensive, oblivious to those around her. She is lost in her inspiration about the novel she is writing, which, in case we might miss the moment of inspiration, is given to us in a voiceover of her thoughts, "She's going to die. That's what's going to happen. She'll kill herself. She'll kill herself over something that doesn't seem to matter." As with most of the moments of her inspiration in the film, her genius is tied to her illness and suicide, the scene of which opens the film.

When near the end of the film, Virginia pleads with Leonard to leave Richmond, where they are living, and to return to live in London. He argues that London will only make her illness worse.

Virginia: I'm dying in this town.
Leonard: If you were thinking clearly, Virginia, you would recall it was London that brought you low.
Virginia: If I were thinking clearly? If I were thinking clearly?
Leonard: We brought you to Richmond to give you peace.
Virginia: If I were thinking clearly, Leonard, I would tell you that I wrestle alone in the dark, in the deep dark, and that only I can know. Only I can understand my condition. You live with the threat, you tell me you live with the threat of my extinction. Leonard, I live with it too.

Only she can understand her "condition." And we are meant to understand that her "condition" is both her illness and her genius. If she were to be made "well," she would lose her authorial gift. He wants her to be well, to be normal, but if she becomes well, she will no longer have the insights and inspirations she does through her illness. We are supposed to side with her in this argument. We are supposed to side with genius over the pedestrian concerns of ordinary people.

In one of the other narratives lines in the film, another ordinary person, Clarissa Vaughn (Meryl Streep) is drawn to Richard Brown because of his passion and his genius. Brown is irascible, anguished, and dying of AIDS. He is also a poet about to be given a prestigious award for his work. She is an editor, again a person who works with other people's words rather than authoring her own, and the person who takes care of other people, including her daughter and Brown. Yet Brown is relentless in his criticism of her life. She is, in his view, mundane and incapable of the greater insights he possesses into the human condition. He scorns the party she is planning to celebrate his award, referring to her as the Woolf character who also misses what is important in life while planning for parties. "Ah, Mrs. Dalloway," Brown says, "Always giving parties to cover the silence." As a poet, on the other hand, he is able to see and experience life in its truest essence beyond the trivialities of daily events such as shopping or parties. He laments his imminent death, "I wanted to write about it all. Everything that happens in a moment. The way the flowers looked when you carried them in your

136 *Popular culture and representations of literacy*

arms. This towel—how it smells, how it feels. This thread. All our feelings. Yours and mine. The history of it all. Who we once were. Everything in the world." We are left in no doubt that this passionate outburst marks him as the Romantic author in the Wordsworth tradition. It is also clear that he will die before the end of the film, and he does indeed leap from a window to his death.

By contrast, Clarissa Vaughn, like Leonard Woolf, has her common-place, routine life brought into strong relief by the exceptional artist she cannot ignore. In both situations the ordinary people, though pained and frustrated by the tormented authors in their lives, must attend to their needs so that the artists can breathe life into their mundane existences. They put up with the madness to be close to the genius, even as they know that the illness and genius will eventually consume the people they love. Although there are films where the ordinary person is transformed or saved by the author's work, in many of these films, there is a cautionary note for all of us ordinary people in the audiences. Sacrificing for art may be noble, but it can be the path to madness and destruction. Perhaps it is best we, the aver-age people, are not so simultaneously blessed and cursed. We may not be geniuses, but at least we have our mental health.

THE MUSE AND REDEMPTION

Though authors in films are usually distinctive and troubled characters, they are not necessarily doomed. For if the tragic and tormented author is a common narrative in contemporary Hollywood films, the author who is saved from failure by another person is equally as common, particularly if the author is male. In films from *Finding Neverland* (2004) to *Shake-speare in Love* (1998) to *Wonder Boys* (2000) to *Finding Forrester* (2000) to *Field of Dreams* (1989), an author who is unable to write, for reasons of varying severity, meets someone who rescues him from his problems and makes him productive again. The redemption of the author's connection to life and to others is entwined with the ability of the author to find inspira-tion and create art. The author remains distinctive, quirky, different from the common person. Yet through his interactions with the other people in these films he rediscovers his connections to humanity and, quite often, his capacity for love. As a result, he not only can write again, but he invariable produces great art from this newfound inspiration.

Finding Neverland (2004) and *Shakespeare in Love* (1998) are two criti-cally acclaimed, popular films that adopt this narrative, one in the genre of tragic melodrama and the other in romantic comedy. As with many of these films, each begins with the author unable to write. In *Finding Neverland*, J.M. Barrie (Johnny Depp) is shown at the beginning of the film at the open-ing of his latest play, a play which it becomes quickly clear is a commer-cial and critical failure. His producer, Charles Frohman (Dustin Hoffman)

The passions of the romantic author 137

though disappointed commissions another play from Barrie. While Barrie promises him "we'll get them next time" it's also clear that he does not have an idea in mind. In a similar way, the first shot of Shakespeare (Joseph Fiennes) in *Shakespeare in Love* is of him scribbling away, but we soon realize that he is only practicing his signature, and that the room is littered with the crumpled results of his futile attempts to write. He is blocked, he complains, with all his ideas "locked" in his head. "Words, words, words," he laments. "Once I had the gift. I could make love out of words as a potter makes lumps from clay." We see his writing now, however, as a purely commercial enterprise from which he takes no joy nor finds inspiration. Even his little pre-writing ritual does not work. He will write true art again, "as soon as I find my muse." Yet, in need of money, he has promised plays to two different theatres, even though he cannot write them.

For both these characters, as for so many authors in film, they cannot write because they are incomplete. They lack the love, the human connection to another that can inspire their work. These films, and so many others about authors, rest on the assumption that the author cannot produce art without a person to act as a muse. Barrie lives in a loveless marriage, and Shakespeare is involved in passionate trysts, but not in love. They are writing only to make money, and because of this their work has become both corrupted and commonplace. Authors who do not write from their souls, inspired by their muses, have betrayed their gifts. Writing only for commerce cannot result in art but only in debased works. What is necessary for these authors is to find love, not in order to live happily ever after, but in order to tap the dormant passions that will fuel their inspirations. Only then can their genius flower as it should.

The finding of a muse and the rebirth or writing genius is the central narrative of these films. Consequently, in these films, it is not long before the author meets his muse. For Shakespeare his muse comes in the form of Viola de Lesseps (Gwyneth Paltrow). We initially see her complaining that "all the men at court are without poetry. I will have poetry in my life, and love." Yet once they meet they are captivated with one another. After having their own balcony scene of passion and infatuation, we see Shakespeare inspired and turning out page after page of the writing that will become *Romeo and Juliet* (with a sonnet thrown in here and there for good measure).

The transformation from frustrated hack to inspired artist happens after Shakespeare and Viola make love. In a scene not long after, we see them stealing kisses back stage as she rehearses for the role of Romeo (in disguise as a boy). He pulls himself reluctantly from her embrace. She pleads with him "Do not go," but he answers "I must, I must" and he dashes off to write, springing to his writing desk with the obsessed enthusiasm of the real author. He begins to write the balcony scene, which begins in voiceover, and then cuts to Viola reading the scene with Will as they lie in bed together, which then cuts to her speaking the final lines of the scene

138 *Popular culture and representations of literacy*

at rehearsal as the rest of the cast looks on transfixed at the poetry they are hearing. Now we see what a true muse does for an author. The passion of true love liberates his genius, igniting a passion to write that even transcends his love. He cannot stop writing. In addition we now see a writer who is not only not blocked, but who seems to no longer need to write drafts or to revise. He can race from his lover's embrace to pour his artistic revelations on the page in a single sitting that then are recognize by all who hear them as the gift of true genius. Of course, Shakespeare is a genius, and we all know that eventually he would get around to displaying it for us. But we also want to see that genius spring forth in the passion and brilliance of a true artist who needed only to find his muse.

Barrie, in *Finding Neverland*, is also an author in need of a muse. Rather than finding it in one woman, he finds it in a widow (Kate Winslet) and her four sons. He comes across them in the park, the day after his disastrous experience with the play that opens the movie. In fact, he see them through the hole of his newspaper where the bad review of his play had been before being cut out by his housekeeper. Through the void left by his failure, then, he spots the family that will inspire him to again be a success. We soon see him in a series of scenes playing with the boys—as pirates, in the Wild West—that move from imaginary settings back to the daily lives of the children. In these moments of play, because we know that Barrie is the author of *Peter Pan*, we begin to recognize the elements he will start to bring together to write that work. When we see him turning to his journal and writing, we know that he has found his inspiration and is now tapping in to the innate genius that marks him as an artist. We also recognize that he is an artist because of his idiosyncratic nature, such as his willingness to dress in children's costumes, or his hanging a spoon from his nose to amuse the boys during a formal dinner party, much to the horror of his proper Victorian wife.

For both Barrie and Shakespeare, once they have found their muses, they are able to take the mundane events of their daily lives and turn them into art. In *Shakespeare in Love* this is played for in-jokes as, for example, Shakespeare walks past a street preacher calling out "a plague on both your houses" and we know that will show up later in *Romeo and Juliet*. In *Finding Neverland* it is played for sentiment as Barrie watches the boys jump up and down on their beds and then imagines them flying out the window as we know he will later write in *Peter Pan*. Just in case we miss the connection, the scene of the boys flying is accompanied by the lyrical music that always accompanies authorial inspiration and a thoughtful and trancelike look on Barrie's face. Despite the difference in tone, however, the effect of such scenes is a similar representation of the author as the person with the distinctive insight to take the dross of daily life and spin it into the gold of literature.

Barrie is, at least, one step closer to the portrayal of a working writer in that he keeps a journal where he says that he's "just making notes. I'm never really certain what they're about until I've read them over later." There is at least a nod here to the possibility that a writer does not sit

The passions of the romantic author 139

down and produced inspired, single-draft masterpieces. Though we never see Barrie struggling in having to turn the notes from the journal into his play. In fact, late in the film when Barrie's wife (Radha Mitchell) reads his journal she tells him, "It's the best you've written, James" as if she is reading finished work.

In both films, even after the author has found his muse, there is a set of inconvenient obstacles that must be overcome before the triumph of the artistic vision is complete. Because these are both films about plays, the obstacles have to do with uncomprehending producers and inflexible laws. Yet, even as others around them, including the producers and actors, find themselves baffled by the author's work, they still somehow trust his vision. Of course, their trust is rewarded when the play becomes an enormous and transcendent success with the audience. We are also left with the sense that this work was not simply a fluke, but that the author has been transformed by these experiences and will henceforth produce similarly transcendent work. We also see that the author's work has been recognized by those in power. In *Shakespeare in Love,* Queen Elizabeth commissions a new play, and in *Finding Neverland*, Frohman, the producer is seen looking admiringly at the play and murmuring "genius."

It is clear that as an artist the author has reached a turning point, and will now be more confident and in touch with his genius. It is also clear that the author has been made a better man. In order to find a muse, he had to find love. The discovery of love, of a contact and investment in human relationships, is the key not only to becoming a better person, but to releasing the artist within. After the premiere of the play, Barrie asks Peter Llewellyn Davies (Freddie Highmore) what he thought of the play:

Peter: It's about our summer together, isn't it?
Barrie: It is.
Peter: About all of us.
Barrie: That's right. You like it?
Peter: It's magical. Thank you.
Barrie: No, thank you. Thank you, Peter.

At the same time, the authors are able to offer their muses a reflection of their lives that allows them to overcome their struggles. For Viola de Lesseps, in *Shakespeare in Love,* the true love she finds in Will Shakespeare and hears expressed in his poetry, gives her the strength to defy convention and survive a loveless arranged marriage.

In *Finding Neverland*, Barrie provides Peter with the gift of writing that allows the boy to overcome the death of both of his parents. When Barrie meets the boy at the beginning of the film, he is reserved and literal-minded, unable to deal with the death of his father. Though Peter is resistant to the imaginative games Barrie plays with the family, Barrie is persistent and gives Peter a journal of his own.

140 *Popular culture and representations of literacy*

Peter: I still have no idea what to write.
Barrie: Write about anything. Write about your family. Write about the
    talking whale.
Peter: What whale?
Barrie: The one that's trapped in your imagination and desperate to get out.

Peter later attempts to write a play, but tears the book to pieces when he learns his mother is ill. Just before she dies she returns the book to her son, loving pieced back together. The final scene in the film, after the success of the play and the death of the mother, is Barrie and Peter sitting together on a park bench, with Peter's journal, now filled with writing. Peter admits that he "just started writing and I haven't been able to stop," to which Barrie replies that Peter's mother would be pleased to know that. Barrie has given Peter the gift of writing, the ability to withstand tragedy, and in turn has freed his imagination. When Peter says he thought his mother would always be with him, Barrie replies, "In fact she is, because she's on every page of your imagination. You'll always have her there. Always."

A successful play, genius awakened, love discovered, it all sounds like the making of a happy ending. In finding his genius, however, the author in these films also often finds that his relationship with the muse must change. The author cannot be fully contented. If he was, he would not still be set apart, different from the rest of the world. If the author had no pain, no source of suffering, he would not be able to be a true artist. The author can become a better man, but not a completely happy man. In *Finding Neverland*, Barrie has found his muse, but Sylvia Llewellyn Davies has died, Barrie's wife has left him, and though he will be the co-guardian for her sons along with their grandmother, we know he will never be able to fill the void left by the death of their parents. The last shot of the film is Barrie and Peter, sitting on the bench in the park, remembering Sylvia and mourning. Barrie still has his love for the boys, but he will not be completely happy.

Similarly, in *Shakespeare in Love*, though Viola de Lesseps rejects her arranged husband, she is not able to marry Shakespeare. He can never be completely happy with her. In their parting scene the pain is almost too much for Shakespeare to bear:

Shakespeare: I am done with the theatre. The playhouse is for dreamers.
    Look where the dream has brought us.
Viola de Lesseps: It was we ourselves did that. And for my life to come I
    would not have it otherwise.
Shakespeare: I have hurt you and I am sorry for it.
Viola de Lesseps: If my hurt is to be that you will write no more, then I
    shall be the sorrier.

Even as she feels the pain of losing her love, she will not stop acting as his muse. It is more important that he continue to write, that he continue

The passions of the romantic author 141

to be an author, than it is that he become a contented man. She tells him that the Queen has commissioned him to write a play for twelfth night and together, in their farewell, she helps him think through the central plot and characters, drawing them from their own frustrated love. We see that, even as Shakespeare suffers her leaving, she will continue to inspire him. Their final words to each other are not just of lovers, but of artist and muse:

Shakespeare: You will never age for me, nor fade, nor die.
Viola de Lesseps: Nor you for me.
Shakespeare: Good bye my love, a thousand times good bye.
Viola de Lesseps: Write me well.

We then see Shakespeare sitting at his desk and beginning to write Twelfth Night. He will not find true contentment, few authors in films do, but has found his muse and his genius and he will, from his solitary room, continue to write great art. The film ends with Shakespeare's voiceover, not quoting from the play, but describing how he will write it. In the final lines of the film he says, "It will be a love story for she will be my heroine for all time. And her name will be...Viola."

THE SOLITARY ARTIST

There are, of course, variations on the theme of the author and muse. It does not always require romance. In *Finding Forrester* (2000), for example, the author is William Forrester (Sean Connery), a J.D. Salinger-like character who has followed up his youthful successes by becoming a curmudgeonly recluse. He is saved by a young African American student, Jamal Wallace (Rob Brown), who he, in turn, helps become a better writer and student. The film ends with Forrester leaving his apartment, writing a new book, and, because he can be completely contented, dying. Nor is every author required to suffer in the end. At the end of *Wonder Boys* (2000), we see Grady Tripp (Michael Douglass), who has been the burned out, blocked writer through most of the film, in the last scene writing meaningful work in a beautiful country home with his new wife and child.

Yet, in all these films, the focus is on a male author. He can find his muse in a woman, as in *Shakespeare in Love*, or in younger male protégés, as in *Finding Forrester* or *Finding Neverland*, or in both, as in *Wonder Boys*. But it is almost always a "he" who does the finding. Women authors on film, such as Sylvia Plath or Virginia Woolf or Iris Murdoch, as we noted above, are much more like to have their narratives end tragically. Men, in these films, are more likely to abuse or fail the women than to inspire them. In part this difference in the narrative of the author for women has to do with the gendered construct of the muse. It is also possible to see the narrative of the tragic woman author as a subtle, cautionary tale about the price

142 *Popular culture and representations of literacy*

paid by successful women. In films where a woman is inspired by a man, it is usually not because of his love or kindness, but because of the pain he has caused her. In films such as *Something's Gotta Give* (2003) and *Under the Tuscan Sun* (2003), the central characters are women authors who do not find their inspiration until they are deeply hurt or rejected by the men they loved. Once the woman author has been hurt and gained independence from the man, she finds a way to thrive as a writer. It is also interesting that this narrative is more common in romantic comedies than in dramas.

Regardless of the differences in films about authors, the constant is the treatment of the author as a person imbued with a special gift. The author may need to be inspired, but the product of that inspiration comes not from hard work or from instruction, but from innate genius. Near the end of *Wonder Boys*, Grady Tripp, who, in addition to being an author, is also a professor of creative writing, makes the following speech to his editor:

> Nobody teaches a writer anything. You tell them what you know. You tell them to find their voice and stay with it. You tell the ones that have it to keep at it. You tell the ones who don't have it to keep at it too, because that's the only way they're going to get where they're going. Of course it does help if you know where you want to go. Helping my students figure that out, that and Sara, that's what made these last years worthwhile.

Nobody can teach an author anything because authors are born, not made. When a real author is inspired, and creates art, it is a magical moment that must remain a mystery to the rest of us. That kind of inspiration, that kind of writing, is something that the rest of us will never know.

The representation of writing as the production of cherished texts by a gifted few stands in contrast to the representation of writing in most films. As we have noted throughout this book, in most films are filled with ordinary people writing in ordinary settings and producing work that is treated as both ordinary and disposable. Across genres and across characters, people writing in other films are not represented as writing from genius or as creating transcendent work. From a thriller like *Mission Impossible* (1996) to a fantasy film such as *Harry Potter and the Chamber of Secrets* (2002) to a drama such as *Changing Lanes* (2002) to a romantic comedy such as *Serendipity* (2001) to many, many others, writing is an action that is done to accomplish a task. Writing is an activity that gets things done and is then forgotten. Writing is not an activity that consumes characters' identities and lives. It certainly is not represented as requiring a more special genius or inspiration than cooking or driving a car.

Recent theories of literacy and writing, however, have emphasized that writing, rather than the result of inspired innate genius, is the product of social interactions and cultural acquisition (Street 1995; LeFevre 1987; Gee 1989, 2004) Whether done to accomplish a daily task or to compose a son-

The passions of the romantic author 143

net, writing has been conceived as a social and teachable practice. There has been a great deal of research and theorizing done about the social nature of writing in daily settings (Barton and Hamilton 1998; Gregory and Williams 2000; Heath 1983) and in the literacy or composition classroom (Trimbur 2000; Bruffee 1984; Faigley 1993). These scholars and others argue persuasively that writing is connected to culture, to other people, to public discourses. As Ede and Lunsford (2001, 355) note, recent scholarship in literacy has been grounded in "the socially constructed nature of writing—its inherently collaborative function." The writer adapts and molds the discourses from the surrounding culture, but is always part of the larger conversation. Although for all of the scholarly conversation about the social and collaborative nature of writing, Ede and Lunsford point out that actual professional work valued in the academy usually continues to be considered the product of individual scholars. "Despite vigorous debates over theories and methods surrounding issues of subjectivity and authorship, ideologies of the individual and the author have remained largely unchallenged in scholarly practice" (358). If the concept of the writer as the individual crafting unique work in relative isolation can remain entrenched in the writing produced in literacy studies, where there has been theorizing and research about the social nature of writing, it is not difficult to see why it maintains an even stronger hold on beliefs about writers in creative writing and in the culture at large.

In general, the scholarship and discussion of the writing practices of creative writers, of authors, has been more limited than the study of other literacy practices. Less time and scholarship has gone into the study of how novelists and poets and playwrights learn their craft and work within the larger culture as writers. There are certainly those who have discussed how creative writers work through the same processes as all writers (Murray 2004; Bishop 1997; Bishop and Ostrom 1994). Nobody is simply inspired to produce perfect manuscripts, these scholars argue, without working through the same struggles, the same questions of invention, the same attention to revision, as all writers.

The culture in general, then, and certainly mainstream literary culture, clings to the conception of the gifted, tortured author. An example of this is the continuing debate about whether creative writing programs and workshops, particularly in the United States, are turning out "too many" writers. If literary writing is the domain of genius, then, so the argument goes, it cannot be spread among the ungifted without diluting the pool of pure genius. According to these critics, such creative writing programs are defrauding untalented students by promising them that they can learn to write, and cluttering the world of true "authors" with writers who are only pretenders to such an exalted title. A recent interview with Lan Samantha Chang, the new director of the venerable Iowa Writers' Workshop at the University of Iowa, centered around her discussions of whether writing could indeed ever be "taught" or was it an innate gift that could only be liberated. Chang

144 *Popular culture and representations of literacy*

came down squarely on the side of the latter (*The Connection* 2005). A lamentable point of view for someone at an educational institution.

The division between the romantic conception of the author and the literacy studies conception of everyday writers can be seen in the split in schools between creative writing courses and courses devoted to basic or academic writing. The former are intended to reward the best—or "gifted" —students by helping them create art and feed their souls, while the latter are intended to inculcate the masses in schools and offer them "useful" skills. Such a split influences who gets to take such courses, with more affluent students being the majority in creative writing classrooms, which operate more on the artist-apprentice workshop model, while poorer and working-class students are taught more instrumental approaches to writing in more traditional teacher-student structured classes (Schweitzer 2004). Teachers and students alike don't expect passion and art to come out of basic and academic writing courses. Students are usually there because they have to be and, like taking bad-tasting medicine, they just try to get over it. But students in the creative writing courses are expecting to be treated like budding authors, who will have to suffer and struggle but whose genius will eventually be recognized as innate.

For those of us who are merely writers and teachers of writing, we will simply have to struggle on with our mundane lives and limited talent. Like the people sitting around us in the cinema, we will write when we have to, but we will rarely think of ourselves as authors. It is not our writing, or our struggles and passions about writing, that will define our lives and set us apart from those around us. Meanwhile, up on the screen, the authors will continue to struggle with their gift and their curse. We will watch as they are marveled at, envied, and pitied by those around them. In *The Hours* (2002), Virginia Woolf's sister, Vanessa Bell (Miranda Richardson), comes to visit with her children. Bell clearly loves and admires her troubled sister, even as she fears and does not understand her. Bell says to her daughter, "Your aunt is a very lucky woman, Angelica. She is because she has two lives. She has the life, she is leading and also the books, she is writing, which makes her very fortunate indeed."

8 The triumph of the word
Literacy as salvation and commodity

"How little we know about learning—and about teaching, too," Harvey J. Graff (1987, 324) exclaims in "Literacy, Myths, and Legacies: Lessons from the History of Literacy." Graff is astonished by simplistic definitions and inflated claims that are regularly put forward in the name of literacy, promoting, for example, assumptions that literacy is a simple concept, that literacy learning is a linear process, or that the effects of literacy are always the same in every context (324). Such definitions and claims about literacy circulate in innumerable forms in educational policy, public opinion, and the media, including films. In previous chapters, we have been interested in the diffuse images of literacy that appear in films that do not explicitly declare an interest in literacy. We have largely been concerned with images of literacy that are easy to miss because they appear unannounced, as markers of film characters' identities or embedded in narratives that focus thematically on something different. In this chapter, however, we look at how literacy itself is defined or represented and at consequences ascribed to literacy in the movies. We turn to the films we have been calling triumph-of-literacy films because they so often convey the message that literacy results in positive developments such as political empowerment, social mobility, material gain, moral enlightenment, and individual agency.

A wide array of popular films has taken up education as a dominant theme over the years, and teachers naturally find these films interesting. Discussions on writing program listservs such as WPA-L and wcenter reflect this interest, exchanging ideas about how to use film in the classroom or to reflect on teaching. When we have presented our own project at conferences, audience members readily suggest long lists of films that address education, teachers, and teaching. The list includes such varied titles as *Goodbye Mr. Chips* (1939 and 1969), *To Sir with Love* (1967), *Educating Rita* (1983), *Ferris Bueller's Day Off* (1986), *Stand and Deliver* (1988), *The Dead Poets' Society* (1989), *Il Postino* (1994), *Dangerous Minds* (1995), *Mr. Holland's Opus* (1995), *The Mirror has Two Faces* (1996), *Anna and the King* (1999), *Wonder Boys* (2000), *The Emperor's Club* (2002), and many more besides. In still other films, literacy and education are not explicitly foregrounded, but are present as powerful subtexts, as in *My Big*

146 *Popular culture and representations of literacy*

Fat Greek Wedding (2002) or *The Shawshank Redemption* (1994). Some of these titles have already been singled out for critique by literacy scholars such as Henry Giroux (1997), Dale Bauer (1998), Jo Keroes (1999), and Keith Gilyard (1999).

We view triumph-of-literacy movies in the light of two theoretical conversations. First, we consider them in relation to the idea of literacy that accompanies the so-called strong theories of literacy in all of its myriad forms. Strong theories tend to define literacy in broad and universally positive ways, claiming that there is a deep divide between literate and illiterate, and also assuming that literacy is simple and easy to learn. Strong theories also tend to assume positive transformations result from the acquisition of literacy: acquiring literacy can perform an act of salvation on individuals or whole societies. Second, we consider the movies in relation to the idea that literacy functions as a commodity in our society, a form of cultural capital owned by some individuals and not by others. As a commodity, literacy gets subjected to the forces that shape all commodities: access to literacy is limited.

LITERACY AS SALVATION

All too often, triumph-of-literacy films work to perpetuate the mass of common conceptions about literacy and its consequences that literacy historian Harvey Graff (1987, 324) has termed the "literacy myth" because of its widespread hold in the minds of the public and policymakers, a myth that still remains, even after its ideas have come in for considerable criticism from scholars and educators. Graff's work on the myths of literacy provides a rich framework for studying literacy as it is represented in popular films. He has distilled a number of "lessons" to be learned from his decades of historical research into the concepts and practices of literacy and schooling in the West, work that he has presented in keynote addresses, conference presentations, and works such as "Literacy, Myths, and Legacies: Lessons from the History of Literacy."

According to Graff, the literacy myth constitutes a bewildering array of assumptions and claims, made in the name of literacy, but having little to do with the real nature of literacy or actual uses to which it is put: "These wholesale claims rarely stand up to either empirical or conceptual probing historically or contemporarily" (324). He attributes the "complications" of Western traditions of literacy, first, to conceptions and conceptualizations of literacy that are, in his terms "extraordinarily frail" and, second, to consequences expected to follow from the acquisition of literacy that are, on the other hand, overly exaggerated and often inaccurate. First, the literacy myth fails to take into account the slippery and contradictory nature of literacy as a social practice. Graff asserts that the weakness of the terms in which literacy has generally been conceptualized allow it to be imagined as a simple and unproblematic notion that is uniform, universal, and always the same (324). Assuming that literacy is a simple notion in turn feeds the myth that it is easy to learn, in spite of all of the evidence showing that the process of acquiring literacy is actually "*hard work*" (328). Another myth is that "subjects such as literacy, learning, schooling, and education are simple, unproblematic notions," even though, he notes, these are fundamentally complex, in reality (323).

Theories that conceive of literacy as simple and uniform in turn support expectations that literacy will have a broad range of strong, positive effects on individuals and societies. Among the consequences that have been attributed to the acquisition of literacy, Graff lists "psychological , cognitive, attitudinal, social-relational, behavioral, symbolic, motivational, participatory, and productive" effects. In terms of the individual, he notes: "Literate persons...are said to be more empathetic, innovative, achievement-oriented, cosmopolitan, media and politically aware, identified with a nation, aspiring to schooling, "modern," urban in residence, and accepting of technology" (324). In broader, social terms, high levels of literacy have been correlated with "economic growth and industrialization, wealth and productivity, political stability and participatory democracy, urbanization, consumption, and contraception" (324). Finally, Graff has observed that the condition of literacy has virtually been equated with "the *condition of civilization*," and literacy has become associated with moral concerns such as "character, discipline and order, security," and even democracy (320).

According to Graff, such claims are not based in empirical study, and do not stand up to scrutiny. He asserts that literacy is difficult to define and extremely contradictory in its effects, and points out that facile assumptions about literacy fall apart quickly when confronted by the "morass" of empirical and historical evidence. Despite its hold on popular and policy opinions, the "strong" theory of literacy "turns out to be much weaker, with literacy's impacts seldom so direct, unmediated, abstract, or universal" (324). His own historical research prompts him to argue vehemently against claims put forward by "strong" theories of literacy because they imply a sense that individual well being and the health of the social order depend on high levels of literacy (320). To ward off the dangers of illiteracy, literacy programs and campaigns are prescribed by experts. Sometimes, Graff says, "great damage is done to the individuals and larger collectivities...in the name of 'development' stemming from expectations about mass provision and possession of literacy in the world's developed and the underdeveloped" (325).

Triumph-of-literacy films often echo the meta-narratives that permeate literacy education from kindergarten through college. Images in some triumph-of-literacy films, such as *Fame* (1980) and *Dangerous Minds* (1995), reinforce the myth that literacy is an autonomous set of skills that one can, and should, adopt to join the dominant culture. In triumph-of-literacy films, literacy also offers learners not just a tool, or a skill that is useful in

148   *Popular culture and representations of literacy*

the world, but a more fundamental kind of personal transformation. They differ from films about literary authors: while authors may experience psychological resolution or change their life circumstances, the changes they experience are of a different quality than those experienced by characters in triumph-of-literacy films, who tend to undergo more radical forms of transformation. As we discussed in Chapter Seven, film images of authors tend to portray them as individuals who possess innate creative abilities that set them apart from the general run of the population. The qualities authors possess are represented as already inherent in them, not something they learn, and the struggles they face in film narratives involve learning how to express their creative gifts in the world. But in triumph-of-literacy films, the characters acquire, or hope to acquire, something that they didn't have before, and they become, or hope to become, renewed, different people.

In *Educating Rita* (1983), a working-class woman (Julie Walters) finds her life deeply changed by the process of gaining a literary education, a project she pursues at Open University with boundless determination. Jo Keroes (1999) reads *Educating Rita* as a revision of the Pygmalion myth, because the story reconfigures the relationship between professor and student: unlike the mythical Galatea, Rita is not the professor's creation come to life, but an outspoken, self-directed woman, who actually brings a sense of rejuvenation to her tutor (Michael Caine), a disillusioned poet with a drinking problem (107–115). Rita is a hairdresser and is unhappily married. As her education progresses, her marriage falls apart, and her relationships with her family and with her tutor become strained. In the end, however, after she has finished college, she is more confident, more independent, and more sophisticated in her ability to engage with the world from a position of strength.

IMAGES OF NONLITERACY

In *Nanny McPhee* (2005), a young scullery maid, Evangeline (Kelly Macdonald), falls in love with Cedric Brown (Colin Firth), the recently widowed master of the household where she works. Evangeline is beautiful and kind, and she loves his brood of seven, very naughty children. Even though her master must remarry quickly or lose the allowance that supports the family, Evangeline knows that it would never occur to him to recognize a potential marriage partner in her (in spite of his attraction to her and her excellent qualities), because she cannot read or write. Evangeline enlists the help of one of the children to teach her "sounds," and she retires to out-of-the-way corners of the house to practice reading in guilty solitude. Nanny McPhee (Emma Thompson) intervenes to disrupt Brown's marriage to the wrong woman, and to bring him together at the altar with Evangeline instead. "But I haven't found out how the story ends yet," Evangeline says. "You *are* the story," Nanny McPhee reassures her, ushering her up the aisle.

The triumph of the word 149

We are used to seeing movies that end with a wedding, and even to seeing unfortunate matches interrupted at the last possible instant before the knot is tied, but we are not used to seeing characters like Evangeline. It is extremely unusual for films to center on characters that do not read or write, or even to represent them in minor roles—a fact that is telling, since it effectively renders this part of the population invisible, at least in cinematic terms. In this broad sense, film replicates the marginalization of nonliterate people in society. Strong or "great leap" theories that posit uniformly positive consequences for literacy invite negative portrayals of the nonliterate by rhetorically constructing a huge difference between "literate and nonliterate persons, societies, and civilizations" (Graff 1987, 325). Such concepts of literacy are even played for laughs in a movie such as *Zoolander* (2001), where the title character, Derek Zoolander (Ben Stiller), a vacuous male model criticized for his lack of intelligence and trivial obsessions, vows to prove his critics wrong by opening the "Derek Zoolander Center For Children Who Can't Read Good And Want To Learn To Do Other Stuff Good Too." A desire to find ways to study and teach literacy that do not perpetuate stereotypes of human difference has been an important impetus for new literacy researchers to discredit the idea that a great leap occurs with the acquisition of literacy. Some researchers also point to the ways that negative portrayals of illiteracy are linked to ideas about literacy itself that they can no longer support.

In "How to Eradicate Illiteracy without Eradicating Illiterates?" and other writings, Munir Fasheh (2002) discredits common perceptions about illiteracy and links these same discredited perceptions to forms of education that theorize and practice literacy as an autonomous skill, forms that he says construct a profoundly alienating experience for the literate person. For him, both aspects are linked. Fasheh's reflections are grounded in his own educational experiences and in his ever-evolving understanding of the life of his mother, who never learned to read or write. Fasheh, who directs the Arab Education Forum at the Center for Middle East Studies at Harvard, describes how long it took him to "discover" that his "illiterate" mother, a seamstress, had knowledge, including knowledge of mathematics. "Her knowledge was embedded in life (like salt in food) in a way that made it invisible to me as an educated and literate person," he writes (3).

> The realization of my mother's knowledge challenged several assumptions, which are usually embedded in official discussions on literacy: that a literate person is better than an illiterate person; that an illiterate person is not a full human being; that s/he is ignorant; that by becoming literate, a person would be magically transformed and poverty and ignorance would be wiped out; that a literate person is freer than an illiterate person; and so on and so forth. The fact is that my illiterate mother was neither inferior in her knowledge nor was less human or less free. (3)

150 *Popular culture and representations of literacy*

In his writing and in his work as a teacher, Fasheh challenges common representations not only of illiteracy but of literacy as well. "Giving literacy magical powers and claims is simply a false promise," he states (3). "Discovering" his mother's knowledge meant recognizing at the same time that dominant educational structures and terminology undermine diverse ways of learning and knowing; imposing one meaning and form of literacy is "inhuman and disruptive" (10). Fasheh's account indicates how deeply strong theories have organized general consciousness and determined general perceptions of literate and nonliterate persons alike.

Images of nonliteracy that turn up in Hollywood movies—generally through minor or peripheral characters—reinforce strong theories of literacy. In *Holes* (2003), for example, a nonliterate boy is nicknamed "Zero" to emphasize his insignificance in the eyes of others. In terms of society, he is merely a cipher, an empty person, until he begins to learn how to read and write and he claims his real name, Hector. *Il Postino* (1994) gives us a rare film portrait of an adult acquiring literacy, and may be the best known such depiction in recent years. Even though it is not a product of the Hollywood film industry, this film was successful enough and repeats common film narratives to be relevant to our discussion. *Il Postino* tells the story of a fisherman's son, Mario, who meets the poet Pablo Neruda, in exile from his native Chile and living near Mario's village on a rustic Italian island. Mario is reluctant to follow in his father's footsteps and become a fisherman, but his world offers few options for other work. When Neruda and his wife move to the island, Mario gets the job of bicycling up to the poet's villa to deliver their mail. The cosmopolitan poet in their midst excites admiration and curiosity among the islanders. They say that his sensual poems make him very attractive to women. When Mario falls in love, he asks Neruda to compose something to make the woman, Beatrice, return his love. Mario's move into literacy comes through his desire to become a poet himself, first to win Beatrice, and later for political expression. Neruda gives him a blank notebook, and Mario begins by drawing a large circle—a "poem" to the full moon. Mario marries Beatrice, and also begins to speak out against the corrupt government that exploits the people in his village. He is invited to read one of his political poems at a rally in a distant city, and when the rally turns violent, Mario is killed.

Neruda uses his power as a celebrity to impress Beatrice in Mario's favor, and *Il Postino* similarly uses the powers of film to create a profoundly sympathetic image of a poor, barely-literate man. While *Il Postino* is sympathetic in its portrayal of Mario, it clearly privileges literacy over nonliteracy. Acquiring literacy is unquestionably a form of salvation for Mario, and the adulation he feels for the poet matches the passion he feels for his wife. The differences in his life as he learns to become a poet are characterized visually as a change from dark to light. Early scenes of him at home with his father are dark and dingy, and their conversation is halting and one-sided. Mario speaks in stumbling fragments, and appears to be simple-minded;

The triumph of the word   151

his father is unresponsive and mute. Their lives seem impoverished in spiritual and emotional realms as well as in an economic sense. The possibilities for Mario are depressingly confining in the "before" part of his life—before his encounter with Neruda. The "after literacy" of Mario's before-and-after portrait shows him as more free in a political sense, more fulfilled in his personal life, and more confident of his own worth as a human being. Later scenes are light-filled and often take place in the breathtakingly beautiful outdoors, rather than in the dark interior spaces.

In some respects, the film appears to undermine great leap theories by portraying a friendship between Mario and Neruda, two men who are as far apart as possible on opposite sides of the supposed gap between literate and nonliterate. Neruda, the consummate poet, cosmopolitan diplomat, and winner of a Nobel Prize, listens thoughtfully to Mario, responds generously to his questions and requests, and even consults Mario for advice on a poem in progress. The literacy that Mario acquires emerges from his own needs and is grounded in his world: he wins Beatrice by expressing his emotions eloquently, and he creates a "letter" to Neruda composed of tape-recorded sounds of the island. His new-found literacy deepens his ability to function in his home world and sharpens appreciation of his own experiences. But in this film, literacy is represented only as a means of expression and communication that is emotionally fulfilling and socially empowering; lack of literacy is represented only as a form of blindness to the world and lack of political discernment. In these respects, *Il Postino* does perpetuate the strong theories of literacy by reiterating the uniformly positive consequences commonly cited as results of crossing over form nonliteracy into literacy (and the negative consequences cited for failing to do so).

Another film, *The Shawshank Redemption* (1994), also presents an illuminating contrast between a highly literate man and one who is barely literate, or who at least is not considered to be literate by conventional measures. In this prison film (based on a book by Stephen King), one of the prisoners, a minor character (Gil Bellows), works to attain a GED, a diploma granted for passing tests to show he has attained the equivalent of a high school education outside of the mainstream educational system. Like Mario, this character is portrayed in a highly sympathetic light. He is young, high-spirited, and clearly intelligent. The life he can look forward to as a person without an education, however, is indicated in the movie as promising nothing but more crime and longer imprisonments. The GED represents a figurative door out of prison for him. When this prisoner is lured into a trap by the prison administrator and shot by guards who claim he was attempting to escape, his death is portrayed as being much more poignant because of the goal he has just accomplished of winning his GED, as if the loss of his life then becomes greater than it would otherwise have been before.

At the same time, Andy Dufresne (Tim Robbins), the main character of *The Shawshank Redemption* does, indeed, use his high level of literacy to

152   *Popular culture and representations of literacy*

escape from prison. Andy is accused of murdering his wife, but insists that he is innocent. He serves many years of a murder sentence before he finds a way to escape. Andy is a professional accountant, and his high degree of literacy sets him apart in prison society more than any other characteristic. On one hand, his outsider status exposes him to violence at the hands of other prisoners, who brutally beat and rape him. On the other hand, literacy serves as a sign of his adaptability, intelligence, and even moral integrity. In spite of the questions about his past, he is portrayed as someone who seems to be made of some finer stuff than any of the other characters—inside or outside the prison bars. His literate abilities help him survive during his years on the inside. He campaigns relentlessly to establish a library for the prisoners and initiates the GED program. The prison administrators also become dependent on his services as an accountant, a position that he uses for his own benefit by systematically defrauding the corrupt organization of money, cash that he eventually redeems after his escape. Literacy literally becomes a form of redemption for this prisoner and for others that he coaches inside the prison: the Shawshank redemption *is* literacy.

LITERACY AS COMMODITY

Researcher Deborah Brandt (1998), like Harvey J. Graff, works to widen the picture of literacy as it exists as a social phenomenon, not just as an individual concern. She points out that a great deal has already been theorized about the "embodied moments" of individual literacy learning, but individual conditions of literacy have rarely been connected by theorists to larger social forces in specific or dynamic ways (166). In "Sponsors of Literacy," Brandt analyzes observations drawn from literacy narratives collected from a wide range of individuals in an American community. Her research involves in-depth interviews with over one hundred participants. By studying conditions that cut across these many individual accounts, she seeks to "connect literacy as an individual development to literacy as an economic development" (166).

> Literacy, like land, is a valued commodity in this economy, a key resource in gaining profit and edge. The value helps to explain...the lengths to which people will go to secure literacy for themselves or for their children. But it also explains why the powerful work so persistently to conscript and ration the powers of literacy. (169)

Literacy skills are "fragilely, contingently within an economic moment" (165). Economic conditions exist not simply as a general context in which literacy practices operate, but much more specifically to determine the kinds of literacy that are valued, and the opportunity or lack of opportunity for literacies to develop.

The triumph of the word   153

An increase in the economic value of literacy during the twentieth century has done much to "set the terms for individuals' encounters with literacy," Brandt claims. "This competition shapes the incentives and barriers (including uneven distribution of opportunity) that greet literacy learners in any particular time and place" (167). Brandt suggests the concept of sponsorship as a mechanism that regulates "individuals' encounters with literacy" (169). She defines sponsors of literacy as "any agents, local or distant, concrete or abstract, who enable, support, teach, model, as well as recruit, regulate, suppress, or withhold literacy—and gain advantage by it in some way" (166). Through the concept of sponsorship, Brandt underlines the ways that structured inequalities continue to operate to give some people access to literacy and restrict it to others, even when official school literacy appears to have begun to address problems of difference. Institutions such as schools may attempt to address unequal performance of literacy that are clearly correlated to unequal social privilege. But "despite ostensible democracy in educational chances, stratification of opportunity continues to organize access and reward in literacy learning" (166).

The role of literacy sponsorship shows up clearly in two of the films we have discussed in the previous section. In *Il Postino*, Neruda clearly serves as a sponsor of literacy for Mario. He responds thoughtfully to Mario's questions, explains metaphors to him, and presents Mario with a gift in front of other villagers in the local restaurant: a beautiful notebook with embossed leather covers, autographed ostentatiously by Neruda on the first page. The notebook bestows on Mario the permission he needs to be recognized as a genuine poet in his own eyes as much as in the eyes of others. In *The Shawshank Redemption*, Andy serves as a literacy sponsor to other men in the prison by campaigning to bring them a higher quality library, and by building the prison teaching program that allows prisoners to earn their high school diplomas while they are in jail.

Literacy sponsorship also figures importantly in two films directed by Gus Van Sant, *Good Will Hunting* (1997) and *Finding Forrester* (2000). In *Finding Forrester*, Jamal (Rob Brown) is a high school boy who has a brilliant mind, but is stuck in a poor neighborhood with a less-than-adequate public school. High test scores and a talent for playing basketball earn Jamal a scholarship offer to attend the best high school in the city. But access to the school by itself is not enough to equalize the chances Jamal has of acquiring the commodity of a fine education. It is Jamal's private encounters with William Forrester (Sean Connery), a reclusive writer who lives in Jamal's neighborhood, that really teach him what he needs to learn about how to write well. And, when Jamal is accused of plagiarism by a teacher at the school, Forrester emerges from his seclusion, and uses his considerable authority to vouch for Jamal's integrity. Without the sponsors he finds in Forrester and in his girlfriend at the new school (Anna Paquin), it is clear that Jamal would have failed. Similarly, in *Good Will Hunting*, a young janitor (Matt Damon) with a genius for mathematics is discovered

154 *Popular culture and representations of literacy*

by a professor (Stellan Skarsgard) at the prestigious Massachusetts Institute of Technology, who mentors him and helps him find the one man (Robin Williams) who can provide him with the psychological counseling that he needs to benefit from his intellectual gifts.

COMPETING PURPOSES FOR LITERACY

Drama is generated in some films by tensions that build up in characters who must balance competing theories of literacy in their lives. *The Dead Poets' Society* (1989), for example, puts a theory of literacy as salvation on a collision course with a theory of literacy as commodity. The action takes place in an American boys' boarding school catering to the wealthy and those aspiring to wealth. The school emulates the visual character and educational practices of more venerable English institutions in the boys' uniforms, the stone colonnades and wooden paneling of its buildings, and its highly choreographed assemblies. School administrators are rigidly devoted to providing literacy as a commodity to their students, whose parents are paying, in the view of the administration, to acquire a carefully defined educational product that will ensure a strong financial future for their sons.

When John Keating (Robin Williams), a former student at the academy, returns to its classrooms as an English teacher, he is aggressive in his challenge to this literacy status quo. Keating enlists all of his performative talents to hold up a different ideal to students, promoting a form of literacy as salvation, and urging them to write original poetry and express their individuality. His promotion of emotion at the expense of logic begins when he commands students to rip a head note on the analysis of poetry out of their textbooks and continues with a series of unconventional assignments designed to get students in touch with their inner drummer. His charismatic appeal promotes the success of his competing theory and inspires students to revive the "Dead Poets' Society," a secret society of readers and writers that meets clandestinely in the woods at night. Keating's challenge precipitates growing disruption and dissatisfaction among the students and administrators.

The tension between the two different aspirations for literacy culminates in one boy's suicide. Neil (Sean Robert Leonard) dreams of participating in theater, and wins a leading role in a production of *A Midsummer Night's Dream*. His father (Kurtwood Smith), who has decided that his son will become a doctor, views Neil's acting as a distraction that will weaken his school work and threaten his chances for medical school. He forbids Neil to act in the play, but Neil disobeys. After a confrontation with his parents, Neil uses his father's gun to take his own life. The competing expectations for literacy sets up an either/or situation for Keating, for the school administrators, for Neil's parents, and even for Neil himself. The lessons in

The triumph of the word   155

literacy that Keating gives hold out the promise of emotional and intellectual transformation, of "finding a voice" and escaping from an ostensibly convention-bound world. The lessons of literacy endorsed by the school and Neil's parents hold out the promise of ensuring survival and the possibility of a good life in a competitive marketplace. These are two different variants of the literacy myth, offering different kinds of personal salvation though literacy. In *The Dead Poets' Society*, the competing expectations for literacy seem to be mutually exclusive: one actually cancels out the other. Underlying both of them, however, is fear—a fear of being deprived of the hoped-for consequences.

My Big Fat Greek Wedding (2002), a romantic comedy, is structured around an equally complex set of competing literacies. The film centers on the character of Toula Portokalis (Nia Vardalos), a woman from a family of Greek immigrants who live in a large American city and own a Greek restaurant. Toula's parents (Michael Constantine and Lainie Kazan) are concerned about her because she is not married yet, and shows no promise of getting married any time soon. She lives at home, works as a hostess in the family restaurant, and associates primarily with her own family—an extensive group of siblings, aunts, uncles, nieces, nephews, and a grandmother dressed in black from head to toe. Her parents discuss options for getting her married, but Toula has other dreams: her secret ambition is to attend computer school.

For Toula, the great struggle is to integrate the values and expectations of her Greek home identity with the values and expectations of her American public identity. These conflicting identities show up in the two parallel but separate forms of schooling that Toula received as a girl. In the American public school, Toula is left out by the blonde, self-consciously Anglo-Saxon girls, who make fun of her for being "different"—her hair is long and dark, she speaks a foreign language at home, and she brings homemade Greek food for lunch. When Toula brings *moussaka* one day, the other girls snicker about her lunch of "moose caca." On Saturdays, Toula attends Greek school with other immigrants' children, who do not relish devoting their weekends to memorizing Greek sentences about goats and other exasperatingly unmodern subjects. Toula's father, intensely proud of the family's Greek culture and heritage, claims that every English word can be traced back to an original Greek root. Toula's American friends slyly tease Mr. Portokalis by demanding to know the Greek origins of words like "kimono," and he obliges them with highly original, but false etymologies.

By the time she reaches thirty, the tensions between Toula's two identities have brought her to a crisis point. While the warm embrace of her family ensures that most of her physical and emotional needs are well cared for, Toula's family also constricts some of the possibilities for her life by dictating its parameters and by assuming that their expectations for her are the same as her own. While she goes along with the script written for her by her family, Toula still harbors other desires that don't fit in with that

156   *Popular culture and representations of literacy*

script, and this prevents her from feeling content. In this situation, Toula's life assumes a drab and predictable stasis, a condition that is reflected in the drabness of her physical appearance—in her shapeless restaurant uniform, unflattering haircut, and large glasses. Toula's dream of learning about computers can be considered an expression of her American identity; in any case, it challenges her father's old country ideas of what is appropriate for his daughter. To take classes at the local college, Toula has to push against the limits the family has inscribed for her life and persuade her father to accept her new venture into schooling. At computer school, Toula appears to come into her own as a person. She is a good student. She buys contact lenses, and starts to wear make up and dress stylishly. Unlike at grade school, at college, the other girls ask Toula to sit with them at lunch. Toula begins to blossom while she is a college student, and continues to quietly, but firmly, challenge family rules and expectations, first by taking a job at her aunt's travel agency, and then by dating and falling in love with a man who is not Greek. As in so many of these narratives, the value of education is displayed not in the knowledge but in physical and social transformations. None of her courses are telling her to dress differently, but she is, though her literacy practices at the school, gaining the cultural capital that makes her recognize the social class limitations of her performance of self. This is a narrative that is particularly common with women in films, such as *Working Girl* (1988), where Tess (Melanie Griffith) not only has to learn about high finance to move from secretary to executive, but also has to learn how to change her fashion and hairstyle in ways that don't mark her as working class.

While not explicitly foregrounding literacy, Toula's experience at college does clearly reinscribe the popular myth of literacy as salvation, and this underlying narrative may have contributed to the film's exuberant success. An independently produced movie, *My Big Fat Greek Wedding* instantly attracted large audiences, earned many nominations and awards, and inspired a TV series of the same name. Toula's story follows a distinctly before-and-after pattern, and the film images exploit this to comic effect. In the opening scenes, Toula's father tells her that she is starting to look *old*, and indeed, she does look worried, distracted, and indifferent to the world around her. After she goes to college and gets the job at the travel agency, Toula sparkles as she scoots happily between the phone and the computer in her tiny office. It is here that she attracts the attention of the man who will become her husband.

In terms of literacy, it is significant that the man Toula marries, Ian Miller (John Corbett), happens to be a high school English teacher. His own background is distinctly white, Anglo Saxon, and Protestant; when Toula's father meets Ian's parents for the first time, he despairingly describes his future in-laws as "dry toast." Ian's family had hoped that he would become a lawyer, but, like Toula, he had gone against his parents' wishes and studied literature, instead. Ian is Toula's lover, not her teacher,

The triumph of the word 157

but he also serves as a literacy sponsor for her. Toula's relationship with Ian provides a catalyst for resolving the tensions in her life. Before meeting him, neither her experience in public school nor her experience Greek school has helped her make sense of the richness of her own Greek American identity. Simple access to these two parallel forms of education does not actually enhance her life. While Toula's mother and her aunt provide some support for her when she needs to obtain her father's consent to go to college and to marry Ian, they aren't able to help her reconcile the discordant parts of her identity. Ian helps her do that. After her marriage, Toula accepts both parts of her identity, and, in the closing scene of the movie, Ian and Toula are walking their own little girl to her lessons at the Greek school.

My Big Fat Greek Wedding is a love story that ends in a wedding. But just beneath the surface lies another story—a story of literacy that also has a happy ending. All too often, however, this happy ending is not the case for literacy in real life. Munir Fasheh (2002) argues that more crucial than being literate is being "rooted in the cultural soil and in daily living," a factor that the imposition of literacy can actually eradicate, not foster (2). It is important to look "not only at what literacy adds (in the way it is conceived and implemented) but also at what it subtracts and makes invisible" (3). In "From the Soils of Culture," Fasheh (2001) writes:

> In general, the current dominant language in education, knowledge, development, the professions, and mass media...ignores these soils...It is often divorced from history, life, and ethics....It is usually handicapped in its ability to express and reflect the richness and complexity in life and cultural traditions, the diversity in human experiences, and the multiplicity of ways of living and making sense.

It is only with some difficulty that Toula succeeds in finding a way to become literate in mainstream culture, without eradicating the world of her own community. Toula's success makes her a sponsor in turn, when she inspires her brother, Nick (Louis Mandylor), to follow in her footsteps. He is determined to study art, even though his efforts have been unceremoniously dismissed by their father. Nick says Toula has shown him to "Go as far as you like, but don't ever forget where you came from." Toula is moved by his beautiful sentiment, even after she finds out that it is not original—he is quoting it from "Dear Abby."

RELATIONSHIPS OF LITERACY LEARNING

Viewing these triumph-of-literacy films as a group leaves us with a strong composite image of the literacy myth in operation. In film after film that we have reviewed for this chapter, it is the idea, the promise, and the possibility

158 *Popular culture and representations of literacy*

of literacy, as much as—or more—than actual practices of literacy that have engaged powerful emotions in the characters and elicited their most powerful allegiances. In these films, literacy brings liberation, love, personal fulfillment, and security to its learners. Brandt observes that economic conditions set the conditions and create or destroy opportunities for individuals to obtain the commodity of literacy. In "triumph-of-literacy films," however, it is personal relationships that bring about the most transformative possibilities promised by the myth of literacy. Highly charged connections between those who have literacy and those who desire it are depicted again and again, and they form the most compelling relationships in many of these movies. The power of these relationships doubtlessly emerges from the fact, which Brandt (1998) observes, that literacy has always required permission. She makes the unsettling point that while we clearly see that learners seek literacy, often very passionately, it is less obvious to us that literacy (in the service of economic needs) is also is seeking learners. For Brandt, recognizing this condition induces a sense of ambivalence in teaching. But in these films, even if problems and ambiguities may come up along the way, they are quieted, in the end, by the resoundingly positive consequences of learning.

It is, however, these same relationships, of sponsor and protégé, teacher and learner, that make these films so powerful for those in literacy education. The films in this chapter are invariably the first movies offered by our colleagues in literacy education when we mention this project. Rarely do other literacy educators and scholars even discuss movies about solitary authors, such as we discussed in Chapter Seven. The idea of the solitary author, innately gifted with the ability to create great writing, may be a myth that is powerful among the general public. The myth on the screen of innate literacy skills and the ability to create art through moments of inspiration fulfills a desire of the general audience for such talent. We've heard the results of this myth from students who come into our classes telling us they dislike writing because they have no talent for it. If only they were gifted, they would write more. Movies about literary authors reinforce the myth that only a few gifted, and odd, people can truly be writers.

Yet though the myth of the author interests movie goers in general, it does not interest our colleagues in literacy and composition studies, perhaps because we can see past the myth of the solitary author, and understand the struggle, drafting, revising, and editing that goes into any written work. A different myth has a grip on the imagination of those of us in this field: a myth about *providing* literacy to those who do not have it. It is a myth of teaching literacy that allows us to believe that, while we may not get paid much for what we do, we can transform the lives of those in our classes. We have known many teachers who, even as they complain about the weary hours spent reading student papers, can turn around in the next moment and talk with conviction about the honorable and life-changing pursuit of teaching writing and reading. Because we often believe in the

The triumph of the word   159

myth of literacy as salvation, we believe that what we can teach students is more inherently important and valuable than what they will learn in other courses, such as science or mathematics. What we would like to believe we offer is the possibility of becoming a better person through literacy. All you have to do is watch a teacher talk with joy about the student whose writing has finally come alive to see the belief in teaching literacy as a noble cause. And, having seen this happen with our own students, you won't find us disagreeing about the nobility of what we do.

The appeal of triumph-of-literacy films, then, isn't only that characters become better, more fulfilled people through literacy; it is also that the characters *need* a sponsor to be able to acquire the literacy and then become new people. They need Pablo Neruda or John Keating or Andy Dufresne. Without the guidance and encouragement of their sponsor they would not be able to see new possibilities, take new chances, overcome institutional or cultural biases, or even find romance. The new abilities and perspectives offered by the sponsor are often illustrated, late in the film, by a gesture or speech by the literacy learner. In *Finding Forrester*, Jamal stands his ground in the face of plagiarism charges. In *The Dead Poets' Society* the students stand on their desks in protest as John Keating leaves the class-room. The sponsor of literacy in the triumph-of-literacy film does more than teach better ways to read and write. The sponsor offers life lessons along with the literacy that imbue the protégé with cultural capital as well as psychological well being. It is this kind of individual metamorphosis that distinguishes triumph-of-literacy films from the other movies we discuss in this book. In other movies we may see social forces such as race, class, or gender work to shape literacy practices but we don't necessarily see literacy employed as a metaphor for individual transformation.

The narrative of individual transformation, of remaking of the self, seems in many ways a very American narrative, so it is little surprise that it has become popular in contemporary Hollywood movies. After all, if these movies only appealed to literacy scholars and teachers they would be enormous financial failures. It is the myth of transformation, of salvation as something that can be gained, not just displayed from an innate gift, that appeals to audiences who aren't teachers. Besides, who of us, as students, has not wished to have had a wise and dedicated mentor who could oversee an almost magical transformation of the self into someone smarter, braver, and even better looking.

The relationship between the teacher and learner in triumph-of-literacy films is often intense and moving, but does not need to be romantic, and very often is not. Unlike the romance novel, it is not necessary that the teacher marry the student in the end. As teachers, we don't have to fall in love with our students. We just want to be important in their lives, to make them better people. And, like Nanny McPhee escorting another woman up the aisle, we send our triumphant students on their way, satisfied we have done our jobs.

Conclusion

Winona Ryder in Girl, Interrupted (1999). ©Columbia Pictures/Everett Collection.

9 Life is not like the movies (or is it?)

Literacy on film and in our lives

As we have come to the close of this volume, we have been struck again by the power of literacy and film in shaping identity, in reproducing culture, in making sense of the world. Of course we probably shouldn't be surprised. Film and literacy have been central parts of both of our lives.

Bronwyn's passion for film came from his father, who had been an usher in the only movie theatre in his small town in the 1930s, and the countless hours they spent watching movies together. Growing up, Bronwyn's friends didn't always understand his references to *The Maltese Falcon* (1941) or *Casablanca* (1943). He learned about romance from Cary Grant, cool from Paul Newman, and dancing from Fred Astaire. Now, with his own sons, he has Friday Family Film night every week that combines pizza with classic movies.

For Amy, a fascination with movies emerged at a later age. Having grown up outside of the United States in a family that rarely went to the movies and did not own a television, her early experiences with film were few and far between. This made her highly conscious of the shared language of film images, expressions, and narratives of her classmates in American universities. At first an insatiable viewer of the old movies and foreign films offered by university film programs, she eventually entered the mainstream, becoming a regular at the multiplexes, as well.

In many ways, then, this book has been a dream project for us in the way it connects our passions for movies with our ongoing interest in literacy research and education. Clearly for us literacy and film are powerful and constructive in their relationships to identity and culture. What this research has reminded us is how powerful a practice and metaphor literacy is in our culture as well as how forcefully and thoroughly popular film shapes and reflects that culture. It has also reminded us that popular culture has both an intellectual as well as an emotional impact on all of us. Even as we would study films for their representations of literacy, we would at times find ourselves having to deal with our affective responses to the films we were watching. The power of film is such that we could find ourselves swept up in an emotional moment, or annoyed at a piece of bad filmmaking, regardless of its relevance to our project. Even as we studied the films, we could be unexpectedly caught up in the suspense or

164   *Popular culture and representations of literacy*

sentimentality of a scene or film. Such moments were important reminders of the emotional and symbolic force of film for all of us and why even short and mundane representations of literacy can be invested with a power beyond what we might rationally expect.

A SOCIAL PRACTICE OF INDIVIDUALS

There are three ideas about how literacy is represented in contemporary films that we came back to time and again in every chapter of this book.

The first of these is the idea that literacy is a social phenomenon. It is easy to find representations of literacy in movies because it is such pervasive social practice. Given that movies are most often about social situations and interactions it is almost impossible to imagine films that would not have to incorporate literacy in some way. Even in the film *Cast Away* (2000), during the lengthy segment where Chuck Noland (Tom Hanks) is alone on a tropical island, he is portrayed using writing on rock walls as a way of continuing to try to stay connected to a social world from which he has been separated. Of course, within the social sphere the definitions and practices of literacy are fluid and contextual. Sometimes literacy is portrayed as an instrumental way of accomplishing a task, sometimes a matter of displaying social status, sometimes as a way of building relationships. It is portrayed as a material and economic practice as well as a moral and societal good. Still, in all of these practices, and others, it is a social activity engaged in with a sense that the reading or writing has been influenced by or will have an effect on others.

There is no doubt that literacy is often represented as an integral part of the economic well-being of the society. In an "information" or "knowledge" economy, literacy becomes a key component of what allows the capitalist system to function. Although economic forces may have driven literacy education as far back as the mid-nineteenth century, when the growth of industry required a workforce and a middle management that could read and write at a certain level, the shift in affluent economies toward the commodification of communication and information has led to an "inexhaustible demand for literacy that seems built into the production imperative" (Brandt 2004, 500). Contemporary movies reinforce the message that literacy is essential to economic well-being and power. Films such as *My Big Fat Greek Wedding* (2002) or *Office Space* (1999) remind us that literacy practices have economic consequences on a social level and repeat the message that for society to remain "productive" literacy is essential.

At the same time, literacy is still often portrayed as a social good as practiced by a moral society. In the movies, literacy not only has the potential to get you a better job, but it will make you a better member of society. What Deborah Brandt (2004) notes about literacy in general can also be connected to representations of literacy in the movies:

Life is not like the movies (or is it?) 165

Good children read to get ahead in school and ahead in life. Good parents read to children. Corporate sponsors and good-neighbor universities, not to mention First Ladies, create social goodwill by supporting literacy programs in school and communities. Reading is regarded as morally superior to just about all of its leisure-time competitors. Illiteracy is still seen as the road to crime. (487).

Literacy bolsters social relationships as well as connects the moral citizen into civic life. In melodramas such as *The Majestic* (2001), we see how literacy, in the reading of letters or of the Constitution, is a moral act that moves a cynical man to take a principled stance.

Because literacy is part of the society's moral as well as material well being, it is often regulated and shaped by a culture's dominant social institutions. In contemporary films, literacy practices still often take place in schools, courts, churches, hospitals, bureaucracies, and other institutions that order and define public life. Of course, social institutions define and reproduce social hierarchies. They decide which literacy practices are legitimate, which bring power, which are subversive. The power and order maintained by dominant social institutions may be explicit in a film such as *Changing Lanes* (2002) with its scenes in courtrooms and law offices. But is no less important, even if more submerged, in a film such as *As Good As It Gets* (1997), where, in just one example, the lives of both main characters, Carol (Helen Hunt) and Melvin (Jack Nicholson), are disciplined by the literacy practices of doctors and hospitals in ways they cannot ignore or resist. Carol cannot get the necessary medical care for her son, even though she has all his medical records in her hands, until she is helped by a doctor who can make them meaningful within the medical institutions and cultures. Movies show us time and again that literacy practices in our society are central to the accumulation and display of both economic and cultural capital, as defined by the dominant culture.

If contemporary films reinforce the social nature of literacy, they also focus their representations on how literacy works for individuals as both a means of human connection and a manifestation of identity. In the movies people use literacy to fall in love (*As Good As It Gets* (1997), *You've Got Mail* (1998)) to express their souls (*Finding Neverland* (2004), *Sylvia* (2003)) or to stake a claim to their identity in resistance to the dominant culture (*Finding Forrester* (2000), *Girl, Interrupted* (1999)). We should not find it surprising that the representations of literacy practices in movies often center around their effects on individuals. After all, most Hollywood films are based on ideologies of individualism. They focus on the lives and concerns of specific characters and how events change or influence the lives of those characters. If we accept that Hollywood movies are character-driven narratives that rely on images to communicate much of their information, then we should expect to find many of the actions and images in films employed to establish identity.

166 *Popular culture and representations of literacy*

It is often important in a film to quickly introduce or reinforce a character's identity location, in terms of culture or gender or class. A movie does not have the luxury of taking pages to accomplish such a point. Instead, movies often portray practices that are simultaneously observable and recognizable in terms of identity location such as eating, or dressing, or driving a particular kind of car. Clearly, literacy practices, in the way they are coded by class, gender, and culture, serve this purpose effectively. A character walks into an office and sits at cubicle. Another character pulls papers from a briefcase. Still another pulls a well-regarded novel from a purse. And another labors over writing at a kitchen table. In each instance the audience uses the cultural markers connected to literacy practices to situate the character's identity. Movies often use literacy practices for creating these shorthand identity markers. Consequently, films prove an excellent place to explore the nature of the culture's dominant conceptions of literacy and identity. For if the audience won't recognize it quickly, then it is of little use to the filmmaker in terms of character and identity.

At the same time, while literacy practices represented on film are patterned by social hierarchies and institutions, they are also often used to represent the triumph of an individual over these same institutions. Literacy practices are most explicitly acknowledged by characters in films, and praised by critics watching them, when they enable characters to employ them for personal growth, empowerment, freedom, and so on. When literacy helps a person overcome obstacles, or rebel (a little) against conformity, or challenge acceptable injustices—in a movie such as *Erin Brockovitch* (2001), for example—it plays to movies' celebration of individualism. Literacy practices in such films are portrayed as powerful individual attributes, rather than social phenomena.

As products of a culture deeply invested in myths of individualism and self-sufficiency, it is easy to see why literacy is glorified as an attribute of individual control and achievement. This individualistic conception of literacy is shaped by the culture, but also then helps shape further ideas about what literacy is, who can employ it and toward what kinds of ends.

Literacy's existence as a social practice and its celebration as an individual attribute contribute to the final concept that we found in many of the films we studied: literacy's power as a cultural commonplace. It is difficult to understate the deep emotional resonance literacy has for characters in movies. Literacy is often submerged and unacknowledged in movies, a testament in part to its pervasiveness in the culture. Yet, when literacy is acknowledged by characters in films, it is often asked to do more than simply advance a plot or enable an action. Literacy is just as often asked to serve a symbolic or metaphorical function. A woman finds her self-esteem in her writing after being abandoned by a man. A boy rebels against institutional injustice by defending his writing before small-minded teachers. A cynical man is redeemed by teaching a teenager to write. A government's treachery is exemplified in a secret file. An evil genius uses literacy to threaten the world, and an icono-

Life is not like the movies (or is it?) 167

clastic hero undoes the plan by finding a weakness in the reading and writing. Literacy as empowerment, as healing, as grace, as threat, as redemption, as power: The metaphors may vary, but the common connection is idea that literacy is imbued by the culture with more meaning than simply the ability to decode words on a page. As literacy operates as metaphor in the culture, it is represented and reproduced on the movie screen.

This final idea raises two questions that we have not been able to address in this volume. In our focus on contemporary films we have, by necessity, had to limit our study in terms of the age of the films we included. Yet we have talked about and wondered how the representations of literacy practices have changed over the years. What metaphors and motifs have remained powerful over the years? Which have faded from view to be replaced by others? Along with a desire to broaden our focus to films outside of Hollywood and to other areas of popular culture such as television, this is an area that could be fascinating to explore.

In addition, we have watched these films and seen these patterns and concepts of literacy represented over and over again. In presenting this material at academic conferences the response from those in the audience has encouraged us to believe that we are not seeing connections that make no sense to others. However, what we do not yet know is how audiences read the representations of literacy on film, and how it may or may not influence their perceptions and definitions of literacy and possibly even their literacy practices. What is the effect of age, culture, gender, class in such audience interpretations? Studying the way audiences read and interpret these representations is an area of research that we hope will be fruitful in the future.

DOES IT MATTER WHAT HAPPENS AT THE MOVIES?

Even if we accept that literacy practices in film are ubiquitous and can be seen to fit certain patterns, we're left with the question of what difference this makes. Does it matter how literacy practices are portrayed in movies?

To answer that question is to think again about the larger cultural considerations of what literacy is, who uses it, and why. Recent scholarship has argued persuasively that literacy is both a product of culture as well as a significant force in shaping and reproducing that culture (Brandt 2001). As we think about literacy as a set of culturally situated practices, rather than a set of a-contextual skills, we realize that such practices are going to be an important part of a culture's representations of itself. Movies, like all forms of cultural representation, may not be "real life" but they draw on the recognizable elements of culture and daily life to construct narratives that are appealing and meaningful to their audiences. In the popular culture of a capitalist society that relies on persuading the largest possible audience to consume products such as films, it is all the more important to

168 *Popular culture and representations of literacy*

portray cultural practices that hew as closely as possible to the dominant culture, and thus appeal to the largest potential number of customers. Film, and other forms of mass popular culture, then offer us ways of examining the practices that have been normalized by the dominant culture as representing "literacy" as a practice and as a means of establishing identity. That these may be idealized or limited representations does not mean that they are not powerful and recognizable to the culture at large. If we want to imagine and examine literacy in daily practices, we must consider how those practices are reflected back to us in our most popular cultural products. Films are a recognizable but idealized and intense view of life and culture. By studying them we attain a sense of what we want to have happen in life as well as a view of what does. We have all at one time or another wished life were more like the movies. That the metaphor of Hollywood as a "dream factory" has become a well-worn cliché does not mean that movies have lost their power to portray as well as shape our desires and anxieties.

Representations of literacy practices in popular movies also provide us with a sense of how the desires and anxieties about literacy get reproduced in the culture at large. It is important to be mindful of how ideology works with popular culture to both produce and reproduce cultural norms. Film offers us both lens and mirror through which we can regard our culture. Filmmakers do not simply create their portrayals of literacy practices without reference to the way such practices operate in the culture. Indeed most filmmakers probably give little explicit thought to how they are portraying literacy, drawing instead almost instinctively on its power as commonplace, metaphor, and identity trope. At the same time, what we see represented on film, particularly when it becomes a common, sometimes almost invisible, element in plot and character development, has an effect in establishing the limits and contours of any cultural practice. If our cultural concepts of romance, family, politics, and other social practices are shaped by their representations on film, then so must our concepts of literacy as a social practice.

Such popular conceptions of literacy have important political implications for public conversations about reading and writing. Few government panels or legislative committees or local school boards make overt references to literacy practices in the movies when they talk about literacy policies. They don't have to. The values we see enacted on the screen reflect assumptions so deeply embedded in the public conversations about literacy that there is no need to address them explicitly. These assumptions are powerful in the way they shape the discourse and debates about literacy and literacy education. What we see reflected in film, such as the divides of literacy practices in terms of gender, or race or class, or the vision of writing as a gift of genius, or the distrust of institutionalized literacies, are also reflected in the assumptions that dominate the cultural discourse about literacy. Again, the persistence of such representations in popular culture means that these are the portrayals of literacy people see over and over.

Life is not like the movies (or is it?) 169

Yet, unlike concerns about sex and violence in the movies, people pay little attention to the ideology or effects of literacy practices, they just accept the values encoded in them and repeat them in their daily lives. In the conversations and debates about literacy education, questions of the goals of literacy, who should teach it, how it should be taught and why, are grounded in many of the same essentially unexamined assumptions.

In a similar way, the representations of literacy in popular movies are internalized by the young people who become our students. We might like to believe that the attitudes and beliefs toward literacy evinced by teachers are the most influential factors in students' perceptions and attitudes toward reading and writing. If, however, we accept that their attitudes toward gender roles, or political issues, or family dynamics, or war might be influenced by the films they watch, then we have to include literacy in that list. The idea that the portrayals of literacy practices we describe in this book might be important influences on students may seem in some ways disheartening, though certainly not all the portrayals are negative. We would like to think of such influences as an opportunity rather than as solely a problem.

Film offers us a compelling medium through which we can engage students in conversations about literacy practices. Students are comfortable and experienced in talking about movies, in part because they can simultaneously identify with characters on the screen, yet detach themselves from the events and discuss them with less resistance and defensiveness. It may be difficult for students to recognize, or admit in class, how identity or institutions or cultural expectations shape their literacy practices. Yet commenting about what happens to people reading and writing on the screen can be done with a certain level of safety. Students also have a familiarity with film that gives them confidence in being able to talk about what they are seeing. They are used to talking about movies, and arguing about them, with their friends, and this experience can carry over into the classroom in positive ways. (It is important that, even as we ask students to discuss and analyze what they watch, we also respect their experience and assure them that our goal in the classroom is not to rob them of their pleasure in going to the movies.)

One use we have made of popular culture representations of literacy practices is fairly straightforward. We show clips of different literacy practices to students and then discuss with them the values and assumptions represented in the clips. Like many of us, students at first miss the reading and writing happening in a given scene. But if we ask them to pay attention to who is reading, for what ends, and with what constraints, they are quickly able to recognize and discuss the literacy practices. If we show them a range of clips, students can use the comparisons and contrasts as a useful step in helping them reflect on their own uses of reading and writing and how those are shaped by culture. Such classroom conversations can be linked to writing assignments such as Literacy Autobiographies of

170   *Popular culture and representations of literacy*

ethnographic-style observations of literacy practices in students' communities to open up for students ways of thinking more creatively and critically about literacy, identity, and culture. Film representations allow us to step back from these practices and reflect on their role in the culture and the assumptions on which they rest, which is a useful reading practice for students to learn regardless of the texts they encounter

THE FINAL REEL

Researching this book has altered the way we watch movies. Sure, we're still able to watch a movie for the pleasure of the narrative, of the characters, of the imagery. Even so, when a character opens a book or pulls out a pen, we notice it in ways we had not before and notice how it connects into similar moments in other films. Nor do we look at literacy practices as we did before. For as our students and friends and colleagues read and write, we see reflections of the practices we have been watching on the screen for months. The representations we have seen on the screen have helped us identify in daily life the cultural and ideological forces that shape our perceptions and practices of reading and writing. We have become more aware of the narratives and assumptions we make about literacy, as well as the ones that dominate in our students' lives, and that has helped us as teachers and scholars in reflecting on our work.

If this were a movie, perhaps we could offer a more definitive conclusion at this point, some kind of snappy and inspiring ending, full of drama, pathos, and humor. Failing a final kiss, a stirring song, or a ride off into the sunset, however, we will instead simply have to sit back, turn our attention to the screen, and roll the credits.

References

Althusser, L. 1971. "Ideology and ideological state apparatuses." In *Lenin and philosophy and other essays*, ed. L. Althusser, trans. B. Brewster, 127–188. New York: Monthly Review Press.

Altman, R. 1999. *Film/Genre*. London: British Film Institute.

Appelo, T. 2001. "A simple twist of fate." *The Nation*. 5 November 2001.

Applebaum, S. 2003. "Jane Campion: *In the Cut*." BBC Interview. 14 October 2003. Available at <http://www.bbc.co.uk/films/2003/10/14/jane_campion_in_the_cut_interview.shtml> (accessed 2 August 2005).

Barthes. R. 1968. "The death of the author." In R. Barthes *Image, Music, Text*, ed. R. Barthes, trans. S. Heath, 142–148. New York: Hill and Wang. 1977.

Barton, D., and Hamilton, M. 1998. *Local literacies: Reading and writing in one community*. London: Routledge.

Bauer, D. M. 1998. "Indecent proposals: Teachers in the movies." *College English*, 60: 301–317.

Belenky, M., ed. 1988. *Women's ways of knowing*. New York: Basic Books.

Benshoff, H. M., and Griffin, S. 2004. *America on film: Representing race, class, gender and sexuality at the movies*. Malden, MA: Blackwell.

Birkerts, S. 1994. *The Gutenberg elegies: The fate of reading in an electronic age*. Boston: Faber and Faber.

Bishop, W. 1997. "Crossing the lines: On creative composition and composing creative writing." In *Teaching lives: Essays and stories*, ed. W. Bishop, 221–235. Logan, UT: Utah State University Press..

Bishop, W., and H. Ostrom 1994. *Colors of a different horse: Rethinking creative writing theory and pedagogy*. Urbana, IL: NCTE.

Blakesley, D. 2003. "Introduction: The rhetoric of film and film studies." In *The terministicscreen: Rhetorical perspectives on film.*, ed. D. Blakesley, 1–16. Carbondale, IL: Southern Illinois University Press.

Bodnar, J. 2003. *Blue-collar Hollywood: Liberalism, democracy, and working people in American film*. Baltimore, MD: Johns Hopkins University Press.

Booth, D. 2002. *Even hockey players can read*. Markham, Canada: Pembroke Publishers.

Bourdieu, P. 1984. *Distinction: A social critique of the judgement of taste*, trans. R. Nice. Cambridge, MA: Harvard University Press.

Brandt, D. 1998. "Sponsors of Literacy." In *Literacy: A critical sourcebook*, eds. E. Cushman, E. R. Kintgen, B. Kroll, and M. Rose, 555–571 (2001) Boston: Bedford/St. Martin's..

———. 2001. *Literacy in American lives*. Cambridge: Cambridge University Press.

———. 2004. "Drafting U.S. literacy" *College English*. 66: 485–502.

172 *References*

Bruffee, K. A. 1984. "Collaborative learning and the conversation of mankind." *College English*, 46: 635–652.

Byars, J. 1991. *All that Hollywood allows: Re-reading gender in 1950s melodrama*. Chapel Hill: University of North Carolina Press.

Carby, H. 1993. *"Grand Canyon*—A narrative for our times." In *Race, identity, and representation in education*, eds. C. McCarthy and W. Crichlow, 236–247. New York: Routledge.

Chodorow, N. 1978. *The reproduction of mothering: Psychoanalysis and the sociology of gender*. Berkeley: University of California Press.

Cixous, H. 1975. "The laugh of the Medusa," trans. K. Cohen and P. Cohen. *Signs* 1: 875–893.

Clifford, J., and Marcus, G. E. 1986. *Writing culture: The poetics and politics of ethnography*. Berkeley: University of California Press.

Coles, N. 2001. "Joe Shakespeare: The contemporary British worker-writer movement." In *Popular Literacy: Studies in Cultural Practices and Poetics*, ed. J. Trimbur, 189–208. Pittsburgh: University of Pittsburgh Press.

Collins, J. 2002. "Genericity in the Nineties: eclectic irony and the new sincerity." In *The film cultures reader*, ed. G. Turner, 276–290 London: Routledge.

The Connection. 2005. [Radio Broadcast] National Public Radio. 17 May.

Cushman, E., Kintgen, E. R., Kroll, B., and Rose, M. (eds.). 2001. *Literacy: A critical sourcebook*. Boston: Bedford/St. Martin's.

De Lauretis, T. 1987. *Technologies of gender: Essays on theory, film, and fiction*. Bloomington: Indiana University Press.

DeSalvo, L. 1996. *Vertigo*. New York: Dutton.

Doane, A. W., and Bonilla-Silva, E. (eds.). 2003. *White out: The continuing significance of racism*. New York: Routledge.

Dyer, R. 1997. *White*. London: Routledge.

Ede, L., and Lunsford, A. A. 2001. "Collaboration and concepts of authorship." *PMLA*. 116: 354–369.

Faigley, L. 1993. *Fragments of rationality: Postmodernity and the subject of composition*, Pittsburgh: University of Pittsburgh Press.

Fasheh, M. 2002. "How to Eradicate Illiteracy without Eradicating Illiterates?" Paper for the Unesco Roundtable on "Literacy as Freedom." 9–10 September 2002. Available at <http://www.swaraj.org/shikshantar/fasheh_illiteracy.htm>(accessed 15 October 2004).

———. 2001. "From the soils of culture: The Qalb El-Umour project in the Arab world." Available at <http://www.multiworld.org/multiversity_files/decolonisation/qalb.htm> (accessed 15 October 2004).

Fine, M., Weis, L., Powell, L. C., and Wong, L. M. (eds.) 1997. *Off white: Readings on race, power, and society*. New York: Routledge.

Fish, S. 1980. "Interpreting the *Variorum*." In *Is there a text in this class? The authority of Interpretive communities*, 148–173. Cambridge: Harvard University Press.

Foucault, M. 1972. *The archeology of knowledge*, trans. A. M. Sheridan Smith. New York: Pantheon.

———. 1969. "What is an author?" In *Contemporary literacy criticism: Literary and cultural studies*, eds. R. Davis and R. Schleifer, 341–353. New York: Longman. 1994.

Frankenburg, R. 1993. *White women, race matters: The social construction of whiteness*. Minneapolis: University of Minneapolis Press.

Garcia Marquez, G. 1997. *Love in the time of cholera*, trans. E. Grossman. New York: Knopf.

References   173

Gee, J. P. 1989. "Literacy, discourse, and linguistics: Introduction." In *Literacy: A Critical Sourcebook*, E. Cushman, E. Kintgen, E. R. Kroll, and M. Rose, eds. 525–544. Boston: Bedford/St. Martin's. 2001.

———. (2004) *Situated language and learning: A critique of traditional schooling* London: Routledge.

Gilbert, S., and Grubar, S. 1979. *The madwoman in the attic: The woman writer and the nineteenth-century literary imagination* New Haven: Yale University Press.

Gilligan, C. 1982. *In a different voice: Psychological theory and women's development*. Cambridge, MA: Harvard University Press.

Gilyard, K. 1999. "*Higher Learning*: Composition's racialized reflection." In *Race, rhetoric, and composition*, ed. K. Gilyard, 44–52. Portsmouth, NH: Heinemann.

Giroux, H. 1997. "Race, pedagogy, and whiteness in Dangerous Minds." Cineaste, 22: 46–49.

Goldberg, D. T. 1993. *Racist culture: Philosophy and the politics of meaning*. London: Blackwell.

Goody, J. 2004. "What the West stole from the East." Paper presented at the Center for Arab and Middle Eastern Studies. American University of Beirut.

Graff, H. J. 1987. "Literacy, myths, and legacies: Lessons from the history of literacy." In H. J. Graff (1995), 318–349. *The labyrinths of literacy: Reflections on literacy past and Present*. Pittsburgh: University of Pittsburgh Press.

Gregory, E., and Williams, A. 2000. *City literacies: Learning to read across generations and cultures*. London: Routledge,

Griffin, S. 1982. *Made from this earth: Selections from her writing, 1967–1982*. London: The Women's Press.

Hall, S. 1981. "The whites of their eyes: Racist ideologies and the media." In *Gender, race and class in media.*, eds. G. Dines and J. M. Humez (1995), 18–22. Thousand Oaks, CA: Sage.

———. 1996. "Introduction: Who needs identity?" In *Questions of cultural identity* , eds. S. Hall and P. du Gay, 1–17. London: Sage.

———. (ed.) 1997. *Representation: Cultural representations and signifying practices*. London: Sage.

Hallam, E., and Street, B. 2000. *Cultural encounters: Representing 'otherness.'* London: Routledge.

Heath, S. B. 1983 *Ways with words: Language, life, and work in communities and classrooms*. New York: Cambridge University Press.

hooks, b. 1994. *Outlaw culture: Resisting representations*. London: Routledge.

Jenkins, T. 2005. "James Bond's "pussy" and Anglo-American cold war sexuality." *The Journal of American Culture*, 28: 309–317

Kendall, C. 2005. *The worlds we deliver: Confronting the consequences of believing in literacy*. PhD thesis. Miami University of Ohio.

Keroes, J. 1999. *Tales out of school: Gender, longing, and the teacher in fiction and film*. Carbondale, IL: Southern Illinois University Press.

Lankshear, C., and McLaren, P. (eds.) 1993. *Critical literacy: Politics, praxis, and the postmodern*. Albany: State University of New York Press.

LeFevre, K. 1987. *Invention as a social act*. Carbondale, IL: Southern Illinois University Press.

Light, A. 2003. *Reel arguments: Film, philosophy, and social criticism*. Boulder, CO: Westview Press.

MacIntosh, P. 1992. "White privilege and male privilege: A personal account of coming to see correspondences through work in women's studies." In *Critical White Studies: Looking Behind the Mirror*, eds. R. Delgado and J. Stefancic (1997), 291–299. Philadelphia: Temple University Press.

174   *References*

Mayne, J. 2002. "Paradoxes of spectatorship." In *The film cultures reader*, ed. G. Turner, 28–45. London: Routledge.

Meade, T., and Wiesner-Hanks, M. E. (eds.) 2004. *A companion to gender history*. Malden, MA: Blackwell.

Mills, C. 1997. *The racial contract*. Ithaca: Cornell University Press.

———. 2003. "White supremacy as sociopolitical system: A philosophical perspective." In *White out: The continuing significance of racism*, eds. A. W. Doane and E. Bonilla-Silva, 35–48. New York: Routledge.

Mitchell, C., and Walker, K. (eds.) 1991. *Rewriting literacy: Culture and the discourse of the other*. New York: Bergin and Garvey.

Morse, M. 1998. *Virtualities: Television, media art, and cyberculture*. Bloomington: Indiana University Press.

Murray, D. 2004. *A writer teaches writing*, 2nd ed. Boston: Heinle.

Newkirk, T. 2002. *Misreading masculinity: Boys, literacy, and popular culture*. Portsmouth, NH: Heinemann.

Omi, M. and Winant, H. 1993. "On the theoretical status of the concept of race." In *Race, Identity, and Representation in Education*, eds. C. McCarthy and W. Crichlow, 3–10. New York: Routledge.

Plath, S. 1961. *Ariel*. New York: Harper & Row.

Postman, N. 1985. *Amusing ourselves to death: Public discourse in the age of show business*. New York: Penguin.

Powell, Linda C. 1997. "The achievement (k)not: Whiteness and 'black underachievement'" In *Off white: Readings on race, power, and society*, eds. M. Fine, L. Weis, L. C. Powell, and L. M. Wong, 3–12. New York: Routledge.

ProLiteracy America. 2003. *U.S. adult literacy programs: Making a difference*. Syracuse, NY: ProLiteracy America.

Ramdas, L. 1989. "Women and literacy: a quest for justice." In (2001) *Literacy: A critical sourcebook*, eds. E. Cushman, E. Kintman, B. M. Kroll, and M. Rose, 629–643. Boston: Bedford/St. Martin's.

Richardson, E. 2003. *African American literacies*. London: Routledge.

Roman, L. G. 1993. "White is a color!: White defensiveness, postmodernism, and anti-racist pedagogy." In *Race, identity and representation in education.*, eds. C. McCarthy and W. Crichlow, 71–88. New York: Routledge.

Said, E. 1978. *Orientalism*. New York: Pantheon.

Sanchez-Escalonilla, A. 2005. "The hero as a visitor in hell: the descent into death in film structure." *Journal of Popular Film & Television*, 32:149–156.

Schweitzer, L. 2004. *Writing in the crossroads: Examining first-year composition and creative writing*. PhD thesis. University of Louisville.

Scribner, S. 1984. "Literacy in three metaphors." In (eds.) *Writing lives: Exploring literacy and community*, eds. S. Garnes, D. Humphries, V. Mortimer, J. Phegley, and K. Wallace, 34–49. Boston: Beford/St. Martin's. 1996.

Smith, M.W., and J. D. Wilhelm. 2002. *"Reading don't fix no Chevys" Literacy in the lives of young men*. Portsmouth, NH: Heinemann.

Street B.V. 1984. *Literacy in theory and practice*. Cambridge: Cambridge University Press.

———. 1993. "Introduction: The new literacy studies." In *Cross cultural approaches to literacy*, ed. B.V. Street, 1–21.Cambridge: Cambridge University Press.

———. 1995. *Social literacies: Critical approaches to literacy in education, development and ethnograph*. London: Longman.

———. 2001. "Introduction." In Literacy and development: Ethnographic perspectives, ed. B. V. Street, 1–7. London: Routledge.

Stroud, S. R. 2001. "Technology and mythic narrative: *The Matrix* as technological hero-quest." *Western Journal of Communication*, 65:416–441,

References   175

Stuckey J. E. 1990. *The violence of literacy.* Portsmouth, NH: Heinemann Boynton/Cook.

Tinkcom, M., and Villarejo, A. 2001. "Introduction." In *Keyframes: Popular cinema and cultural studies,* eds. M. Tinkcom and A. Villarejo, 1–30. London: Routledge.

Trafton, S. 2004. *Egyptland: Race and nineteenth-century Egyptomania.* Durham: Duke University Press.

Trimbur, J. 2000. "Composition and the circulation of writing." *College Composition and Communication* 52:188–219.

Vera, H., and Gordon, A. M. (2003) "The beautiful American: Sincere fictions of the white messiah in Hollywood movies." In *White out: The continuing significance of racism,* eds. A. W. Doane and E. Bonilla-Silva, 113–125. New York: Routledge.

Welsh, J. M. 2000. "Action films: The serious, the ironic, the postmodern." In *Film genre 2000: New critical essays,* ed. W. W. Dixon, 161–176. Albany NY Suny Press.

Williams, B. T. 2002. *Tuned in: Television and the teaching of writing.* Portsmouth, NH: Heinemann Boynton/Cook.

———. 2004a. "A puzzle to the rest of us': Who is a 'reader' anyway?" *Journal of Adolescent & Adult Literacy,* 47:686–689.

———. 2004b. "Are we having fun yet? students, social class, and the pleasures of literacy." *Journal of Adolescent & Adult Literacy,* 48:338–345.

Woolf, V. 1927. *To the lighthouse.* New York: Harcourt Brace.

Wordsworth, W. 1993. "Preface to *lyrical ballads.*" In *The Norton anthology of English literature* (vol. 2, 6th ed.), eds. M. H. Abrams et al., 140–151 New York: W.W. Norton..

Zender, S. M., and Calvert, S. L. 2004. "Between the hero and the shadow: developmental differences in adolescents' perceptions and understanding of mythic themes in film" *Journal of Communication Inquiry,* 28:122–137.

Filmography

10 Things I Hate About You (1999). Director: Gil Junger, USA, Touchstone Pictures.
2001: A Space Odyssey (1968). Director: Stanley Kubrick, USA, MGM.
About Schmidt (2002). Director: Alexander Payne, USA, New Line.
Adaptation (2002). Director: Spike Jonze, USA, Columbia.
Air Force One (1998). Director: Wolfgang Petersen, Columbia.
Ali (2001.) Director: Michael Mann, USA, Columbia.
Alien (1979). Director: Ridley Scott, USA, 20th Century Fox.
Amadeus (1984). Director: Milos Forman, USA, Warner Bros.
American Splendor (2003). Directors: Shari Springer Berman/Robert Pulcini, USA, Warner Bros.
America's Sweethearts (2001). Director: Joe Roth, USA, Columbia.
Anna and the King (1999). Director: Andy Tennant, USA, Fox.
As Good As It Gets (1997). Director: James L. Brooks, USA, Columbia.
Atlantis (2001). Directors: Gary Trousdale and Kirk Wise, USA, Disney.
Austin Powers: International Man of Mystery (1997). Director: Jay Roach, USA, New Line Cinema.
Bamboozled (2000). Director: Spike Lee, USA, 40Acres and a Mule.
Barton Fink (1991). Director: Joel Coen, USA, Fox.
Beauty and the Beast (1991). Directors: Gary Trousdale and Kirk Wise, USA, Disney.
Behind Enemy Lines (2002). Director: John Moore, USA, Fox.
Beverly Hills Cop (1984). Director: Martin Brest, USA, Paramount.
The Birth of a Nation (1915). Director: D.W. Griffith, USA, D.W. Griffith Corp.
Blade Runner (1982). Director: Ridley Scott, USA, Warner Bros.
Body Heat (1981). Director: Lawrence Kasdan, USA, Warner Bros.
The Bourne Identity (2002). Director: Doug Liman. USA. Universal.
The Bourne Supremacy (2004). Director: Paul Greengrass, USA, Universal.
Boys Don't Cry (1999). Director: Kimberly Pierce, USA, Fox.
Brazil (1982). Director: Terry Gilliam, UK, Fox.
Bridget Jones' Diary (2001). Director: Sharon Maguire, UK, Miramax.
Bullets Over Broadway (1994). Director: Woody Allen, USA, Miramax.
Cast Away (2000). Director: Robert Zemeckis, USA, Fox/Dreamworks.
Catch Me If You Can (2002). Director: Steven Spielberg, USA, Dreamworks.
Central Station Changing Lanes (2002). Director: Roger Michell, USA, Paramount.
Chinatown (1974). Director: Roman Polanski, USA, Paramount.
Cinderella Man (2005). Director: Ron Howard, USA, Universal.
Clear and Present Danger (1994). Director: Philip Noyce, USA, Paramount.
Con Air (1998). Director: Simon West, USA, Touchstone.
Crash (2004). Director: Paul Haggis, USA, Lions Gate.
Dangerous Minds (1995). Director: John N. Smith, USA, Buena Vista.

178   *Filmography*

The Dead Poets' Society (1989). Director: Peter Weir, USA, Touchstone.

Deconstructing Harry (1997). Director: Woody Allen, USA, New Line.

Delirious (1991). Director: Tom Mankiewicz, USA, MGM.

Diamonds Are Forever (1971). Director: Guy Hamilton, UK, United Artists.

Die Another Day (2002). Director: Lee Tamahori, USA, United Artists.

Die Hard (1988). Director: John McTiernan, USA, Fox.

Dirty Harry (1973). Director: Don Siegel, USA, Warner Bros.

Divine Secrets of the Ya-Ya Sisterhood (2002). Director: Callie Khouri.USA, Warner Bros.

The Door in the Floor (2004). Director: Tod Williams, USA, Focus.

Dr. No (1962). Director: Terence Young, UK, United Artists.

Dreamchild (1985). Director:Gavin Millar, UK, Universal.

Educating Rita (1983). Director: Lewis Gilbert, UK, Columbia.

The Emperor's Club (2002). Director: Michael Hoffman, USA, Universal.

Erin Brokovitch (2001). Director: Steven Soderbergh, USA, Columbia.

Eternal Sunshine of the Spotless Mind (2004). Director: Michael Gondry, USA, Focus.

The Evil Dead (1981). Director: Sam Raimi, USA, Renaissance Pictures.

Executive Decision (1995) Director: Stuart Baird, USA, Warner Bros.

Fame (1980). Director: Alan Parker, USA, MGM.

Fear and Loathing in Las Vegas (1998). Director: Terry Gilliam, USA, Universal.

Ferris Bueller's Day Off (1986). Director: John Hughes, USA, Paramount.

Field of Dreams (1989). Director: Phil Alden Robinson, USA, Universal.

Finding Forrester (2000). Director: Gus Van Sant, USA, Columbia.

Finding Neverland (2004). Director: Marc Forster, UK/USA, Miramax.

Five Easy Pieces (1970). Director: Bob Rafelson, USA, Columbia.

Forbidden Planet (1956). Director: Fred M. Wilcox. USA. MGM.

French Kiss (1995). Director: Lawrence Kasdan, USA, Fox.

From Russia With Love (1963). Director: Terence Young, UK, United Artists.

The Fugitive (1993). Director: Andrew Davis, USA, Warner Bros.

Girl, Interrupted (1999). Director: James Mangold, USA, Columbia.

Goldeneye (1995). Director: Martin Campbell, USA, MGM.

Goodbye, Mr. Chips (1939). Director: Sam Wood, USA, MGM.

Goodbye, Mr. Chips (1969). Director: Herbert Ross, USA, MGM.

The Green Mile (1999). Director: Frank Darabont, USA, Warner Bros.

Harriet the Spy (1996). Director: Bronwen Hughes, USA, Paramount.

Harry Potter and the Chamber of Secrets (2002). Director: Chris Columbus, USA/UK, Warner Bros.

Hellboy (2004). Director: Guillermo Del Toro, USA, Columbia.

Higher Learning (1995). Director: John Singleton, USA, Columbia.

Holes (2003). Director: Andrew Davis, USA, Disney.

The Hours (2002). Director: Steven Daldry, USA, Miramax.

I Know What You Did Last Summer (1997). Director: Jim Gillespie, USA, Columbia.

I, Robot (2004). Director: Alex Proyas, USA, Fox.

I Spy (2002). Director: Betty Thomas, USA, Columbia.

Ice Princess (2005). Director: Tim Fywell, USA, Disney.

Il Postino (1994). Director: Michael Radford, France/Italy/Belgium, Blue Dahlia.

In The Cut (2003). Director: Jane Campion, USA, Pathe.

Independence Day (1996). Director: Roland Emmerich, USA, Fox.

Indiana Jones and the Last Crusade (1989). Director: Steven Spielberg, USA, Paramount.

Indiana Jones and the Temple of Doom (1984). Director: Steven Spielberg, USA, Paramount.

Filmography 179

Iris (2001). Director: Richard Eyre, UK/USA, Miramax.
King Kong (1933). Directors: Merian Cooper and Ernest B. Shoedsack. USA, RKO.
King Solomon's Mines (1937). Director: Robert Stevenson, UK, Gaumont British.
Legally Blonde (2001). Director: Robert Luketic, USA, Fox.
Lethal Weapon (1987). Director: Richard Donner, USA, Warner Bros.
Lethal Weapon 2 (1989). Director: Richard Donner, USA, Warner Bros.
Licence to Kill (1989). Director: John Glen, UK, United Artists.
Loaded Weapon (1993). Director: Gene Quintano, USA, New Line.
The Lord of the Rings: The Fellowship of the Ring (2001). Director: Peter Jackson, USA/New Zealand, New Line.
Love Actually (2003). Director: Richard Curtis, UK/USA, Universal.
The Majestic (2001). Director: Frank Darabont, USA, Warner Bros.
The Maltese Falcon (1941). Director: John Huston, USA, Warner Bros.
Man on Fire (2004). Director: Tony Scott, USA, Fox.
The Man With The Golden Gun (1974). Director: Guy Hamilton, UK, United Artists.
Master and Commander: The Far Side of the World (2003). Director: Peter Weir, USA, Miramax.
Matewan (1987). Director: John Sayles. USA, Cinecom.
The Matrix (1999). Directors: Andy and Larry Wachowski, USA, Warner Bros.
Memento (2000). Director: Christopher Nolan, USA, Columbia.
Men in Black (1997). Director: Barry Sonnenfeld, USA, Columbia.
Million Dollar Baby (2004). Director: Clint Eastwood, USA, Warner Bros.
Minority Report (2002). Director: Steven Spielberg, USA, Dreamworks/Fox.
The Mirror Has Two Faces (1996). Director: Barbra Streisand, USA, Columbia.
Misery (1990). Director: Rob Reiner, USA, Castle Rock/Columbia.
Mission Impossible (1996). Director: Brian De Palma, USA, Paramount.
Moonraker (1979). Director: Lewis Gilbert, USA, United Artists/MGM.
Mrs. Parker and the Vicious Circle (1994). Director: Alan Rudolph, USA, Miramax.
Mr. Holland's Opus (1995). Director: Stephen Herek, USA, Buena Vista.
The Mummy (1999). Director: Steven Sommers, USA, Universal.
My Big Fat Greek Wedding (2002). Director: Joel Zwick, USA, Warner Bros.
Nanny McPhee (2005). Director: Kirk Jones, USA, Universal.
Nell (1994). Director: Michael Apted, USA, Fox.
Nora (2000). Director: Pat Murphy, Ireland/UK, Road Movies/Volta.
Norma Rae (1979). Director: Martin Ritt. USA. Fox.
Office Space (1999). Director: Mike Judge, USA, Fox.
On the Waterfront (2004). Director: Elia Kazan, USA, Columbia.
One Flew Over the Cuckoo's Nest (1975). Director: Milos Forman, USA, United Artists.
Out of Time (2003). Director: Carl Franklin, USA, MGM.
Paris is Burning (1990). Director: Jennie Livingston, USA, Off-White Productions.
Paycheck (2003). Director: John Woo, USA, Paramount/Dreamworks.
The Peacemaker (1997). Director: Mimi Leder, USA, Dreamworks.
Pollock (2000). Director: Ed Harris, USA, Sony Pictures.
Possession (2002). Director: Neil LaBute, USA/UK, Warner Bros.
The Producers (1968). Director: Mel Brooks, USA, MGM.
Quills (2000). Director: Philip Kaufman, USA/Germany/UK, Fox.
Raiders of the Lost Ark (1981). Director: Steven Spielberg, USA, Fox.
The Royal Tennenbaums (2001). Director: Wes Anderson, USA, Touchstone.
Rush Hour (1998). Director: Brett Ratner, USA, New Line.
Secret Window (2004). Director: David Koepp, USA, Columbia.
Serendipity (2001). Director: Peter Chelsom, USA, Miramax.

180   *Filmography*

Se7en (1995). Director: David Fincher, USA, New Line.
Shakespeare in Love (1998). Director: John Madden, USA/UK, Miramax/Universal.
The Shawshank Redemption (1994). Director: Frank Darabont, USA, Columbia.
She's All That (1999). Director: Robert Iscove, USA, Miramax.
The Shining (1980). Director: Stanley Kubrick, USA, Warner Bros.
Signs (2002). Director: M. Night Shyamalan, USA, Touchstone.
Sky Captain and the World of Tomorrow (2004). Director: Kerry Conran, USA, Paramount.
Sleepless in Seattle (1993). Director: Nora Ephron, USA, Columbia.
A Soldier's Daughter Never Cries (1998). Director: James Ivory, France/USA, Capitol/October Films.
Something's Gotta Give (2003). Director: Nancy Meyers, USA, Columbia/Warner Bros.
Spiderman 2 (2004). Director: Sam Raimi, USA, Columbia/Sony Pictures.
The Spy Who Loved Me (1977). Director: Lewis Gilbert, UK/USA, United Artists.
Stand and Deliver (1988). Director: Ramon Menendez, USA, Warner Bros.
Stanley and Iris (1990). Director: Martin Ritt, USA, MGM.
Star Wars: a New Hope (1977). Director: George Lucas, USA, Fox.
Stargate (1995). Director: Roland Emmerich, USA/France, MGM.
The Sum of All Fears (2002). Director: Phil Alden Robinson, USA, Paramount.
Superman (1978). Director: Richard Donner, USA, Warner Bros.
SWAT (2004). Director: Clark Johnson, USA, Columbia.
Sylvia (2003). Director: Christine Jeffs, UK/USA, Capitol/Focus.
The Terminator (1984). Director: James Cameron, USA, Orion Pictures.
Thelma and Louise (1991). Director: Ridley Scott, USA, MGM.
Three Kings (1999). Director: David O. Russell, USA, Warner Bros.
To Sir, With Love (1967). Director, James Clavell, UK, Columbia.
Tom and Viv (1994). Director: Brian Gilbert, UK/USA, Miramax.
Tomorrow Never Dies (1997). Director: Roger Spottiswoode, UK/USA, MGM.
Top Gun (1986). Director: Tony Scott, USA, Paramount.
Tootsie (1982). Director: Sydney Pollack, USA, Columbia.
Under the Tuscan Sun (2003). Director: Audrey Wells, USA/Italy, Touchstone.
Undercover Brother (2002). Directors: Malcolm D. Lee; Gregory Dark, USA, Universal.
Van Helsing (2004). Director: Steven Sommers, USA, Universal.
Vanilla Sky (2001). Director: Cameron Crowe, USA, Paramount.
Vertigo (1958). Director: Alfred Hitchcock, USA, Paramount.
Vincent and Theo (1990). Director: Robert Altman. Netherlands/UK, Hemdale Films.
When Harry Met Sally (1989). Director: Rob Reiner, USA, Castle Rock.
The Wizard of Oz (1939). Director: Victor Fleming, USA, MGM.
Wonder Boys (2000). Director: Curtis Hanson, USA, Paramount.
Working Girl (1988). Director: Mike Nichols, USA, Fox.
The World is Not Enough (1999). Director: Michael Apted, UK/USA, MGM.
X2-Xmen United (2003). Director: Bryan Singer, USA, Fox.
X-Men (2000). Director: Bryan Singer, USA, Fox.
You Only Live Twice (1967). Director: Lewis Gilbert, UK/USA, MGM.
You've Got Mail (1998). Director: Nora Ephron, USA, Warner Bros.
Zoolander (2001). Director: Ben Stiller, USA, Paramount.

Index

A

Abdegnale, Frank, 54–60
Action films
  action hero omnipotent literacy
    skills, 85–86
  anti-establishment hero, 91
  began with Bond movies, 88
  characteristics, 88
  class, 94–96
  discourse, 94–96
  file-on-the-desk moment, 89–91
  hero characterized, 88
  institutional and bureaucratic
    literacy practices rejected, 91–92
  institutional knowledge, 92–93
  literacy, 85–104
  literacy practices, 97
    literacy at pivotal moment, 98–100
    scenes of, 89
  literary villains, 102–104
  literate sidekicks, 100–104
  mythology of the lone hero, 97
  parodied, 88
  pen *vs.* sword, 104
  power, 94–96
  race, 77–81
  supervisor, 89–91
Adventure, race, 77–78
As Good As It Gets, gender, 26–30,
  32–33
Authors
  author-function, 130–131
  female authors, 141–142
  female characters, intimate
    relationships, 32
  film genres, 129
  gendered construct of the muse,
    141–142
  identity, 107–110, 129–131

  contextual, 107
  inspiration, 136–141
  male authors, 141
  male characters, 27–28, 29–30
  myth of, 158
  redemption, 136–141
  as solitary artist, 141–144
  as tragic genius, 132–136

B

Bond films, 85
  bureaucratic exchange, 90–91
  class, 94–96
  gender, 94–96
  homosexual stereotypes, 103
  literacy practices, 90, 91–92, 97
    literacy at pivotal moment, 98–100
  literate sidekick, 101–102
  literate villain, 102–104
  obligatory opening action sequence, 90
  race, 94–96
Bourdieu, P., 52–53, 58
Boxing genre, 38–39
Brandt, Deborah, 152–153, 158,
  164–165
Bridget Jones's Diary, gender, 30–31
Buddy action films, 97

C

Campion, Jane, 33–34, 35, 37
Catch Me If You Can
  class, 54–60
  habitus, 58
Change, literacy practices, 14
Changing Lanes
  class, 44–49
    systems of discourse and power,
      44–49
  race, 46

182 Index

Chat rooms, 119
Class, 25, 166
  action films, 94–96
  Bond films, 94–96
  Catch Me If You Can, 54–60
  Changing Lanes, 44–49
    systems of discourse and power,
      44–49
  conformity, 60–62
  dress, 55, 56–57, 59
  information, 60–62
  literacy, 41–62
    gaining the upper hand, 50–51
    history, 44
    institutional literacy demands, 57
    institutions of power, 44–50
    perceptions of, 52–54
    performance, 54–60
    reinforcing class status, 42–43
  literacy education, 50
  Love Actually, 51
  Office Space, 61–62
  Serendipity, 50–51
Comic book heroes, 93–94
Commodification
  of communication and information,
    164
  of literacy, 152–154
Communication, multimodal, 10
Conformity, class, 60–62
Crash, 65–66
Creative writing programs, 143–144
Cultural capital, 52–53
  exhibiting, 55–56
  performance, 55–56
Cultural context, 4, 12
Cultural markers, 166
Cultural studies film criticism, 5,
  23–24

D

Dangerous Minds
  economic empowerment, 41
  race, 68–69, 70, 76
The Dead Poets' Society, 154–155
Dehumanizing system, 61–62
DeSalvo, Louise, 21
Diaries
  female characters, 30–31
  male characters, 31–32
Discourse, action films, 94–96
Domains of life, 12
Dress, class, 55, 56–57, 59

E

Economic empowerment
  Dangerous Minds, 41
  Educating Rita, 41
  literacy, to deny, 49
  Stanley and Iris, 41
Educating Rita, 25, 26, 148
  economic empowerment, 41
Erin Brokovitch, 42
The Evil Dead, 106

F

Fame, race, 67–68, 76
Fantasy, 106–110
Fasheh, Munir, 149–150
Female characters, *see also* Gender
  diaries, 30–31
  images, 23–26
  letter writing, 28–29, 30
  professional authors, intimate
    relationships, 32
  thank-you notes, 28–29, 30
Feminist film critics, 23–24
Film genres, 86
  authors, 129
  development, 86–87
  fulfillment of genre expectations, 86
  gender, 25
  history, 86
  intertextual references, 87
  predictability *vs.* variety, 87
  symbolic usage of key images, 87–88
Films
  about literacy, 9
  as cultural export, 8, 9–10
  explicit narratives, 10–11
  global power of, 8–11
  images of nonliteracy of, 148–152
  narrative, naturalistic conventions
    of, 8
  observing culture on, 5–8
  reproducing culture in, 163
  selection of, 11
  significance of, 8
  variety of purposes of, 8
Finding Forrester, 134, 141, 153–154
Finding Neverland, 136–137, 138–140
Foucault, M., 130–131

G

Garcia Marquez, Gabriel, 36
Gender, 166
  Bond films, 94–96

Bridget Jones's Diary, 30–31
genres, 25
Girl Interrupted, 31
As Good As It Gets, 26–30, 32–33
literacy, 21–39
    challenging images, 33–38
    theory and research, 23
    using literacy for critical action,
       38–39
Girl Interrupted, gender, 31
Good Will Hunting, 153–154
Graff, Harvey, 146–147

H
Habitus, 58
    Catch Me If You Can, 58
    defined, 58
Hall, Stuart, 21–23
Harry Potter films, literacy practices,
    103–104, 110–122
    author as fraud, 111–117
    critical theorist position, 115–116
    deception of young readers by older
       writers, 120–122
    difficult, forbidden, and dangerous
       literacies, 117–122
    *Harry Potter and the Chamber of
       Secrets,* 106
Hellboy, 101
Holes, 150
    race, 70–76
Hollywood Homicide, race, 63–64
Homosexual stereotypes, Bond films,
    103
hooks, bell, 37
Horror films, 106–110
    race, 77–81
The Hours, 133, 134–135, 136

I
Identity
    concept, 21–22
    literacy
       perceptions of, 52–54
       representation, 23
    literacy and film's power in shaping,
       163
Il Postino, 150–151, 153
Individualism, 127–144, 166
Information
    class, 60–62
    commodification of, 164
Inspiration

authors, 136–141
    gendered construct of the muse,
       141–142
Instant messaging, 119
Institutional knowledge
    action films, 92–93
    The Peacemaker, 92–93
In the Cut, 33–38
    Serendipity, 34–35
    To the Lighthouse, 35–36

L
Language, ambiguity, 109
Legally Blonde, 25–26
Letter writing, female characters,
    28–29, 30
Literacy
    action films, 85–104
    always requires permission, 158
    autonomous model, 11
    class, 41–62
       gaining upper hand, 50–51
       history, 44
       institutional literacy demands, 57
       institutions of power, 44–50
       perceptions of, 52–54
       performance, 54–60
       reinforcing class status, 42–43
    as commodity, 152–154
    competing purposes, 154–157
    contextual nature, 11
    counter-narratives, 5
    as danger, 105–123
    danger of trust, 119–120
    definitions, 9, 10, 12
       defined by cultural norms, 6
       simplistic, 145
    economic development and
       prosperity, 41
    economic empowerment, to deny, 49
    gender
       challenging images, 33–38
       gender roles, 21–39
       theory and research, 23
       using literacy for critical action,
          38–39
    historically situated, 13–14
    identity
       manifestation of, 165
       perceptions of, 52–54
    as individualism, 127–144
    inflated claims, 145
    institutional definitions, 9

184 *Index*

Literacy (*continued*)
  lack of access to, 25
  means of human connection, 165
  mystical and ambiguous power, 106
  narratives, 5
  perils of misreading, 105–123
  power, 85–104
    as cultural commonplace, 166
  product of ideology, 6
  race, 63–82
    assumptions about literacy itself,
      76
    collective and embodied, 65–70
    dominant versions of literacy,
      68–70
    othering literacies, 77–81
    underachievement, 67
  relationships of literacy learning,
    157–159
  as salvation, 146–148
  shaped by culture's dominant social
    institutions, 165
  situated nature, 11, 61
  as social good of moral society,
    164–165
  as social practice of individuals, 164
  social theories, 11–14
  traditional perception of, 52–54
  unschooled, 106
  uses, 41
  valuing, 52
Literacy education, 158
  class, 50
  myth about providing literacy,
    158–159
Literacy events, 4
  concept, 12
  context, 4
  creating narrative about literacy,
    10–11
  literacy practices, relationship, 12
  meaning shifts, 4
Literacy myth
  characterized, 146–147
  triumph-of-literacy films, 146
Literacy policies, 168–169
Literacy practices, 4
  action films, 97
    literacy at pivotal moment, 98–100
  Bond films, 90, 91–92, 97
    literacy at pivotal moment, 98–100
  change, 14
  defined, 11–12

economic consequences, 164
embedded in broader social goals
  and cultural practices, 13
fluid and dynamic, 14
Harry Potter films, 110–122
  author as fraud, 111–117
  critical theorist position, 115–116
  deception of young readers by
    older writers, 120–122
  difficult, forbidden, and dangerous
    literacies, 117–122
literacy events, relationship, 12
personal qualities, 56–57, 58
popular culture, 5
representations, 4–5
significance, 167–170
triumph of individual over
  institutions, 166
Literacy sponsorship, 153–154
  triumph-of-literacy films, 158–159
Lone hero, 97
*The Lord of the Rings: The Fellowship
  of the Ring,* 109
Love Actually, class, 51
Love in the Time of Cholera, 36

M
Male characters, *see also* Gender
  diaries, 31–32
  images, 23–26
  professional authors, 27–28, 29–30
  public literacy, 32
Matewan, 42
Memento, 105–106
Million Dollar Baby, 38–39
Misinterpreted document, 105–123
The Mummy
  race, 77–81
  texts, 79, 80
Muse, *see* Inspiration
My Big Fat Greek Wedding, 155–157

N
Narrative
  about literacy, 10–11
  of individual transformation, 159
Nicholson, Jack, 26–27
Nonliteracy, images of, 148–152
Norma Rae, 42

O
Objectification of women, 24, 25
Office Space, class, 61–62

Index   185

Opportunity, 42
Orientalism, 81
Othering, 26–27
Othering literacies, 77–81
  race, 81–82

P
Patriarchy, 23
The Peacemaker, institutional
      knowledge, 92–93
Performance, cultural capital, 55–56
Plagiarism, 116
Plath, Sylvia, 132–134
Popular culture
  lamentable rise, 52
  literacy practices, 5
  not uniform, 7
  popular culture membrane, 7
Power
  action films, 94–96
  literacy, 85–104
  relationships, 13

R
Race, 25
  action films, 77–81
  adventure, 77–78
  Bond films, 94–96
  Changing Lanes, 46
  color blind approach, 66
  as constructed reality, 65
  critical theories, 64–65
  Dangerous Minds, 68–69, 70, 76
  Fame, 67–68, 76
  Holes, 70–76
  Hollywood Homicide, 63–64
  horror films, 77–81
  identifying whiteness as category of
      identity, 65, 66
  influence on films, 67
  literacy, 63–82
    assumptions about literacy itself,
      76
    collective and embodied, 65–70
    dominant versions of literacy,
      68–70
    othering literacies, 77–81
    underachievement, 67
  marked as racialized, 64
  The Mummy, 77–81
  objectified, 65, 69
  othering literacies, 81–82
  writing others, 81–82

Redemption, authors, 136–141
Representation
  identity, 23
  of literacy
    extrapolations from film, 9
    means of exclusion, 42–43
    means of representation, 10
    uses, 169–170
    variations in extent, 10
Rhetoric, 6–7
Rhetorical conventions, 6–7
Romantic author, 127–144
Romantic individualism, writing,
      127–144

S
Science fiction, 106–110
Scientists, 93
Secret files, 4
Self-sufficiency, 166
Serendipity, 36
  class, 50–51
  In the Cut, 34–35
  Love in the Time of Cholera, 36
Shakespeare in Love, 131, 137–138,
      139, 140–141
The Shawshank Redemption, 151–
      152, 153
Situated acts of expression, 6
Social institutions, 13
Social mobility, 54
Something's Gotta Give, 142
Spiderman 2, 94
Stanley and Iris, economic
      empowerment, 41
SWAT, 89–90
Sylvia, 132–134

T
Texts, 12
  difficult, forbidden, and dangerous
      literacies, 117–122
  misreading, 105–123
  The Mummy, 79, 80
  situated nature, 56
  without authors, 107–110
Theories of multiliteracies, 10
To the Lighthouse, In the Cut, 35–36
Triumph-of-literacy films, 9, 145–159
  literacy learning, 157–159
  literacy myth, 146
  literacy sponsorship, 158–159
  meta-narratives, 147–148

186 *Index*

Triumph-of-literacy films *(continued)*
   personal relationships, 158
   teacher-learner relationship, 159
2001: A Space Odyssey, 107

U
Under the Tuscan Sun, 142
Uniforms, 56–57
University writing courses, 50

V
Van Helsing, 101
Vertigo, 21

W
White American self-concept, 77–78
White messiahs, 78, 79
Wonder Boys, 141, 142
Woolf, Leonard, 134–135, 136

Woolf, Virginia, 35, 133, 134–135, 136
Working-class characters, 42
Working Girl, 41–42
Writing
   process, 142–144
   representation of, 127–144
   Romantic individualism, 127–144
   social nature, 143
   teaching, 142–144
Writing others, race, 81–82
Writing spaces, 29

X
X-Men, 3–4, 12–13

Y
You've Got Mail, 31